THE RUSSIAN RESEARCH CENTER

The Russian Research Center of Harvard University is supported by a grant from the Carnegie Corporation. The Center carries out interdisciplinary study of Russian institutions and behavior.

Russian Research Center Studies

1. *Public Opinion in Soviet Russia: A Study in Mass Persuasion,* by Alex Inkeles

2. *Soviet Politics — The Dilemma of Power; The Role of Ideas in Social Change,* by Barrington Moore, Jr.

3. *Justice in Russia: An Interpretation of Soviet Law,* by Harold J. Berman

4. *Chinese Communism and the Rise of Mao,* by Benjamin I. Schwartz

5. *Titoism and the Cominform,* by Adam B. Ulam

6. *A Documentary History of Chinese Communism,* by Conrad Brandt, Benjamin Schwartz, and John K. Fairbank

7. *The New Man in Soviet Psychology,* by Raymond A. Bauer

8. *Soviet Opposition to Stalin: A Case Study in World War II,* by George Fischer

9. *Minerals: A Key to Soviet Power,* by Demitri B. Shimkin

10. *Soviet Law in Action: The Recollected Cases of a Soviet Lawyer,* by Harold J. Berman and Boris A. Konstantinovsky

11. *How Russia Is Ruled,* by Merle Fainsod

12. *Terror and Progress USSR: Some Sources of Change and Stability in the Soviet Dictatorship,* by Barrington Moore, Jr.

13. *The Formation of the Soviet Union: Communism and Nationalism, 1917–1923,* by Richard Pipes

14. *Marxism: The Unity of Theory and Practice,* by Alfred G. Meyer

15. *Soviet Industrial Expansion, 1928–1951,* by Donald R. Hodgman

16. *Soviet Taxation: The Fiscal and Monetary Problems of a Planned Economy,* by Franklyn D. Holzman

17. *Soviet Military Law and Administration,* by Harold J. Berman and Miroslav Kerner

SOVIET MILITARY LAW AND ADMINISTRATION

SOVIET MILITARY LAW

AND ADMINISTRATION

Harold J. Berman
and
Miroslav Kerner

HARVARD UNIVERSITY PRESS · CAMBRIDGE · 1955

©

Copyright, 1955, by the President and Fellows of Harvard College

Distributed in Great Britain by Geoffrey Cumberlege,
Oxford University Press, London

This volume was prepared under a grant from the Carnegie Corporation of New York. That Corporation is not, however, the author, owner, publisher, or proprietor of this publication and is not to be understood as approving by virtue of its grant any of the statements made or views expressed therein.

Library of Congress Catalog Card Number 55–5383
Printed in the United States of America

PREFACE

Although it is generally realized that the Soviet military establishment is of crucial importance in the Soviet social, economic, and political order, relatively little scholarly effort has been devoted to the study of its internal structure. D. Fedotoff White's excellent historical treatise, *The Growth of the Red Army* (Princeton, N. J., 1944), is devoted largely to developments prior to World War II. More recent studies, of which the best is the chapter on the armed forces in Merle Fainsod's *How Russia Is Ruled* (Cambridge, Mass., 1953), are concerned largely with one aspect of Soviet military administration — the nature and extent of Communist Party and police controls. (See also Zbigniew Brzezinski, ed., *Political Controls in the Soviet Army*, New York, 1954.) Raymond Garthoff's monumental work, *Soviet Military Doctrine* (Glencoe, Ill., 1953), contains but a brief appendix on the organization of the Soviet armed forces and has little to say about the standards and procedures by which Soviet military life is ordered.

The present work does not purport to constitute a complete study of the internal order of the Soviet military establishment but only an analysis of its administrative and legal structure. More specifically, we deal with Soviet military administration, the regulation of military discipline, the law of military crimes and punishments, and the organization and procedure of military courts and of military prosecution. In order that the reader may have available the sources upon which the analysis is based, and in order that future studies relating to the Soviet military establishment may have the benefit of documents otherwise not easily accessible, we have prepared a companion volume, *Documents on Soviet Military Law and Administration* (Cambridge, Mass., 1955), consisting of translations of the most important statutes, codes, cases, and other legal materials affecting the Soviet military system. Included in those materials are some reports of former Soviet citizens who have experienced Soviet military life at first hand.

Of course no study based as this is on published Soviet materials and on reports of émigrés can answer certain questions which have an important bearing on the subject under investigation. To what extent there is illegal exercise of power within the armed forces at various levels, how well disciplined Soviet troops in fact are, what their attitudes are on various subjects, whether or not there is serious opposition to the Communist Party within the armed forces — such questions as these could be conclusively answered, if at all, only from the extensive first-hand and up-to-date experience of a large number of Soviet soldiers and administrators.

Nevertheless, a study of the administrative and legal structure of Soviet military life does reveal much that is of importance for our understanding of the realities of the Soviet system — both the military system and the Soviet social system as a whole. Since diverse sets of conclusions may undoubtedly be derived from the materials upon which this study is based, and since these materials for the most part have never before been made available, we have thought it best to proceed by interpreting the laws, regulations, cases, and other materials, rather than by arranging them in such a way as to demonstrate our own conclusions. However, we have presented in an introductory chapter a brief statement of certain general propositions which seem to us to emerge from the materials, and we have set forth in a concluding chapter our general evaluation of the significance of Soviet military administration and military law — its significance for Soviet military life as well as its general significance for American scholars, lawyers, soldiers, and citizens. The concluding chapter includes the personal impressions of one of the authors, Mr. Kerner, a former Czechoslovak lawyer, derived from his one and one-half years of service with the Czechoslovak armed forces in Russia during World War II.

The authors are grateful to the Russian Research Center of Harvard University for providing necessary financial support as well as a congenial environment for the writing of this book. Special thanks are due also to Taras Butoff for his careful, critical examination of the manuscript and for his many excellent suggestions for its improvement; to Ada Dziewanowski for her expert and patient secretarial assistance; and to Ann Twombly for her help in preparing the charts.

We gratefully acknowledge the permission of N. Semenov, to quote from his book, *Sovetskii sud i karatel'nia politika* (The Soviet Court and Penal Policy; Munich, 1952); and of the Research Program of the USSR to quote from Z. Brzezinski, ed., *Political Controls in the Soviet Army* (New York, 1954).

As this book goes to press, important changes are taking place in the top leadership of the Soviet Government and the Ministry of Defense. The date of this preface is the last opportunity the authors have had to note such changes in the text.

H.J.B.
M.K.

Cambridge, Massachusetts

February 13, 1955

CONTENTS

CHARTS

SOVIET MILITARY LAW AND ADMINISTRATION

HYPOTHESES

Certain general propositions concerning Soviet military law and administration are offered here as hypotheses to guide the reader through the materials presented in the following chapters. The authors' over-all appraisal of the Soviet system of military law and administration is reserved for the final chapter; the following propositions are intended to serve rather as an introduction than as a conclusion.

First, although the Soviet military establishment is subject to strong ideological pressures from the Communist Party organizations within it, and strong security pressures from the Committee on State Security of the Council of Ministers, nevertheless the Ministry of Defense (which operates the armed forces) has succeeded in achieving considerable administrative autonomy and stability. The relative deficiency of clear-cut jurisdictional boundaries at the higher levels is part of a system of government by personal influence and autocratic power, in which the military leaders play an important secondary role. At the intermediate and lower levels, however, there is a fairly well understood division of functions, with military authorities having considerable independence in military matters.

Second, the Soviet system of military service and civil defense is effective in maintaining the population in a permanent state of semimobilization. On the whole the system of conscription and service is founded on the principle of equality of sacrifice.

Third, a theory of military discipline founded on revolutionary ideas of class struggle, socialism, internationalism, camaraderie of all troops, and deëmphasis of distinctions of military rank was tried in all earnestness by the Soviet leaders in the first years of their power and was found wanting. The restoration of traditional Russian military institutions, and indeed the establishment of a "Prussian" rigor, motivated primarily by patriotism, ceremoniousness, and ideals of loyalty and self-sacrifice, rather than by revolutionary ideology, has been carried out systematically and by means intelligently adapted to the given ends.

Fourth, the strictness of Soviet military discipline as declared in the disciplinary and criminal codes is susceptible to conflicting explanations: one is that the Soviet soldier is amenable to rigorous discipline; another is that he is basically undisciplined and therefore, from the official standpoint, requires severe control. Official sources provide no basis for forming a judgment on this matter. The authors incline to the second of the two views, for reasons given in the concluding chapter.

Fifth, the military courts and organs of law-enforcement have achieved a large measure of independence in matters not concerning politics, but are subservient to Party and security agencies in matters which *those agencies* consider political.

Sixth, the trial of serious political offenders (such as Beria) by the Military Division of the Supreme Court under a 1934 statute which explicitly denies to the accused the right to counsel, the right to appeal, the right to be present at the trial, and other rights which are essential to due process of law, shows that the Soviet lawmakers understand full well what due process of law means and choose to do without it in certain types of cases.

Seventh, since Soviet military courts try cases of political crimes — a reversion to a practice which was eliminated in most Western countries in the eighteenth and nineteenth centuries, and in Tsarist Russia in the 1860's — they are bound to be corrupted to a certain extent even in the trial of nonpolitical military offenses.

Eighth, the Soviet system of military criminal law, though harsh in its prohibition of deviations, is nevertheless founded on principles designed to resolve the eternal dilemma of all criminal law: finding means for convicting the guilty which at the same time secure the acquittal of the innocent.

Ninth, Soviet military courts, like Soviet civilian courts, though bound by general statutory provisions, have a high degree of freedom of decision because of the emphasis on subjective standards of guilt and because of the doctrine of analogy, which permits, within certain defined limits, conviction in the absence of a statute directly prohibiting the particular act of the accused.

Tenth, Soviet military law is characterized by extremes of ruthlessness on the one hand and leniency on the other. Relatives of servicemen who desert to the enemy may be punished though they had nothing to do with the crime. On the other hand, very large scope is given to extenuating circumstances, not only in mitigating punishment but in exonerating the accused altogether. Periods of severity in criminal administration have occasionally been followed by general amnesties.

Eleventh, Soviet criminal law permits a very wide range of punishments, ranging from the death penalty and sentence to penal battalions (which in wartime was often equivalent to a death sentence) to very liberal provisions for suspension of sentence and annulment of convictions. Such a range of punishments requires a judiciary of very high caliber. One means whereby the Soviets seek to achieve a good military judiciary is through the institution of permanent tribunals independent of military command; however, judging by decisions in the Supreme Court of the USSR which reverse lower military tribunals, and by émigrés' reports, the caliber of Soviet military judges in general is not very high, though it is probably higher than that of the Soviet civilian judiciary.

Twelfth, the procedure in Soviet military courts *in peacetime* permits a high degree of protection of the rights of the accused, with the explicit exception of political offenders. The possibility of review of decisions by the Military Division of the Supreme Court, and ultimately by the Plenum of the Supreme Court, is a safeguard to the accused and also promotes the harmony of military and nonmilitary law.

Thirteenth, in World War II the Soviet military courts, by resorting to a summary procedure in which neither defense counsel nor prosecutor was permitted and the right of appeal was severely limited, restricted their efficacy as instruments of justice but enhanced their efficacy as instruments of discipline.

Fourteenth, it is questionable whether even in peacetime it is possible, from a military point of view, to maintain elaborate procedural guarantees and objectivity of decisions in the military courts without a complementary allocation of very large powers of nonjudicial "company" punishment. The Soviet system of military law is characterized by this dualism.

Fifteenth, the cases involving nonpolitical military crimes which reach the Supreme Court of the USSR indicate a high degree of concern both for the justice of the decision in the particular case and for the strengthening of military discipline. When there is a conflict between these two goals, the latter is given primary importance. However, the Soviet Supreme Court has in many of the cases shown its awareness that ultimately a system of military law and discipline cannot flourish without meeting the need for individual justice.

I

SOVIET MILITARY ADMINISTRATION

1. WHO RULES THE SOVIET ARMED FORCES?

Who rules the Soviet armed forces? Is it the Supreme Soviet of the USSR, which, according to the Soviet Constitution, is "the highest organ of state authority" (Article 30), and is entrusted with "questions of war and peace" as well as with the organization of military defense and the direction of the country's armed forces (Article 14, *b* and *g*, Article 31)? [1] Despite the language of the Constitution, the answer is clearly no; for the Supreme Soviet is a body of some 1350 elected representatives that generally meets for a few weeks twice a year, with deliberations consisting largely in speeches in support of bills presented, which in practice are unanimously approved.

Is it the Presidium of the Supreme Soviet (not to be confused with the Presidium of the Central Committee of the Communist Party, formerly called the Politburo) — a body of thirty-three persons chosen from the Supreme Soviet to conduct its affairs between sessions (Constitution of the USSR, Articles 48 and 49)? According to the Constitution, the Presidium of the Supreme Soviet has these four specific military functions: the appointment and removal of the supreme command of the armed forces, proclamation of war during times of recess of the Supreme Soviet, declaration of general or partial mobilization, and proclamation of martial law (Article 49, *l*, *m*, *n*, and *r*). In addition it is impowered to issue legislation in the form of edicts (*ukazy*); a large part of the military legislation translated in the companion volume to this book, *Documents on Soviet Military Law and Administration*, consists of such edicts. Nevertheless it may be doubted whether the Presidium of the Supreme Soviet has anything more than a ministerial function in the enactment of such legislation or in the exercise of the military functions ascribed to it by the Constitution. This doubt is founded in part on the relative unimportance in the hierarchy of the Communist Party of the thirty-three men who constitute the Presidium of the Supreme Soviet. It is also founded in part on the formal character of much of its activity. Often the Presidium of the Supreme Soviet issues an edict enacting a decree of the Council of Ministers, which may or may not be published as part of the edict.

Is it, then, the Council of Ministers, "the highest executive and administrative organ of state authority" (Constitution of the USSR, Article 64), which rules the Soviet armed forces? The Council of Ministers consists of the heads of the various economic, political, military, social, and other branches of the Soviet state. In 1954 it had fifty-five members, including a chairman and eight vice-chairmen drawn chiefly from the leading members of the nine-man Presidium of the Central Committee of the Communist Party. The economic ministries are the most numerous, comprising thirty-four in 1954; among them are the ministries of agriculture, metallurgy, coal, oil, chemicals, machine construction, and others. Among the noneconomic ministries are those of internal affairs, foreign affairs, justice, health, culture — and defense (Constitution of the USSR, Articles 74–78). It is the Council of Ministers which is referred to as "the Government" of the Soviet Union.

Although the Constitution provides that the Council of Ministers shall be responsible to the Supreme Soviet and to the Presidium of the Supreme Soviet, in fact the "decrees and regulations" of the Council of Ministers are the operative legislation of the Soviet Union. It is the Council of Ministers, for example, which makes and executes the national economic plan (Constitution of the USSR, Articles 65, 66, 68, *b*). Also the Council of Ministers has general authority to "coördinate and direct the work of" its member ministries (Article 68, *a*). Thus it has authority over the particular ministries primarily concerned with military affairs, namely, the Ministry of Defense and the Ministry of Internal Affairs.

In addition, the Constitution gives certain specific military powers to the Council of Ministers. It provides that the Council of Ministers "shall fix the annual contingent of citizens to be called up for military service and shall direct the general organization of the armed forces of the country"; and also that it "shall set up, whenever necessary, special committees and chief administrations under the Council of Ministers of the USSR for economic and cultural affairs and for defense" (Article 68, *e* and *f*). The Council of Ministers also bestows higher ranks upon military personnel, up to and including the rank of general of the army.[2]

We know very little about the actual functioning of this important body. Presumably its members are consulted on matters that affect the interests of the organizations which they represent. Yet it seems unlikely that significant conflicts of interests among the various ministries would be resolved by a majority vote of all members. Basic policy decisions, such as the decision to increase substantially the availability of consumer goods during 1953, and the concomitant decision to expand foreign trade including the export of certain strategic goods — decisions which vitally affect a whole series of ministries, including the Ministry of Defense — are made not by the Council of Ministers but by the Presidium of the Central Committee of the Communist Party. In "executing and administering" such decisions, the Council of Ministers is undoubtedly controlled by its key members, whose influence derives both from the power of the ministries they represent and from their positions of leadership in the hierarchy of the Communist Party.

Is it, then, the Communist Party, and particularly its Presidium, which rules the Soviet armed forces? If the answer seems to be obviously yes, we are still left with the question, what does that answer mean?

The Presidium of the Communist Party has jurisdiction to make all political, economic, social, military, or other decisions affecting the Soviet Union. This jurisdiction derives from its leadership of the Communist Party, which is described by the Soviet Constitution as "the leading core of all organizations of toilers, both social and state" (Article 126). The Communist Party stands behind the entire complex constitutional and organizational structure of the Soviet state; without the Party that structure would be too unwieldy to stand.

Yet the Party structure itself is also complex and unwieldy. Theoretically, the Central Committee of the Communist Party, elected by local, regional, and republican Party representatives, designates a Presidium responsible to it. In fact, the Presidium controls the Central Committee, which in turn controls the subordinate Party organs reaching down through all levels of Soviet political, economic, and social life. These lines of authority seem simple enough: they run straight from top to bottom. The complexity lies in the fact that often important Party members bear direct responsibility for economic, administrative, military, or other matters; the Party chief on any particular level (city, region, republic) may be less influential in fact than the economic, administrative, military, or other official on that level — also a Party member — whom he is "controlling." Only at the very top — at the Presidium level — is there authority unqualified, and even there its distribution is precarious.

The relation between the Communist Party and the armed forces cannot be adequately summarized as a relation between ruler and ruled. In fact, the armed forces play an important role within the Party. This is indicated by the promotion on February 8, 1955, of Marshal Bulganin to the chairmanship of the Council of Ministers. Formerly Minister of Defense, Bulganin, it is true, rose to leadership as a Party bureaucrat rather than as a military expert. Nevertheless his political strength came to depend in part on the success of his military policies and on the efficiency of the armed forces under his direction. A more striking case is that of Marshal Zhukov, who replaced Bulganin as Minister of Defense. Zhukov became a deputy minister of defense in World War II, as a result of his earlier military exploits, and was then made a candidate member of the Central Committee of the Party. After Stalin's death he was made a First Deputy Minister of Defense and was promoted to full membership in the Central Committee. The overlapping of political and military authority may also be seen in the fact that the Central Committee has a Military Section which is apparently identical with the Chief Political Administration of the Ministry of Defense. At the same time, of some 235 members and candidate members of the Central Committee in 1953, twenty-seven were top military leaders, and of these twenty-one were also members of the Supreme Soviet.[3] (See the lists on page 10.)

Perhaps the best answer to the question of who rules the Soviet armed forces is that they are ruled in the last analysis not by any distinct governmental or political body or bodies but by a group of thirty or forty men who have succeeded in rising to positions of political and military leadership through various channels, including the channel of military administration. The channels through which they have risen and through which their authority flows — whether it be the Ministry of Defense, the Ministry of Internal Affairs, the Council of Ministers, the Central Committee of the Communist Party, the Presidium of the Central Committee, or even the honorary and semihonorary channels of the Supreme Soviet and its Presidium — are important means whereby their authority is maintained and conveyed. But their authority is essentially personal rather than organizational.

If this analysis is correct the promotion of Marshal Zhukov from Commander of the Odessa Military District to First Deputy Minister of Defense in 1953, and to Minister of Defense in 1955, is *not* to be interpreted as an indication of the increased political power of the armed forces or as a first sign of Bonapartism. Zhukov's promotion would appear rather as a means of increasing the popularity of the new leadership among all groups of the population (including the armed forces), a means of showing that the new leadership represented, as a unit, all major groups within the country. Similarly the rivalry between Malenkov and Beria in 1953 was not an organizational struggle between the Party and the MVD but a personal struggle for leadership over both. Likewise it would be a mistake, in our opinion, to visualize a struggle between the MVD and the armed forces.

Military leaders who in 1953 were members or candidate members of the Central Committee of the Communist Party and of the Supreme Soviet of the USSR

Marshal Bulganin, Minister of Defense
Marshal Voroshilov (without office in the army)
Marshal Zhukov, First Deputy Minister of Defense
Marshal Vasilevskii, First Deputy Minister of Defense
Marshal Sokolovskii, Chief of General Staff
Marshal Konev, Commander of the Carpathian Military District
*Marshal Bogdanov, Chief of Tank Troops
*Marshal Govorov, Commander in Chief of Ground Forces
*Marshal Budenny, Inspector of Cavalry
*Colonel General Zhigarev, Chief of Air Forces
*Colonel General Gorbatov, Chief of Parachute Troops
*Colonel General Malinin, Chief of Main Staff
*Colonel General Artem'ev, Commander of Moscow Military District
*Colonel General Luchinskii, Commander of Leningrad Military District
Marshal Meretskov, Commander of White Sea Military District
*Marshal Bagramian, Commander of Baltic Military District
*Marshal Timoshenko, Commander of Belorussian Military District
*Colonel General Chuikhov, Commander of Troops in Germany
*Colonel General Grechko, Commander of Kiev Military District
*Marshal Malinovskii, Commander of Primorskii Military District
*Admiral Basistyi, Deputy Minister for the Navy

Military leaders who in 1953 were members or candidate members of the Central Committee of the Communist Party but who were not members of the Supreme Soviet of the USSR

Admiral Kuznetsov, Deputy Minister for the Navy
*Colonel General Kuznetsov, former head of Chief Political Administration of the Ministry of Defense
*Marshal Nedelin, Deputy Commander of Artillery
*Admiral Sakharov, Deputy Minister for the Navy
*Colonel General Shtemenko, former Chief of General Staff
*Admiral Iumashev, former Minister of the Navy

---

* Candidate members.

The MVD, the armed forces, and the Party itself, as organizations, do not, it would seem to us, play independent political roles. The top leaders have the political initiative, and use the organizations to symbolize and to effectuate their policies. This certainly does not mean that the leaders are independent of the organizations through which they rose to power. It does mean that the leaders control the organizations, and not vice versa; further, that an individual leader at the top represents not a separate organizational hierarchy but the totality of such hierarchies; finally, that the relationship of the top leaders to each other is a personal one and is not determined by the relationship of the organizations to each other.

That the relationship of the top leaders is essentially personal rather than organizational may be demonstrated by two facts. The first is the fact that in the crisis of a war the organizational clothing was discarded and the leaders assumed naked personal authority. On June 30, 1941, eight days after the German invasion, as an emergency war measure "the entire plenitude of state power" was concentrated in the hands of a State Committee of Defense, established by decision of the Presidium of the Supreme Soviet, the Central Committee of the Communist Party, and the Council of Ministers. Stalin was named chairman and Molotov vice-chairman of the State Committee of Defense. Malenkov, Beria, and Voroshilov were the other three members originally named. Later Mikoian, Kaganovich, and Voznesenskii were added, and in 1944 Bulganin replaced Voroshilov. All state, Party, and military organs were subject to the orders of this committee, until it was dissolved by an edict of the Supreme Soviet of September 4, 1945.

The second fact which demonstrates that the relationship of the top leaders is essentially personal rather than organizational is that the division of functions among the various ruling bodies is so loose, and the overlapping so great, that the viability of the system can only be explained by the personal fusion of conflicting authorities. This is especially true of the division of military and nonmilitary functions. The armed forces are controlled ideologically and politically by Party organizations and political workers who are under the control of the Central Committee of the Communist Party; they are at the same time permeated with the Counterintelligence Sections of the Committee on State Security of the Council of Ministers; finally, they are subject to the hierarchy of command that culminates in the Minister of Defense. The system would fall apart if these three bodies were not fused by the close personal relations of their representatives at the top.

At the same time, these two examples of the essentially personal or *autocratic* character of Soviet military-political authority also testify to the important secondary role of the organizational or *bureaucratic* element. In normal times even the top levels of authority are clothed in organizational garments, with division of functions and diverging lines of control. At all times the intermediate and lower levels of authority are held in check through such specialization of function and control.

2. THE PLACE OF THE COMMUNIST PARTY IN SOVIET MILITARY ADMINISTRATION

The fusion of political and military authority at the higher levels through the appointment of generals and admirals to leading Party and government positions, and the reciprocal appointment of Party leaders (notably Marshall Bulganin) to the Ministry of Defense, does not necessarily determine the extent to which the armed forces at intermediate and lower levels are independent of, or subject to, Party control. On the whole the tendency both during and after World War II has been toward military self-government, or unity of command; however, in view of the long and complicated history of political commissars in the Soviet armed forces, it would be risky to conclude that the issue has been settled once and for all.

In the early years of the Revolution, an army independent of Party control would have been intolerable to the new regime — and indeed might well have overthrown it. On the other hand, from a military point of view it was absolutely necessary that the majority of the commanders of the new Red Army be drawn from the prerevolutionary officer class. It was thought that this dilemma could be resolved by the appointment of political commissars who would guard the ideology of the armed forces while leaving military matters to the commanders.

Although in 1917 the Provisional Government under Kerensky had introduced the institution of political commissars (then called front commissars), and they had apparently been used from the beginning of the Soviet period, the first document issued by the Soviet government defining their function was an order of the People's Commissar for War dated April 6, 1918.[4] This order stated that the military commissars were the direct political organ of the Soviet government in the army. "The military commissar," it stated, "shall see to it that the army does not become a thing apart from the entire Soviet system and that the various military establishments do not become foci of conspiracies or instruments against workers and peasants." Only orders countersigned by the commissars were to be considered valid. However, the ultimate responsibility for purely military orders was left to the commanding personnel, and the commissars' signature on such orders merely meant that there was no reason to suspect a counterrevolutionary motive behind the intentions expressed in the order. At the same time the commissars were made responsible for the prompt execution of all orders.

"The commissar shall see to it," the order further stated, "that all workers of the Red Army, from the top to the bottom, fulfill their work faithfully and energetically, that all funds are disbursed economically and under the most stringent supervision; that all military property is preserved with all possible care."

As Leon Trotsky, the People's Commissar for Military and Naval Affairs, wrote in 1918, "The military specialists will direct the technical end of the work, purely military matters, operation, work, and combat activities. The political side of the organization, training, and education, would be entirely subordinated to the representatives of the Soviet regime in the presence of its commissar."[5]

However, a few months later Trotsky revealed "a trend toward the interpenetration of the fields of activity of the commissar and the commander, toward the synthesis of these originally opposed elements of Red Army leadership." "Nobody ever prohibited the commissar from expressing his opinion regarding operation problems, giving advice, controlling the execution of an operation order, etc.," he stated, and at the same time, "a good commander cannot fail to take an interest [in political work], as the state of political work has a tremendous influence on the fighting efficacy of the unit." [6]

Even before the order of April 6, 1918, the All-Russian Bureau of Military Commissars was organized to direct and coordinate the work of the commissars.[7] On September 2, 1918, the bureau was replaced by the Political Section of the Revolutionary Military Council of the Republic (which governed the People's Commissariat for Military and Naval Affairs); in May 1919 the Political Section was in turn replaced by the Political Administration of the Republic (PUR). Under the Political Administration of the Republic, political departments were established in fleets, armies, divisions, and military districts. The PUR, with its higher centralized organization, was directly under the Central Committee of the Communist Party.

With the end of the Civil War in 1921–22, the Red Army was drastically reduced in size (it had reached a peak of 5.5 million in 1920) and by 1924–25 was reorganized on a new basis: a cadre army of 562,000 men serving from two to four years existed alongside a territorial militia which received intermittent training for eight to eleven months over a five-year period. (The territorial militia was finally abolished only in 1939.) Now emphasis was placed on securing Party members for responsible military positions. By 1928, 53.6 per cent of all regimental commanders, 71.9 per cent of all divisional commanders, and 100 per cent of all corps commanders were Party members; and more than 55 per cent of the total officer corps were either Party members, candidates for membership, or members of the Young Communist League. The proportion of Tsarist officers in the total officer personnel was reduced to 10 per cent, as contrasted with 76 per cent in 1918.[8]

In the 1924 reorganization of the army under Mikhail Frunze, shortly before he succeeded Trotsky as People's Commissar for Military and Naval Affairs, unity of command was established in principle and the military commissars were subordinated to the commanders.[9] Where the commander was con-

sidered especially trustworthy, he was to take charge of political work himself; otherwise, the military commissar was to
continue but was to confine himself (according to Kliment E.
Voroshilov, who succeeded to Frunze's office after the latter's
death in 1925) to "party-political and cultural-educational
work" and to discontinue the functions of control and observation of commanding personnel. The PUR survived, however,
and remained to a large extent independent of the People's
Commissar for Military and Naval Affairs and the Revolutionary Military Council of the Republic, on the one hand, and
of the local civilian Party organizations on the other.

Thus the Frunze-Voroshilov reform did not eliminate military commissars generally and left the principal responsibility
for political education outside the jurisdiction of the military
commanders. However, it did establish the supremacy of the
military commanders over the commissars.

On August 15, 1937, two months after the announcement of
the execution of Marshal M. N. Tukhachevsky and seven other
high-ranking Soviet generals as spies and traitors, and the
suicide of Ian Gamarnik, Deputy People's Commissar of Defense and head of the PUR, a statute was enacted redefining
the functions of military commissars.[10] This statute was designed to restore the military commissar to a position of equality with the commander and thus to strengthen Party control
over the army at a time when a large-scale military purge was
in progress and when the size of the army was being greatly
increased.

The 1937 statute declares: "For political direction and the
immediate execution of Party-political work in military units
. . . of the Worker-Peasant Red Army, military commissars
shall be appointed by the People's Commissar of Defense of the
USSR upon nomination by the Political Administration of the
Worker-Peasant Red Army" (Article 1). In the specifications
of the responsibilities and functions of the military commissar,
the statute gives him equality with the commander, but not
superiority over him. Article 12 states that all orders shall be
signed by the commander and the commissar, but that "since
the commander is the supreme chief of the unit [that is] subor-

dinate to him," orders shall be issued in his name. The statute further subjects the military commissar to orders and decrees of the People's Commissar of Defense of the USSR, the Political Administration of the Worker-Peasant Red Army, and also to "orders and instructions of those military councils, military commissars, and political organs, to which he is subordinated in service" (Article 11).

Of particular importance in view of the military purges [11] is the provision of the 1937 statute that the military commissar together with the commander "shall attest" the commanding personnel of the unit "and shall compose for each of them a detailed political characterization." "Attestations shall be signed by the commander and the military commissar of the unit" (Article 10). The same article provides that presentation of awards and promotions, as well as demotions, of commanding personnel shall be carried out by the commander and the military commissar jointly.

In August 1940, after the Finnish war, the office of military commissars was abolished and political work was declared to be in the control of the military council of the district. The PUR with its subordinate political departments was transferred into an administration of political propaganda, and the military commissars were renamed Deputy Commanders for Political Affairs.[12] It is commonly believed that this change was a response to the difficulties encountered by the system of dual leadership under combat conditions in Finland.

However, on July 16, 1941, less than a month after the German invasion of Russia, the earlier system was restored, on the consideration that the war "has made it imperative that our political workers do not limit their work to propaganda but take upon themselves the responsibilities of military work at the front as well." [13] (Indeed the mass defections of military units at the outbreak of the war are now a matter of common knowledge.) The 1941 statute stated that the new factors in the task of political workers "call for increasing its role and the responsibilities of the political workers, just as during the Civil War against foreign military intervention." Accordingly, the Political Administration of the Worker-Peasant Red Army and political sections were reintroduced; the institution of military commissars was reintroduced into all regiments and divisions, staffs, military schools and institutions of the Red Army; and the institution of political instructors (*politruki*) was introduced into companies, batteries, and squadrons.

Fifteen months later, in October 1942, however, the Presidium of the Supreme Soviet enacted an edict entitled "The Introduction of Strict One-Man Control and the Abolition of the Institution of Military Commissars in the Red Army." [14] This statute purported "to relieve commissars . . . of their functions" and again appointed them as deputies for political affairs under their respective commanders. It directed the military councils of army groups and armies to bestow upon political workers such military ranks as they were entitled to bestow, and to submit to the People's Commissar of Defense, for the purpose of bestowing commanding ranks, the qualifications of political workers of the rank of Chief Battalion Commander and above. Political workers trained in field operations were generally to be promoted to field posts, especially as company commanders and battalion commanders. Military training courses were to be established for a certain number of former commissars.

The 1942 statute introduced a system of political work in the Soviet armed forces which has remained in effect without basic changes ever since. Under this system, the Chief Political Administration of the Armed Forces is on the one hand the Military Section of the Central Committee of the Communist Party,[15] and on the other hand, part of the Ministry of Defense. Its departments include the following: a Propaganda and Agitation Administration for the supply of cultural and educational materials, for the staffing of certain military publications, and so forth; a section for academies and military instructional institutions which supervises military schools; and a section for work among members of the Young Communist League.[16]

The Chief Political Administration of the Armed Forces has a subordinate branch in each of the military districts into which the country is divided; the chief political administration of a military district works, in turn, through the political sections of the subordinate corps and divisions. The head of the chief political administration of a military district is generally also the deputy commander for political affairs (*zampolit*) of the district and a member of the three-man military council which governs the district. Similarly, the head of the political section of a corps or division is generally the zampolit of the corps or division. The members of the chief political administration of the district, including the zampolit, are appointed from above, and they in turn appoint the members and zampolits of the corps or division political section.

Thus the zampolit is subordinate not only to the commander of his military unit but also to the zampolit of the next higher military unit, who in effect appoints him. This principle of dual subordination runs from top to bottom.

At the levels of military district, corps, and division there exist, in addition, Party commissions, which direct the activities of Party organizations in the corresponding military units. These Party commissions are elected by Party conferences, representing the Party membership of the district, corps, or division. However, the work of these commissions is theoretically and practically under the control of the chief political administration or political section of the corresponding military unit, and the secretary (i.e., head) of the Party commission is invariably the zampolit of the corresponding military unit.

At the level of regiment, the chief political administration operates directly through the regiment zampolit and his assistants. The role of the Party commission is played by the regiment Party bureau, and that of the Party conference by the regiment primary party organ. The regiment zampolit controls the regiment Party bureau and is generally one grade above its secretary in military rank.[17] Although the primary Party organ of the regiment elects the secretary and members of the regiment Party bureau, as well as its own secretary, they are nominated by the regiment zampolit upon the recommendation of the division zampolit.[18]

During the war internal Party democracy was even further restricted than in peacetime. The Party secretaries in the army were replaced by so-called Party organizers, who were appointed, and the members of the Party commissions were also appointed. Instead of general Party conferences, special meetings of delegates were organized. The secretaries were reintroduced and the Party commissions were once again made elective by a resolution of the Central Committee of the Communist Party of August 22, 1946.[19]

At the battalion and company levels, the zampolit works directly through the primary Party organ of the battalion or company — i.e., without a Party bureau or corresponding department. The battalion or company zampolit exercises direct control over the Party activities of Party members and over the political activities of the entire unit. He is, as Major General D. I. Ortenberg wrote in 1948, "the representative of the political administration in the regiment and in the battalion." [20]

The main task of the zampolit is the political education of privates, noncommissioned officers, and officers. This purpose he achieves through political instruction, political information, group and individual discussion, lectures, reports, sessions and meetings, newspapers, and cultural-educational work. The zampolit organizes groups for political education, selects leaders and their assistants for these groups, leads seminars with them, and so on. He chooses subjects of political information and together with the commander prepares and leads gatherings and meetings of the personnel. He personally conducts the training of officers in Marxist-Leninist doctrine.

The tasks of the primary Party organs in the armed forces are, according to Ortenberg, the carrying on of propaganda and organizational work among the masses of the soldiers, the execution of party instructions as well as orders of the command, giving assistance to commanders in all their work, strengthening discipline, caring for the welfare of the soldiers, improving the political standards of the Party members and securing them a leading role in drill and discipline, and "active participation in the economic and political life of the country." "The Party organization secures through its Party influence and by its work an exemplary execution of tasks by the entire unit, and above all by the Communists and the Komsomols," he writes.[21]

Ortenberg lists four distinguishing features of Party organization and activity in the armed forces, as contrasted with Party organization and activity outside the armed forces.[22] First, the principle of election of leaders is abandoned except for the lower echelons. Second, Party organs in the armed forces are organized according to military units and not (as is the case outside the armed forces) according to geographical areas. Third, Party organs of the armed forces are at the same time organs of military command, and their leaders are part of the general military hierarchy — while outside the armed forces, Party organs operate chiefly behind the scenes and are separate from the economic, governmental and other organizations whose activities they are supposed to "guide." Fourth, the tasks of the Party organs in the armed forces are supposed to be limited to propaganda, education, morale, discipline, and similar matters, and do not extend to control of the service activities of commanders. In other words, one does not find the Party organs as such issuing directives regarding military operations — though outside the armed forces one does find Party organs issuing directives regarding (for example) economic operations.

Whether the line between political and military activities can always be maintained in practice is dubious. Ortenberg himself states: "There is not a single part of the unit's life upon which the political organs do not exert their influence. Military drill and political education are inseparably connected in our army."[23] The political officers and the secretaries and other officials of Party organizations in the army inevitably diminish to some extent, if only by their mere existence, the authority of the military commanders. In addition, the political personnel are there to see to it that the military commanders mind their ideological *P*'s and *Q*'s; an unfavorable report from a zampolit might hinder a company commander's chances of promotion.

Nevertheless, the Party units and Party workers within the armed forces are urged to concentrate on improving military discipline within a unified structure of command. An article on Party life in the army published in the newspaper of the armed forces "Red Star" on September 4, 1953, stated: "Party and

Komsomol organizations are obliged to strive for the strengthening of the authority of the commander, to help him in educating soldiers, in mobilizing them toward new successes in military and political preparedness." [24] The article was one of a series emphasizing military discipline and the principle of obedience to military law.

Two principal factors have served to reduce the authority of the political workers in the Soviet armed forces. One is the increase in Party strength within the officer corps as a whole. In October 1952 Marshal Vasilevsky reported to the Nineteenth Party Congress that 86.4 per cent of all officers were Party members or members of the Young Communist League. The experience of thirty-seven years of Soviet rule has shown that political commissars in the armed forces have been used in the past in times of political crisis and that the increased political stability of the armed forces has led to reduction in influence of political workers generally.

The second factor which has served to reduce the importance of the political workers is the existence of a parallel organization of security police, under the Committee on State Security, within all military units. The Chief Political Administration no longer has the functions of apprehending "subversives" but is confined to the task of political education — a task which may safely be subordinated to that of military training so long as the officer corps is politically reliable, but which may not safely be left to the military commanders themselves so long as the Communist Party continues to maintain central control over the circulation of thought in the Soviet Union. ·

3. THE PLACE OF THE SECURITY POLICE AND MVD TROOPS IN SOVIET MILITARY ADMINISTRATION

The Soviet security police play an important role in Soviet military administration by virtue of their almost unlimited power to arrest and denounce individual soldiers of whatever rank, coupled with their virtual independence of military command.

Since March 1954 all Soviet security matters have been under the jurisdiction of a special committee of the Council of

Ministers called the Committee on State Security.[25] From March 1953 to March 1954 they were under the jurisdiction of the Ministry of Internal Affairs (MVD). Prior to March 1953 they had been for some years under the jurisdiction of the Ministry of State Security, which had been established originally as a Chief Administration of the Ministry (then People's Commissariat) of Internal Affairs.[26]

These shifts of jurisdiction at the top have probably not affected substantially the structure of security controls in the armed forces. The Chief Administration for Counterintelligence of the Armed Forces is independent of the Ministry of Defense and operates through a Counterintelligence Administration in each military district and Counterintelligence Sections (called Special Sections, or, in abbreviation, "OO," before World War II, and SMERSH — an abbreviation for *Smert' Shpionam*, "Death to Spies" — during the war) in all armies, corps, and divisions. Apparently there are not Counterintelligence Sections at the regiment level and below; their functions are performed by assigned counterintelligence officers.[27]

According to the report of a former Soviet counterintelligence officer, the Counterintelligence Section in the division in which he served consisted of six officers and a platoon of fifteen to twenty riflemen! [28] He reports further:

> The officers of the OO lead a closed life, and what happens within their circle is rarely known to the rank and file of the army. They have their own Party organization, meetings of which are secret, as OO work is often discussed in them. The OO officers are not subordinated either to the commander of the unit to which they are attached or to the Party secretary of the unit Party organization. Party activities are undertaken separately by the OO Party organization.
>
> As far as is known, the OO head does not interfere in the affairs of the unit commander or his staff and has no influence on their tactical decisions. He does, however, gather information on the military condition of the unit, the political morale of the troops and their material and medical welfare. All this is done with the aim of preventing sabotage and wrecking.[29]

In pursuing this aim, the Counterintelligence Sections keep

in close touch with commanders, zampolits, and military procurators. They study the zampolit's reports on the political morale of the troops, keep dossiers on all officers, and investigate all "extraordinary happenings" such as serious accidents, desertions, self-infliction of wounds, thefts of military property, and the like.[30] The Counterintelligence Section may turn over to the so-called Special Board of the MVD, for secret administrative trial, persons suspected of counterrevolutionary activity. Clearance by the Counterintelligence Sections is a prerequisite to promotion.

The Counterintelligence Sections rely heavily on numerous secret informers, called *seksoty* (an abbreviation for "secret collaborators"), in the various military units.

The system of informing, together with the power of the security organs to arrest suspects and send them to prison or to labor camps by administrative sentence, "generates an atmosphere of insecurity from which even the most thoroughly indoctrinated Soviet military unit is not wholly free." [31] The fear which the security organs can inspire by a mere word is illustrated in the following incident recounted at the Eighteenth Party Congress in 1939 by Lev Mekhlis, the former head of the Chief Political Administration, in discussing some of the abuses of the purges of the late thirties:

> The representative of the Special Section in a certain regiment told the Commissar, Gashinsky, that he was after the club superintendent, a politruk by the name of Rybnikov. Gashinsky passed this on in confidence to the Party organization and Rybnikov was expelled by the Primary Party organization. It soon turned out that Rybnikov was not a bad Bolshevik and that the Special Section was after him . . . to get him to work in their department. The mistake was corrected, but only after Comrade Rybnikov was put to a lot of mental suffering.[32]

It is impossible to ascertain with any degree of precision the effect of the Counterintelligence Sections and informers upon the system of military administration. Their influence is apparently exercised through negative measures such as arrest, denunciation, and withholding of clearance, rather than through any positive formulation of policy or direct control of administration.

In addition to the secret police, there exists a separate organization of military police under the Ministry of Internal Affairs. Border guards, internal guards, and escort guards of the MVD are military personnel, subject to military law, with all the rights and duties pertaining to regular military service. Although they are called up by the Ministry of Defense, and are ultimately responsible to it, their operations are under the immediate supervision of the Chief Administration of Border and Internal Guards of the Ministry of Internal Affairs.

The precise division of responsibility between the Ministry of Defense and the Ministry of Internal Affairs with respect to border guards, internal guards, and escort guards of the MVD is impossible to determine from official sources or, indeed, from unofficial sources available to the authors. The Ministry of Defense customarily conscripts men annually for these troops, together with conscripts for the Soviet army and navy.* However, the day-to-day administration of their activities seems to be under the control of the MVD, to the extent, even, that they are subject to the jurisdiction of special MVD military courts. It should be noted that the MVD is also in charge of the regular civilian police.

4. THE STRUCTURE OF THE MINISTRY OF DEFENSE AND THE HIGH COMMAND

(a) *The Ministry of Defense.* The Party and the security police, each in its own way, exercise certain supervisory functions with respect to the military establishment, but neither can

---

* Some commentators interpreted the order of September 5, 1953, signed by Marshal Bulganin as Minister of Defense, calling up conscripts for the army, navy, and border and internal guard troops, as a sign that the latter troops were no longer under the direct control of the MVD. See *Pravda*, September 6, 1954. However, the same procedure has been followed in the past. See *Pravda*, September 4, 1940. In recent years the order of the Minister of Defense calling up conscripts has not been published, apparently for the reason that customarily this order also discharges military personnel whose term of service has expired. In fact in recent years many such personnel have not been discharged promptly, and it is probable that the Soviet government omitted publication of the annual order to avoid calling attention to this fact.

run it. Neither can give it the fighting power and efficiency which are its main reasons for being. It is only the professional military leadership — combat, technical, and administrative — which can in the long run build a powerful military organization. The gradual recognition of this fact by the heads of the Soviet state has resulted in the building up of a Ministry of Defense and a command structure which, despite pressures from the Communist Party and the security police, have achieved considerable stability and independence. The powers of the Ministry of Defense are declared in a 1934 statute issued by the Council of Ministers, which is still in effect with minor changes.[33] The following summary of these tasks is given in a 1950 Soviet textbook on administrative law.

Drafting plans for the development, construction, and equipment of the Soviet Army; organizing and constructing the armed forces; directing the organization of troop formations of constituent republics; developing and perfecting of all armaments and technical weapons; equipping the Soviet Army with all means of combat and providing it with all types of supplies;

directing the military and political training of servicemen and persons liable to military service, and the operational use of them in time of peace and war;

defense construction and organization of the anti-aircraft defense of the USSR;

induction into active service and the calling of reserves for training periods, assignment of inductees to the various branches of service and to military districts, establishment of the system of length of military service;

directing the medical and veterinary services of the army;

securing pensions and allowances of generals, officers, persons in extraterm service and their families, and various other problems related to the strengthening of the defensive might of the USSR.[34]

The 1934 statute defining the competence and structure of the Ministry of Defense increased the powers of the minister within the ministry, in accordance with the general trend in Soviet administration at that time and thereafter toward increased "one-man control" as contrasted with "collegiate" control by boards. Thus the 1934 statute abolished the Revolutionary Military Council of the USSR which, under the earlier statutes of 1923 and 1929, had been the governing board of the Commissariat.[35] Under the 1934 statute, commanders of troops are immediately subordinate to the Minister of Defense.

However, absolute singleness of control has not been an entirely undisputed principle of Soviet administration, military or civilian. The 1934 statute replaced the Revolutionary Military Council with a new Military Council, whose powers (declared in a separate statute) [36] are quite limited; it is an advisory organ under the chairmanship of the minister, its members named by the Council of Ministers on his recommendation, its meetings convened and adjourned at his order and its decisions issued and executed by him. In 1938, however, with a general restoration of a modified collegiate system in the Commissariats, a Chief Military Council was formed to govern the People's Commissariat of Defense.[37] During the war Stalin and Zhdanov were among its members, and Stalin also assumed the position of People's Commissar of Defense. The Chief Military Council apparently went out of existence at the end of the war, and the Military Council of the Ministry of Defense is apparently now made up merely of the Minister and Deputy Ministers of Defense. In March 1953 Marshals Vasilevsky and Zhukov were named Deputy Ministers of Defense under Bulganin.

On February 1, 1944, the Ministry (then People's Commissariat) of Defense was transferred from an all-union to a constituent republican status. This was a purely formal decentralization, corresponding to the *pro forma* establishment of national military units of the constituent republics. The USSR Ministry has retained jurisdiction over the organization of the defense of the USSR, the administration of the armed forces, and the drafting of basic rules for the organization of the republican military formations. The distinction between an all-union ministry and a constituent republican ministry is that the former acts through its own representatives in the republics and localities, while the latter acts through corresponding ministries of the various republics. The decentralization of the

Ministry of Defense was accompanied by a law conferring powers of foreign relations upon the constituent republics, and transforming from all-union to constituent republican status the Ministry (then People's Commissariat) of Foreign Affairs. These changes paved the way for independent representation of two constituent republics — the Ukrainian and the Belorussian — in the United Nations.

(b) *The High Command*.[38] The Minister and Deputy Ministers of Defense plan and operate the military establishment through a General Staff, which is charged with implementing, through detailed orders, the general directives of the ministry. Coördinate with the General Staff are the Chief Political Administration, referred to above, and the Chief Inspectorate, which is charged with keeping the Ministry of Defense informed on the state of readiness and efficiency of the armed forces.

The General Staff is divided into six sections: the Operations Administration, the Intelligence Administration, the Organization and Mobilization Administration, the Topographic Administration, the Signal Communications Administration, and the Historical Section. The two highest military academies — the Voroshilov Academy and the Frunze Academy — are also represented on the General Staff.

The six sections of the General Staff, as well as the Chief Inspectorate and the Chief Political Administration, are represented on the staff organizations of the headquarters of the various arms and services. These headquarters include Ground Forces Headquarters, Rear Services Headquarters, Army Air Force Headquarters, Long Range Air Force Headquarters, Civil Defense Headquarters, some logistical or technical headquarters for functions pertaining to both army and air force, and some independent administrative agencies, among them the Chief Administration for Personnel, the Chief Administration for Formation and Equipment of Troops, the Chief Administration for Hydrometeorological Service, and the Chief Administration for Military Tribunals.

The headquarters of the arms and services are staff agencies concerned largely with technical training and administration.

Under the ground Forces Headquarters are various administrations concerned with day-to-day administrative operations, as well as an administration for military schools. Under the Rear Services Headquarters are a large number of service and logistics agencies, concerned with transport, supply, finance, medical care, veterinary care, and the like.

The Ministry of Defense, with its General Staff and its arms and services headquarters, plans and operates the military establishment; that establishment itself, that is, the military units, is organized in military districts. A military district is the peacetime equivalent of an army group (a so-called "front") or army — or, correspondingly, a fleet or flotilla. Before World War II the Soviet Union was divided into nine military districts.

The Minister of Defense and his General Staff work through commanders of military districts (or army groups or armies). Though the commander of a military district has a command staff, with a chief of staff, deputy commander for political affairs, and others (such as artillery commander, tank commander, deputy commander for the rear, and others), the members are directly subordinate to him and not to the General Staff or its various headquarters.

(c) *The Military Council of the District.* In governing the military district, the commander of the district is supposed to operate through a three-man military council, of which he is chairman — not to be confused with the military council of the Minister of Defense. Under the 1937 law establishing the military council of the district,[39] that body is stated to be "the supreme representative of military authority in the district (fleet, army)," to which "shall be subordinated all military units and military installations located within the territory of the district (fleet, army)" (Article 3). Further, the military council of the district is stated to be "immediately subordinate" to the Minister of Defense (Article 5), rather than to the commander of the district. The prestige of the military council of the district is enhanced by the fact that the deputy commander for political affairs invariably serves as one of the three members.

Soviet sources do not reveal who the third member of the

military council is or by whom he is nominated. It would be valuable to learn whether he is primarily a military man nominated, perhaps, by the commander of the district or primarily a political figure nominated by the Communist Party leadership.

The military council of the district is charged by the 1937 statute with "full responsibility for the political-moral condition [and] constant preparedness for combat and mobilization of military units and military installations located within the territory of the district" (Article 4). It directs the selection of cadres, and "the education of Redarmymen and all officer personnel in the spirit of unlimited devotion to the Motherland and to the Soviet authority, in the spirit of merciless struggle against enemies of the People — spies, diversionists, wreckers" (Article 6, *c* and *d*). Further, it is in charge of technical and material supplies to military units in the district, civil defense, military training of civilians, and conscription of citizens for active military service (Article 6, *e, g, i,* and *k*).

The 1937 statute on military councils states that all orders for the district shall be signed by the commander of troops, one of the members of the military council, and the chief of staff of the district (Article 7); and that "since the commander of troops of the military district (fleet, army) is the supreme head of all troops and military installations located within the territory of the district (fleet, army)," orders shall be issued in his name (Article 8).

The importance of the district military councils was highlighted by the Edict on Martial Law of June 22, 1941, which vested in them all governmental functions in areas placed under martial law.[40]

Within the districts the Ministry of Defense has its organs of local military administration, which on the one hand are subordinate to the district military councils and on the other hand operate as military sections of the local governing councils.[41] The chief local organs of military administration are — since 1938 — the local military commissariats (as they are still called), which handle the registration and conscription of citizens for military service (see pp. 35 ff.).

CHART I   CONSTITUTIONAL LINKS OF THE SOVIET MILITARY SYSTEM

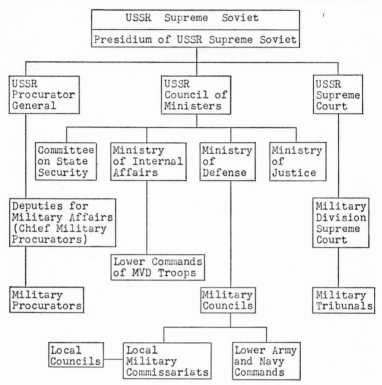

CHART II   THE COMMUNIST PARTY AND THE ARMED FORCES OF
THE SOVIET UNION

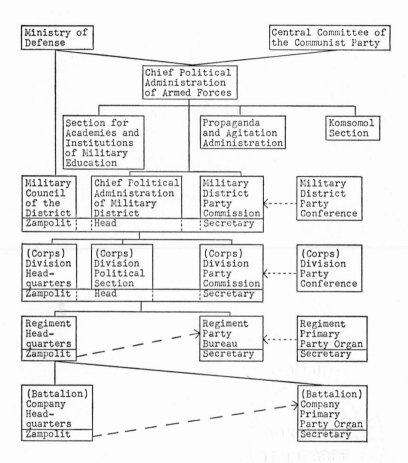

- - - - indicates election.

— — — indicates informal control.

CHART III   THE SOVIET HIGH COMMAND

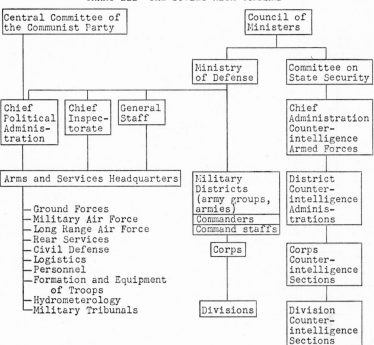

CHART IV THE PROCURACY OF THE SOVIET ARMED FORCES [a]
------indicates informal controls exerted upon the procuracy

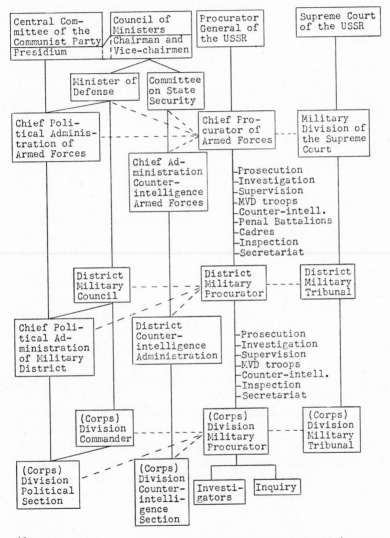

[a] See also N.S. Semenov, *Systema sovetskoi iustitsii* (System of Soviet Justice, Munich, 1953, in Russian), Chart 8.

5. THE MILITARY COURTS AND THE MILITARY PROCURACY

Soviet military administration is complicated by the division of functions among Communist Party organizations (with primary responsibility for political orientation and "morale"), State Security organizations (with primary responsibility for internal security), and the Ministry of Defense (with primary responsibility for military training and operations). This structure is further complicated by the allocation of the functions of prosecution and trial of military crimes to separate organizations — the military procuracy and the military courts — which are independent of the military command and subordinate ultimately to the Procurator General of the USSR and the Supreme Court of the USSR respectively. In addition the system of military law is under the general supervision of the Ministry of Justice of the USSR.

The creation of an independent hierarchy of permanent military courts, culminating in the Military Division of the Supreme Court, and of an independent hierarchy of permanent military prosecutors subordinate to the Deputies for Military Affairs of the Procurator General, reflects a general integration of military and nonmilitary law and a general policy of central control of all aspects of the social order. At the same time it must be recognized that the separation of administrative and judicial functions in the armed forces, and the control of military trials by agencies outside the Ministry of Defense, give to Soviet military law a degree of stability and objectivity which it might otherwise lack.

In terms of military administration proper, the military courts and military procuracy do not play a very significant role. In the administration of military discipline and military law, however, their role is a crucial one. The system of military discipline and law, and the organization and procedure of the military courts and the procuracy, forms the subject of detailed analysis in later chapters.

6. THE LAWS OF MILITARY SERVICE

(a) *The Principle of Universal Military Obligation.* Although the Bolsheviks were ardently antimilitarist before they came to power and, like other socialist parties of the time, called for the abolition of military service, once they established their own regime they immediately called for volunteers, and shortly thereafter for conscripts, to defend the new order against its foreign and domestic enemies. The first law on compulsory universal military service was enacted on May 29, 1918, and on June 12, 1918, a decree ordered the conscription of certain age groups "of workers and of peasants who do not exploit the labor of another." New laws on general conscription were introduced in 1922, 1925, 1928, 1930, 1939.[42] The 1939 law is still in force without substantial changes.

The system of military service worked out in the various laws from 1922 to 1930 imposed military service on "toilers" only, excluding the then disfranchised elements such as persons employing hired labor or leasing land, clergy and sons of clergy, sons of former Tsarist police, and others. The "nontoilers" were required to pay a special tax in lieu of military service. They were subject to mobilization into special work units in time of war.

The 1936 Constitution abolished class distinctions as a basis both of the franchise and of military service. Article 132 states that "universal military obligation shall be law" and that "military service in the armed forces of the USSR shall be an honorable duty of citizens of the USSR." Article 133 states: "The defense of the country shall be the sacred duty of every citizen of the USSR. Treason to the Motherland — violation of the oath of allegiance, desertions to the enemy, impairing the military power of the state, espionage — shall be punished with all the severity of the law as the most heinous of crimes."

The law of September 1, 1939, "on Universal Military Obligation" extends compulsory military service to all able-bodied male citizens of the USSR, without distinction of race, nationality, religious profession, education, social origin, and position (Article 3). Persons are subject to induction in the year of their nineteenth birthday, or, if they have completed secondary school, their eighteenth (Article 14). Privates and noncommissioned officers remain in the reserve up to the age of fifty (Article 10). Women who have had medical veterinary, or other special technical training, may also be called to service by the Minister of Defense (Article 13).

(b) *Active and Reserve Service.* Soviet military service is classified as either active service or reserve service. Different systems of active and reserve service are applicable to officers and enlisted men.

The duration of active service for enlisted men under the law on universal military obligation (Article 7) is as follows: for privates in the ground forces and MVD troops, two years; for noncommissioned officers in the ground forces and MVD troops, three years; for privates and noncommissioned officers in the military and naval air forces and the coast guard, four years; for privates and noncommissioned officers in the navy, five years.*

After completing his term of active service, the private or noncommissioned officer is transferred to the first category or second category reserve (Article 31). The following are assigned to the second category reserve: men who are physically handicapped but nevertheless fit for noncombat service in war time; men who are supporting two invalid or aged parents; able-bodied and eligible men in excess of the annual quota needed for the armed forces; and women who have had medical, veterinary, or technical training and who have registered and been accepted for military service.

Private and noncommissioned reservists are called upon periodically to spend from one to three months in training. The duration of each training period and the number of such calls depends upon the type of reserve (first or second category) and the age group to which the reservist belongs (Articles 33, 36, 37). Both first and second category reserve are divided into three age groups: the first under thirty-five years, the second from thirty-five to forty-five, and the third from forty-five to fifty (Article 32).

* See note *supra*, p. 24.

A different system of division into active and reserve duty applies to junior, field, and general officers. For example, second lieutenants and lieutenants are in active service only until the age of thirty and then go into a first group reserve until forty, a second group reserve until fifty, and a third group reserve until fifty-five; lieutenant colonels and colonels are in active service until forty-five, and spend another fifteen years in reserve evenly divided among first, second, and third groups; active service of generals ends at fifty or sixty and they remain in reserve until sixty-five (Article 41). Active age in the navy is generally five years higher (Article 42). Training periods of officers in reserve are for two to three months, depending upon the reserve group, the total training period not to exceed thirty-six months (Article 44).

(c) *Registration and Induction.* The registration and induction of citizens for military service, under the law of September 1, 1939, is in the hands of county or city military commissariats which work in conjunction with organs of local government but are subject to the officer commanding the military district or army or fleet. The records of all citizens liable for military service and all inductees are kept by military registration boards, which in the cities are connected with departments of the police and in agricultural localities and settlements with the village councils (Article 59). Conscription is carried out by induction boards of the county or city military commissariats; the induction boards are composed of the county or city military commissar as chairman, and the deputy chairman of the county or city executive committee of the local governing council, the head of the county or city section of the Ministry of Internal Affairs, the head of the county or city police, and two doctors assigned by the local health department (Article 21).

Induction starts each year during the months of January and February, when the county or city military commissariats issue warrants to appear before the induction board (Article 17). Medical examinations are performed, applications for deferments are considered, and family allowances are determined at the actual induction, which takes place between September fifteenth and October fifteenth (Article 15). Soviet émigrés report that induction is accompanied with band music and great fanfare.

Only two excuses are accepted for nonappearance before the induction board: illness proved by medical certificate, and "obstacles of a physical character" certified by the village council or the local police authorities (Article 20). An inductee may be three times rejected on medical grounds, but the third time he must be either declared entirely unfit for military service or assigned to the noncombat reserves (Article 24). Students of secondary schools may be granted a deferment until the end of their studies, up to the age of twenty (Article 29). Persons who support two invalid or aged parents may be exempted from active service and may be assigned instead to the reserve of the second category (Articles 26, 27). Persons who are arrested, deported, or banished, as well as persons who have been deprived by court of their electoral rights, may not be inducted during the period of their sentence (Article 30).

The 1939 law says nothing about exemption or deferment of students of higher educational institutions. A decree of the Council of Ministers of September 15, 1943, listed some eighty-five technical schools whose students were to be exempted from military service.[43] The authors have found no other legislation on this subject. Apparently exemptions, and not mere deferments, are given rather generously to students who are engaged in pursuits considered vital for general military purposes, while other students are subject to conscription in their eighteenth year, if they have then completed secondary school, whether or not they are in a higher educational institution.

Appeals from decisions of local induction boards may be taken to higher induction boards of districts, regions, territories, and republics; while the appeal is pending, execution of the decision is not suspended.

(d) *Preservice Training.* During the Civil War of 1918–1921, Trotsky introduced universal compulsory military training. This was probably the first attempt at total mobilization of an entire nation in modern times (though at that time members of the bourgeoisie were exempted). In the emergency of World War II, universal compulsory military training was again introduced. By decree of the State Committee of Defense of September 18, 1941, all men between sixteen and fifty years of age were made liable to military training, called *Vsevobuch* (an abbreviation for universal military training), under a Chief Administration of Universal Military Training.[44] The training was carried on without interfering with the normal occupation of the trainee, who was given a program of 110 hours lasting over a period of several months.

Since the end of the war the functions of the Chief Administration of Universal Military Training are apparently confined to preservice training, with civilian training left to the civil defense organization. The basic statute governing preservice training is the law on military service of September 1939, which prescribes that basic preparatory military drill shall be instituted for all students of the fifth to seventh grades for two hours per week during the school year, and that preservice training shall be instituted for all students from the eighth to the tenth grades, likewise for two hours per week.

According to a decree of the Council of Ministers of August 13, 1946, the primary training established for boys in the fifth through the seventh years of secondary school is confined to physical training and is not directly military training.[45] Students at the college and university level who have not had active military service are also required to take preservice training.

Preservice training is conducted by military personnel under the supervision of the Ministry of Defense. The training is incorporated into the normal school curriculum, and, in addition, the trainees are sent from time to time to camps for a period of five to ten days.

The following program of preservice training appeared on February 14, 1947, in the official periodical of the Chief Administration of Universal Military Training.

In the eighth grade students become acqainted with the organization of the armed forces of the USSR, with the rudiments of military discipline and the rules for the conduct of servicemen. They study the action of soldiers in formation without arms, the mechanism of the carbine, the methods and rules for firing it. In the ninth grade, in addition to the theoretical knowledge, the students acquire the practical training of the rifleman. Whenever the predraftees are assembled for training in camps (from five to ten days) they get practical training in the field under conditions which are very close to those of army service. In the tenth grade, by means of review, the theoretical knowledge acquired in the eighth and ninth grades is improved and the practical training is perfected. In addition, the mechanism of the submachine gun and the rules for firing it are studied and the student is given the fundamentals of military topography. . . . Physical training in the eighth to tenth grades is an inseparable part of the military training of the student and is directed toward the development of the physical qualities required of a soldier. By the character of the exercises the physical training is a continuation of the physical education which began with the first years of school. . . .

The subject matter of the curriculum must be taught in accordance with these basic requirements:

Students must be taught by means of demonstration, and must be taught only such things as are needed by the preservice trainee for the effective and conscientious performance of the soldier's actions within the first days of his military service. The training must go under strict observance of the rules and regulations of the armed forces of the USSR, and actual examples of military exploits of the Soviet soldiers during the great patriotic war must be used. . . .

A rating for each quarter of the academic year is given on the basis of observation of the progress made in each lesson. If the progress of the individual student is not quite clear, the instructor may, by additional assignments, and questions, check up on their knowledge. The review lessons provided for by the schedule should be used for this purpose. The progress in physical training is evaluated on the basis of tables of normal requirements established for basic exercises. . . .[46]

(e) *Military Preparatory Schools.** "On the eve of World War II steps were taken to establish special military and naval preparatory schools with a general educational program corresponding to the eighth through the tenth years of secondary school. Boys of ages fourteen to sixteen were eligible for admittance and, in addition to general subjects, they were to be taught military subjects and trained in military discipline.

* The following quotation is from United States President's Advisory Commission on Universal Training, *Report*, 1947, pp. 348–349.

Upon graduation they were supposed to go to the military academies for two or three years to become officers.

"On August 22, 1943, the establishment of ten additional military schools was ordered. In honor of the famous Russian general of the eighteenth century, these schools were called 'Suvorov Military Schools.' On December 1, 1943, the schools were opened. The schools are organized, as the order states, 'after the pattern of the former (imperial) Cadet Corps.' [47] The boys, primarily the orphans and children of generals and distinguished officers, are admitted at the age of ten years to become professional officers in the future. Thus the purpose of the school is 'to prepare boys for the military service in the capacity of commissioned officers and give them general education equivalent to the secondary school.' The course lasts seven years, during which the students must live in dormitories under conditions coming close to those in military barracks.

"The average capacity of each of the Suvorov Military Schools is 500 students, with a total capacity of 4500 for all schools. In 1943 the first four classes were opened and boys of the ages ten to thirteen were taken. The Suvorov Military Schools are located in Krasnodar, Novocherkask, Stalingrad, Voronezh, Kharkov, Yelets (called *Arlovskoe*), Kalinin, and Stavropol. These schools do not take the place of the numerous military schools which train adolescents to become officers upon graduation, but are established in addition to these to serve as preparatory schools."

In addition, Nakhimov Schools, named after a famous Russian admiral, were established in 1943 as naval preparatory schools, parallel to the Suvorov Schools.

(f) *Civil Defense*.[48] The Soviet civil defense organization is also, in part, an instrument of premilitary training. It is defined in the 1947 edition of the "Great Soviet Encyclopedia" as "a voluntary mass organization of citizens of the Soviet Union — to train mass reserves for the armed forces of the USSR and to strengthen the anti-aircraft and chemical warfare defense of the country." This organization, now called *Dosaaf*, was established in 1926 to popularize military knowledge both in the Red Army and among the population. It was formed from the earlier Military Scientific Society, the Society of Friends of the Air Force, and the Society of Friends of Chemical Defense and Industry, and was originally called *Osoaviakhim* (Society in Aid of Defense and of Aviation-Chemical Construction of the USSR).

In the twenties, Osoaviakhim organized the first Soviet attempts to study the stratosphere. In 1928 it took part in an expedition to save the dirigible "Italy," and in 1929 promoted a propaganda flight from Moscow to New York. It promoted the introduction of chemicals to combat vermin in agriculture, as well as research into defense against chemical warfare. In the early thirties, "study circles" were gradually replaced by training centers, schools, and rifle ranges. In 1929 Osoaviakhim contained 27,000 groups for the study of military science. By 1931, the organization had 14 glider stations, 40 flying fields, and 139 emergency landing fields. Its membership had increased from 2,950,000 in 1927 to 11,000,000. By 1936 it had over 550 towers for parachute jumping, and over 100 parachute stations.

According to Soviet sources, Osoaviakhim trained, prior to 1941, thirty-eight million citizens in the use of antichemical defenses, fire-fighting, and first aid to the wounded. It gave elementary training to tens of thousands of pilots and to hundreds of thousands of glider pilots and parachutists. Yakovlev, the famous Soviet aircraft designer, was introduced to aeronautics in Osoaviakhim. In addition, it is stated that more than six million so-called Voroshilov riflemen were trained by Osoaviakhim in the prewar years. During the war, Osoaviakhim is said to have prepared ninety-eight million Soviet citizens, ages eight to sixty, in anti-aircraft defense. Many of Osoaviakhim's training subdivisions were in the ranks of Partisans. With the expulsion of the Germans, the organization played a leading role in de-mining liberated territory.

In 1947, Osoaviakhim was reorganized into three groups, *Dosarm*, *Dosflot* and *Dosav*, serving the ground forces, the navy, and the air forces, respectively. In August 1951, the three bodies were remerged as Dosaaf. The membership as of 1947 was stated to be 16,000,000. Training in the use of rifles, submachine guns, mortars, and parachutes has been stressed in the postwar period, though sports activities have also continued on a large scale. In 1946 100,000 persons participated in rifle-shooting matches in Moscow, with 9,000 qualifying as sharp-shooters.

Dosaaf is administered by the Civil Defense Headquarters of the General Staff of the Ministry of Defense, and is controlled in each military district by the military council of the district. However, actual anti-aircraft operations are apparently under the immediate control of the Chief Administration of Local Anti-aircraft Defense (MPVO) of the Ministry of Internal Affairs, which during the war directed the local units in factories, buildings, dwelling houses, and so forth. General supervision of MPVO is in the local governing bodies, that is, the executive committees of the city and county councils.[49]

II

SOVIET MILITARY DISCIPLINE

Soviet military law resembles that of the United States and of European countries generally in distinguishing between those military offenses which are punishable only after trial by a court-martial and those which are subject to disciplinary or nonjudicial punishment by a superior officer. The Soviet system differs from that of the United States, however, though not from that of some European countries, in defining disciplinary offenses and punishments in a special so-called Disciplinary Code.

A remarkably vivid picture may be derived from the Soviet Disciplinary Code of the kind of military discipline and military spirit which is officially demanded of the Soviet armed forces. The picture gains perspective through comparison of the most recent Disciplinary Code, that of 1946, with its three predecessors, those of 1919, 1925, and 1940.[1]

Each of these four codes marks an end of a period in the development of the Soviet armed forces. The first was issued in the midst of the Civil War, when the Revolutionary Red Army under the leadership of Leon Trotsky had finally emerged from infancy as an effective fighting force. The second was published under Mikhail Frunze as part of his reorganization of the Soviet armies during the relatively stable period of the mid-twenties; although called "provisional," it remained in force for fifteen years, surviving the succession of Kliment E. Voroshilov as head of the People's Commissariat for Army and Navy Affairs (in 1934 renamed People's Commissariat of Defense). The experience of the Finnish War led to the issuance of a new Disciplinary Code in 1940, under Semen K. Timoshenko's short-lived leadership of the People's Commissariat of Defense. World War II tested this code and apparently it was found wanting; it was substantially revised in the 1946 edition, under Nikolai Bulganin, who in 1946 succeeded Stalin as People's Commissar (later Minister) of Defense. The dates of the two latest codes indicate with what rapidity the Soviet military leaders draw conclusions from combat experience and put them into effect.

The four codes contain elements of marked similarity and elements of marked diversity. Some changes introduced in the 1925 code were abandoned in the 1940 code — only to be restored in the 1946 code. The 1946 code is considerably larger than its predecessors.[2] Nevertheless, there are some important trends which are more or less continuous. These trends may be listed as follows:

The deëmphasis of revolutionary ideas of class struggle, socialism, and internationalism as the basis of military discipline, and the reëmphasis of patriotism and personal responsibility;

The deëmphasis of camaraderie of all troops and the reëmphasis of distinctions of military rank;

The deëmphasis of rights of offenders and the reëmphasis of duties, including the absolute duty of obedience;

The general increase in severity of disciplinary penalties;

The increase in the severity of the procedure for imposing such penalties.

Among the most important features which all four codes have in common are the entrusting of disciplinary powers to non-commissioned as well as commissioned officers, the specification of particular disciplinary powers of individual ranks, and the definition of rewards for meritorious conduct.

1. THE SOVIET THEORY OF MILITARY DISCIPLINE

It was the original Bolshevik theory that the Red Army should be motivated in its conduct by a spirit of revolutionary zeal. This theory was in part a response to the revolutionary situation of 1917. The Bolsheviks sought to disrupt the Russian Army, end the war, and thereby bring on an international proletarian revolution. They recruited many of their supporters from the ranks of disaffected soldiers — and especially deserters from the defeated armies first of the Tsar and later of the Provisional Government, the men who, in Lenin's words, "voted for the Revolution with their feet." Also the tactics of revolution, as taught by Marxism, called for breaking up the discipline of the old military organization and substituting for it a new military organization with a new discipline.

After the abdication of the Tsar in March 1917, the Bolsheviks were among the leaders of those who clamored for drastic changes in military discipline. Partly out of sympathy for such changes but chiefly because of the necessity of meeting the demands of a discontented and half-defeated army, the Provisional Government under Kerensky permitted self-government among the troops, restricted the powers of officers, introduced political commissars to represent the government in the army, abolished the death penalty, permitted enlisted men to sit on courts-martial, and introduced a general spirit of camaraderie into the armed forces.

These reforms were continued and expanded by the Bolsheviks for a brief period after their seizure of power. Within six weeks the new regime introduced the election of officers and abolished all ranks, insignia, and decorations.[3] Early in 1918 a "Workers' and Peasants' Army" was ordered to be formed on a volunteer basis.[4] The official oath of this army, adopted on April 22, 1918,[5] began with the words, "I, son of the toiling people and citizen of the Soviet Republic." "Before the toiling classes of Russia and of the whole world," the new revolutionary soldier pledged himself "to direct all my acts and thoughts to the great goal of liberation of all toilers," and "in the struggle for the Russian Soviet Republic and for the cause of socialism and the brotherhood of peoples to spare neither my strength nor my life itself."

It soon became apparent to the Soviet leaders that revolutionary zeal alone, however, would not win the Civil War, which just at that time, in April and May 1918, began to take on serious proportions. On May 29, 1918, conscription was decreed.[6] It soon became necessary to cope with an immense number of desertions, and on December 25, 1918, in its second decree on desertion, the Soviet government restored the death penalty for that crime.[7] Soldiers' self-government now came to be frowned on by the same leaders who had risen to power on its back.[8] In 1920 Lenin told English newspapermen: "A war is a war; it demands an iron discipline."

The restoration of "iron discipline" ended the experiments started by the Kerensky government, but by no means signified the abandonment of the conception of a revolutionary army. The 1918 oath retained its significance. The leaders continued to demand the allegiance of the troops to the cause of international socialism. The difference now lay in the recognition that no army can function without strict obedience, and that strict obedience cannot be effectively maintained unless a system is established for the punishment of disobedience. These elementary truths were embodied in the 1919 Disciplinary Code, without, however, blurring its main thesis: that underlying obedience and punishment, underlying all military discipline, was the revolutionary class-consciousness of the proletariat-in-arms. "Discipline in the Workers' and Peasants' Red Army," the code stated, "rests upon . . . boundless devotion to the socialist soviet system and upon the consciousness of the necessity of the heaviest personal sacrifices for the sake of total liberation of the entire toiling class from the yoke of the capitalist system." [9]

Similarly, the 1925 code stressed class-consciousness as the basis of Soviet military discipline. "In the armies of monarchies and bourgeois capitalist republics," it stated, "discipline is based upon the class subjugation of the rank and file to the feudal-bourgeois officers' corps. The less class-conscious a soldier of a capitalist army is, the better he complies with the duties of a defender of the capitalist system." [10] On the other hand, "the discipline of the Red Army is a new discipline of a Workers' and Peasants' State; this discipline is not based upon class subjugation but upon the conscious understanding by all servicemen of the aims and importance of the Workers' and Peasants' Red Army. The more [class-] conscious a soldier of the Red Army is, the better he fulfills his duties toward the socialist state, [and] the more efficient is the Workers' and Peasants' Red Army."

In the mid-1930's significant changes took place in the Soviet theory of military discipline — changes which correspond to a fundamental reorientation of Soviet concepts generally. The revival of Russian national military traditions was reflected in a shift of emphasis away from proletarian internationalism and class-consciousness toward Soviet patriotism and toward discipline for its own sake. This shift did not take place all at once. The adoption of a new military oath in 1939, and the 1940 and 1946 Disciplinary Codes mark successive stages in its accomplishment.

The military oath of January 3, 1939,[11] sworn by all units of the Red Army on the following February 23 (Red Army Day), drops the revolutionary appeal of the earlier oath. The Soviet soldier is no longer required to swear as a "son of the toiling people," and his oath is no longer taken in the name of the toiling classes of the "whole world"; nor must he swear to devote himself to the "liberation of all toilers" or "the cause of socialism and the brotherhood of peoples." He now takes his oath simply as "a citizen of the Union of Soviet Socialist Republics," pledging himself to be "dedicated to my people, to my Soviet Motherland and to the Worker-Peasant Government." (The 1947 revision substitutes the word "Soviet" for "Worker-Peasant.") The new text stresses the qualities of a good soldier as such; the Soviet soldier pledges himself "to be an honorable, brave, disciplined, and alert warrior, strictly to guard military and state secrets, to fulfill without demur all military codes and orders of commanders and superiors." He pledges himself to defend his "Motherland" (*rodina*) "manfully, ably, with dignity and honor, not sparing my blood nor my life itself in order to achieve full victory over enemies."

The 1918 oath is a product of a political mind, the 1939 oath of a military mind. Although it may seem verbose to a United States soldier, whose oath of enlistment is not half as long, it is doubtless an effective instrument for the moral education of Soviet troops, each of whom in turn must read it aloud in an elaborate ceremony.[12] Also it is considered to have legal significance, and is cited as one of the basic documents of military law.

The 1940 Disciplinary Code retained some traces of the political concept of the earlier codes. "Soviet military discipline," it declared, "is founded upon the integrity of the class interests of the entire personnel of the Red Army and upon its utmost devotion to its own people and upon the feeling of high responsibility of every man in the service for the defense of the Socialist Fatherland with which he is entrusted. . ." [13] But in this context "class interests" and "socialism" seem to have lost much of their general meaning and to have become terms of art to distinguish the Soviet from the non-Soviet world. "Therefore," the code provision continues, "Soviet discipline must be higher, firmer, and marked with severer and harsher requirements than discipline in other armies based upon class subjugation."

The 1946 code abandons the notion of a special Soviet socialist military discipline. It states: "Military discipline is founded on recognition by each serviceman of military duty and personal responsibility for the protection of his Motherland — the Union of Soviet Socialist Republics." [14] No indication is made that Soviet military discipline differs from that of other countries. The definition and general requirements of military discipline are stated with reference to military discipline as such and not to a special Soviet form of it. The language and style of the general provisions of the code are strongly reminiscent of the latest prerevolutionary Russian model, the Imperial Disciplinary Code of 1869.[15]

2. DISTINCTIONS OF RANK

Although military necessity compelled the reluctant recognition of relationships of superiority and inferiority, the 1919 Disciplinary Code placed heavy stress on the spirit of equality. The terms "officer" and "general," abolished in 1918, remained absent from the code; the commanding personnel continued to be called commander, squad commander, company commander, corps commander, army commander, and so forth, according to the type of job they performed.[16] Saluting was eliminated, and all personnel were addressed as "comrade." Only "a mutual respect and courtesy between all military personnel" was required.[17] All personnel were given the right to wear plain clothes when off duty.[18] It was stated in the code that "a soldier of the new army does not for a single moment lose his membership in the Communist machine." [19] The code provided the same penalties for all personnel,[20] and one of its most important innovations was the institution of "Comrades' Courts" where men charged with lesser disciplinary offenses were tried informally by their fellows.[21]

The trend in all the subsequent Disciplinary Codes has been toward increasing differentiation of rank and insistence upon respect for rank. However, this trend became sharply defined only after 1935, when the traditional military ranks of lieutenant, captain, colonel, and the like, were restored.[22] Only in 1940 was the title "general" reintroduced,[23] and the duty to salute imposed.[24] In July 1943 the title "officer" was restored,[25] together with the traditional Russian officers' insignia of rank, the gold braid epaulets.[26] Also the term "soldier" (*soldat*) has been reintroduced to refer to army privates, instead of the term "Redarmyman" — a change which preceded the adoption of the name "Soviet Army" to replace "Red Army." [27]

The 1946 Disciplinary Code declares the duty of respect toward officers, and specifically includes the requirement of the salute as essential to military discipline.[28]

Perhaps the most striking symbol of the reëmphasis of distinctions of rank is the restoration in the 1940 and 1946 codes of the Tsarist institution of Officers' Courts of Honor. The 1940 code only mentions these courts in passing,[29] but the 1946 code devotes an entire chapter to them.[30] They are instituted "for the guarding of the dignity and honor of the rank of officer," and they have jurisdiction over "offenses unworthy of the rank of officer or degrading to military honor or incompatible with the concept of morality." [31] Generally considered to be representative of a feudal military organization, the Officers' Courts of Honor are the antithesis of the Redarmymen Comrades' Courts, which are mentioned only in passing in the

1940 code [32] and not at all in the 1946 code. The 1925, 1940, and 1946 codes have all distinguished between disciplinary penalties applicable to privates, noncommissioned officers, and officers.

More important than any of the code provisions as an indication of the actual differences between the various ranks, and also of the relationship between officers and men, are the distinctions in privilege and remuneration. During World War II junior officers up to and including the rank of captain lived with the troops in a very close comradeship and enjoyed relatively few advantages in respect to privileges and allowances, although the distinctions in pay were considerable.[33] The main differentiation started with the rank of major. Generals and admirals form a special group, and the 1946 Disciplinary Code consistently refers to "officers, generals, and admirals." [34]

The establishment after the war of special military schools for the sons of officers and others has undoubtedly enhanced the distinction of rank, and may even help to create a hereditary officer class in the Soviet Union.[35]

3. DISCIPLINARY DUTIES

(a) *The Absolute Duty to Obey.* The disorganization of the Russian armies in 1917 had the effect upon the soldiers of making them feel "free," which to them meant that they did not have to obey anybody's orders. In building a new military organization, the Bolsheviks did not immediately impose an absolute duty of obedience. Under the 1919 Disciplinary Code a subordinate was required to execute only "service" orders and perform "service duties," and was excused for refusing to execute "a command which was directed against the Soviet Government" or was "obviously criminal in its nature." [36] The 1925 code dropped the 1919 restriction on types of orders and duties to be performed, but excused refusal to obey an order if it was "criminal in its nature," eliminating the word "obviously." [37]

The 1940 Disciplinary Code started a reverse trend. It provided that every command must be executed regardless of its contents, stating in Article 8 that "subordinates must unconditionally obey their commanders," and in Article 6 that "the order of the commander is law for the subordinate. He must execute it without reservation, precisely and promptly." [38] The 1946 code preserves the language of Article 8 of the 1940 code, though it drops the old Article 6.[39]

Some mitigation of the consequences of disobedience is provided in the 1946 code. Under the 1940 code, failure to execute any order was a crime to be tried by a military tribunal,[40] whereas under the 1946 code minor transgressions may be regarded as disciplinary offenses at the discretion of the commander giving the order.[41] Further, the 1946 code somewhat lightens the 1940 provisions that "in case of disobedience, open resistance, or malicious breach of discipline, the commander has the right to take all measures of coercion, including the application of force and weapons," [42] and that in the event of the exercise of that right the commander "shall not be responsible for the consequences." [43] The newer code states that a commander may use a weapon only in an "extreme case which does not permit delay," and that every such instance must be immediately reported to the next superior officer in the chain of command.[44] Also, the 1946 code modifies the 1940 provision that "a commander who does not . . . take active measures for the restoration of order shall be tried by a military tribunal." [45] The newer code states: "A commander who does not take active measures for the restoration of order and discipline shall bear responsibility for that." [46] This change makes possible the imposition of a disciplinary penalty for such failure, and not (as in 1940) compulsory trial by court-martial.

Together with the trend toward unconditional obedience, there has gone a relaxation of the protection of enlisted men against excesses by commanding officers. The 1919 code stated that a commanding officer who exceeds his power "shall be handed over for trial." [47] The 1926 and 1940 codes made such transgression punishable either by disciplinary action or by court-martial.[48] The 1946 code states merely that an officer who exceeds his powers "shall bear responsibility for that." [49]

(b) *General Duties.* The first three codes dealt only in very general terms with the duties required by military discipline, embracing them in a single article of Chapter 1 (General Principles). The 1919 code listed as general duties the observances of all requirements of law, strict execution of service orders of commissars and commanders, and conscientious and conscious performance of all service duties.[50] The 1925 code added to these the safeguarding of military secrets.[51] The 1940 code was more strongly worded than its predecessors in this respect, providing that "Soviet discipline imposes the duty of solid knowledge and exact execution without any reservation whatsoever of the military oath, military codes and regulations, and all orders and decrees of superiors and seniors; of maintaining strictly the order established in the army and of causing others to abstain from violating it; of executing conscientiously all service duties and assignments; of keeping military and state secrets strictly; of safeguarding military property and the national domain by all means." [52] The 1940 code also imposed on the commander the duty "continuously to inculcate in his subordinates the spirit of execution of all requirements of military discipline," and stated that "the commander is responsible for his subordinates; he must always be exacting, severe, and just to them; he must inflict penalties upon those who are indolent or who violate discipline; and must encourage those who display merit." [53]

On the general duties of all military personnel, the 1946 code requires, in addition to the requirements of the 1940 provision, each serviceman "staunchly to bear all burdens and deprivations of military service, not to spare blood or life itself in fulfilling military duty, to be honorable, truthful, and to study conscientiously the art of war . . . strictly to observe the rules of military courtesy and saluting." [54] The duties of commanders are stated more or less as in the 1940 code, with the omission of the statement that the commander is responsible for his subordinates.[55]

(c) *The Duty to Report Irregularities in the Procurement System.* A new and unusual provision in the 1946 code states that servicemen who discover plunder or spoilage of military equipment, illegal use of funds, or other apparent misdeeds in the military procurement system shall be required to report such matter in the chain of command, "and may send a written report to a superior commander." [56] If by help of such reports abuses or deficiencies are removed, the serviceman is to be given a reward,[57] but if he intentionally makes a false report he "shall be held responsible." [58] On the other hand, "a commander who committed an apparent injustice or illegal act toward a subordinate because of his complaint or report shall be held strictly responsible." [59]

4. DISCIPLINARY PENALTIES AND REWARDS

(a) *Penalties.* A disciplinary penalty is defined in the 1940 code as "a punishment imposed upon servicemen by authority of the direct or immediate commander to whom such men are temporarily or permanently subordinate." [60] This definition is for some reason omitted in the 1946 code and no substitute is offered. In both codes, however, it is stated that disciplinary penalties shall be inflicted for offenses committed by a serviceman which are not subject to trial by a court-martial.[61] The decision whether an act of a serviceman merits a criminal trial and not merely disciplinary punishment rests in part with the superior, who in borderline cases has the right to determine whether a disciplinary punishment is sufficient or whether the delinquent shall be tried by court-martial.[62]

The omission in the 1946 code of the earlier provision that "the disciplinary penalty is an educational measure" [63] indicates the weakening of one of the more significant of the revolutionary ideals. In fact, the severity of the penalties have in general (though not in all respects) increased with each successive code. The 1919 code provided for six types of penalties, of which the last was of a general character.[64] These were applicable to all ranks. In 1925, more than ten types of penalties were listed for each of three groups of personnel,[65] and in 1940 approximately the same number were listed for five groups.[66] The 1946 code presents a less diversified system which corresponds closely to that of the Imperial Code of 1869.[67]

The three latest codes have listed separately the penalties which may be imposed on different ranks. The 1946 code provides separate sets of penalties for privates and privates first class,[68] for sergeants and technical or master sergeants,[69] for noncommissioned officers in extraterm service,[70] for officers,[71] and for generals and admirals.[72]

PENALTIES LISTED IN THE DISCIPLINARY CODES OF 1925, 1940, AND 1946 [a]

1925	1940	1946
Privates and Privates First Class		
1. Warning	1. Personal reprimand	1. Personal reprimand
2. Reminder	2. Personal reprimand in front of unit	2. Restriction to quarters up to one month
3. Reproof	3. Restriction to quarters up to 6 weeks	3. Extra duty (excluding guard or sentinel duty) or extra detail up to 5 assignments
4. Reprimand	4. Extra detail up to 8 assignments	
5. Personal reprimand in front of unit	5. Simple confinement up to 20 days	4. Simple confinement up to 20 days
6. Restriction to quarters up to 1 month	6. Strict confinement up to 10 days	5. Strict confinement up to 15 days
7. Extra detail up to 5 assignments	7. Handing over to Red-armymen's Comrades' Court	6. Reduction in rank (for private first class)
8. Confinement up to 20 days		
9. Reduction or elimination of regular furlough		
10. Placing of name on blackboard for a period up to 1 month		
11. Reading of record of offenses in front of unit		
12. Reading of record of offenses at festival gathering		
Sergeants and Technical or Master Sergeants		
1. Warning	1. Personal reprimand	1. Personal reprimand
2. Reminder	2. Restriction to quarters up to one month	2. Restriction to quarters up to one month [b]
3. Reproof	3. Extra detail up to 8 assignments	3. Extra duty (excluding guard or sentinel duty) or extra detail up to 3 assignments
4. Personal reprimand	4. Reprimand in order of the day	
5. Personal reprimand in front of unit	5. Simple confinement up to 20 days	4. Simple confinement up to 20 days
6. Extra detail up to five assignments	6. Strict confinement up to 10 days	5. Strict confinement up to 10 days [b]
7. Confinement up to 20 days	7. Handing over to	6. Demotion in command
8. Omission of a presentation for promotion		

1925	1940	1946
9. Demotion in command	Sergeants' Comrades' Court 8. Reduction in rank 9. Reduction in command 10. Removal from command with reduction in rank to a private	7. Reduction in rank to private inclusive

Noncommissioned officers in extraterm service

Not in a separate group	1. Personal reprimand 2. Extra detail up to 4 assignments (excluding sergeant majors) 3. Reprimand in order of the day 4. Reduction of a regular furlough by the maximum number of 15 days 5. Simple confinement up to 15 days with the obligation to perform duty and a reduction of 25% of the basic daily pay for every day of confinement 6. Strict confinement up to 10 days with a 50% reduction of the daily basic pay for every day of confinement 7. Handing over to Sergeants' Comrades' Court 8. Reduction in rank for one grade 9. Reduction in command 10. Transfer into reserve	1. Personal reprimand 2. Simple confinement up to 20 days 3. Demotion in command 4. Transfer to reserve for the remainder of term of service

Officers

1. Warning 2. Reminder 3. Reproof	1. Personal reprimand 2. Reprimand in the order of the day	1. Admonition and personal reprimand either oral in the officers' assembly or

1925	1940	1946
4. Strict reproof 5. Personal reprimand 6. Written personal reprimand 7. Reprimand in the order of the day 8. Personal reprimand in officers' assembly 9. Extra detail up to 2 assignments 10. House arrest up to 7 days 11. Confinement up to 20 days	3. Reduction of a regular furlough by the maximum number of 15 days 4. House arrest up to 15 days with the obligation to perform duties and a 50% reduction of the basic daily pay for every day of arrest 5. Postponement of the regular promotion for 1 year 6. Submission to Officers' Court of Honor 7. Loss of seniority allowance for a period up to 6 months 8. Removal from command 9. Reduction in rank for one grade 10. Demotion in command 11. Transfer into reserve or retirement	written in the order of the day 2. House arrest up to 20 days 3. Confinement up to 20 days 4. Warning of inadequate discharge of duty 5. Demotion in command 6. Reduction in rank
	Generals and Admirals	
Not in a separate group	1. Warning 2. Personal reprimand 3. Reprimand in order of the day 4. Loss of seniority allowance for a period up to 6 months 5. Removal from command 6. Transfer into reserve or retirement	1. Admonition and personal reprimand, oral, written, or in order of the day 2. Warning of inadequate discharge of duty 3. Demotion in command

ª The translation is rendered more difficult by the fact that the Russian texts are not consistent in using the same expressions for particular punishments. Certain of the Russian terms do not have a precise meaning; thus the distinctions between warning, reminder, reproof, and reprimand are no clearer in the original than in the translation.

ᵇ Not applicable to technical sergeants and chief petty officers.

It may be seen from the accompanying table that while the 1946 code relaxes some features of the 1940 code, nevertheless, taken together, the penalties of the 1940 and 1946 codes are considerably more severe than those of the two earlier codes. Also, certain educational penalties of the 1925 code applicable to privates are conspicuously absent in the later ones: placing of the delinquent's name on a blackboard for one month or less, and reading of his record in front of the formation or at a festival gathering.[73] The most notable change is the granting of power to a superior to reduce a subordinate (including officers) in rank by way of disciplinary penalty. The 1940 code spoke of reduction to the next lower grade, but the 1946 code removes this limitation.

Finally, the 1946 code introduces for the first time a general authority in officers of the grades of regimental commander or above to remove delinquent subordinates from their commands. The authority is restricted to "urgent cases not permitting any delay"; the action must be reported and explained immediately, and the superior who removes a subordinate from his command without adequate reason is said to be "responsible" for his decision.[74]

The right of a commander to use weapons — that is, to shoot if necessary — in an "extreme case" of open disobedience (Article 7 of the 1946 code) is not listed among disciplinary penalties.

(b) *Rewards.* One of the most significant innovations of the Soviet Disciplinary Codes is the specification of rewards for meritorious conduct. In the first codes the chapter on rewards preceded that on punishments, the emphasis thus being placed on incentives rather than repression. The 1925 code put the chapter on punishments first but in the following chapter listed thirteen rewards, including promotion, a special written commendation certifying the particular accomplishments performed, furloughs, decoration, a personal photograph in front of the unfurled banner of the unit, and a personal engraved firearm.[75] The 1940 code reduced the number of rewards to six, omitting written commendations, photographs, and the like, and introducing rewards of more prosaic character, including a valuable gift or sum of money, promotion, and remission of a previously imposed disciplinary penalty.[76] The 1946 code retains these rewards and restores some of the earlier ones. It also divides rewards into two groups: those for privates, noncommissioned officers and warrant officers, and those for commissioned officers and generals and admirals.[77]

The first of these two groups includes the following rewards: oral commendation in front of the formation or in the order of the day, remission of a previously imposed disciplinary penalty, a pass up to two days, a furlough for up to ten days excluding travel time, testimonials of merit for graduates of training schools or for men released into the reserve, valuable gifts or money rewards, a personal photograph in front of the unfurled unit banner, notification of the man's home town or former place of employment of his exemplary performance and of the rewards granted to him, and military decoration. In addition, the names of graduates of schools may be placed on the honor roll of the school.

5. PROCEDURE FOR IMPOSITION OF PENALTIES

The procedural requirments for "company punishment" are, by the very nature of the punishment, not very elaborate in any system of military law; otherwise, the distinction between judicial and nonjudicial punishment would tend to disappear and the enforcement of discipline speedily and on the spot would be weakened. However, unless certain procedural safeguards are maintained, the imposition of disciplinary penalties may become entirely arbitrary and tyrannical.

Among the most important procedural requirements of the 1946 Soviet Disciplinary Code are these: that a penalty must be imposed within five days after the offense was committed,[78] that the penalty must be executed within one month after its imposition,[79] that the penalty imposed must be proportionate to the importance of the offense,[80] and that a superior who exceeds his disciplinary powers shall himself be liable to disciplinary or judicial punishment.[81] The right of complaint against the imposition of a disciplinary penalty, which is the chief safeguard for the subordinate, is quite restricted. He may complain against the severity of the penalty only if the superior has exceeded his powers.[82] Further, a superior commander may not reduce a disciplinary penalty imposed by a junior commander,[83] but he may increase it although there has been no complaint or appeal.[84] Finally, the provision of the earlier codes that if a complaint is not dealt with by the immediate superior within a certain time (in the 1940 code, fifteen days) the complainant may appeal to the next higher authority [85] is abolished in the 1946 edition.

On the other hand, the 1946 code omits the 1940 provision that a complaint against a disciplinary penalty must be made within one month from the day the illegal or unfair treatment took place.[86] Any serviceman may place a complaint against an illegal decision of his commanders regarding his person, against infringement of his service rights and privileges, and against the withholding of allowances due him.[87] The complaint has to be placed with his superior commander [88] and may be made orally or in writing.[89] Complaints by groups are forbidden.[90] Complaints may not be made while in a formation, on guard or sentry duty, or on detail.[91] Making of an obviously wrong complaint with the intention of discrediting the superior is punishable by disciplinary penalty or by court-martial.[92]

All complaints must be recorded in a special "Book of Complaints," the pages of which must be properly numbered, sewn together, sealed, and certified by the commander of the unit.[93] Apparently the legislators do not have great confidence in the reliability of superior officers in this regard.

The 1946 code omits the earlier rule prohibiting the imposition of a disciplinary penalty upon a delinquent in the presence of personnel subordinate to him,[94] but states generally that humiliation of the offender should be avoided.[95]

(a) *Jurisdiction to Impose Disciplinary Penalties and Rewards.* The right to impose disciplinary penalties rests with commanders, starting with squad leaders and going up to the Minister of Defense. A squad leader may impose on his subordinates the penalties of personal reprimand, deprivation of one regular permit to leave quarters, and assignment of one extra detail. The next higher commander, that is, the deputy platoon commander, has slightly greater powers in that he may deprive a delinquent of two regular permits to leave quarters, and may assign two extra details. Noncommissioned officers and platoon commanders have somewhat greater powers of punishment. Company commanders, who generally in European and American armies are the lowest ranking personnel with disciplinary jurisdiction, may issue a personal reprimand; restrict to quarters for one month; assign five extra details to privates and three to noncommissioned officers; and order ordinary confinement of privates up to ten days, noncommissioned officers up to five days, and noncommissioned officers in extraterm service up to three days, and strict confinement of privates up to four days and noncommissioned officers up to two days. In respect to his junior officers he may issue a personal reprimand orally and place them under house arrest or in the guardhouse for two days.

(b) *Courts of Honor*.[96] Courts of Honor are under the jurisdiction of regimental commanders and above. The court consists of five members and two deputies, elected annually by secret ballot of the officers' assembly. Courts of Honor deciding a case of a junior officer must contain at least one senior officer; the lowest rank eligible is that of captain. No officer may be judged by a lower-ranking officer.

A decision of a commander to turn a case over to the Court of Honor may be made only after a preliminary investigation. Court sessions are public and the presence of the accused is required. The decision is made in a closed session by a simple majority.

The court may impose the following penalties: admonition, personal reprimand, strict personal reprimand, recommendation of postponement of regular promotion, recommendation of demotion in rank or command, recommendation of transfer to another unit, and recommendation of transfer to retirement.

An appeal may be taken to the convening officer only, and if he disapproves the decision a new trial must take place.

(c) *The Disciplinary Functions of Communist Party Organs and of Counterintelligence Sections of the Committee on State Security.* The Disciplinary Code says nothing regarding the disciplinary functions of Communist Party organs and of the Counterintelligence Sections.[97] However, by their nature these organizations exercise considerable control over discipline.

The Deputy Commanders for Political Affairs (zampolits) and the officers of Counterintelligence Sections have several disciplinary functions in common: to guard the political morale of troops, to investigate and report to higher authorities any violations of discipline which may reflect political dissidence, and to investigate and report official laxity in enforcement of discipline. Former Soviet army officers state that the regimental zampolit, to whom company zampolits must report frequently on political morale and opinion in their units, gives a copy of such reports to the chief counterintelligence officer.[98] The counterintelligence officer, on the other hand, "notwithstanding the fact that he receives voluminous reports from his *seksoty* [informers], gives the zampolit merely some extracts from his reports, and this not always but only in the more serious cases." [99] That the counterintelligence officer is beyond the control of the zampolit or the Party organization of the unit is further evidenced by the fact that the Counterintelligence Sections have their own autonomous Party organization.[100]

Because of the informality of the zampolit's work and the secrecy of the Counterintelligence Section's activities, it is impossible to state precisely their role in the maintenance of military discipline. Such information as is available is largely anecdotal, in the sense that it consists of experiences recounted by former Soviet officers, some of them former counterintelligence officers. One may judge from these accounts that the counterintelligence officers and zampolits not only exercise pressure against the expression of political dissent but also serve to channel grievances respecting administrative and other injustices.*

Thus a Soviet displaced person, in an unpublished manuscript, recounts the following episode. The commander of a

* For a more detailed treatment see below pp. 134, 145.

tank regiment of the Belorussian Military District was summoned to the Counterintelligence Section of the corps. "The devil knows what's going on in your kitchen," the head of the Counterintelligence Section said. The regiment commander replied that as far as he knew there were no special irregularities. "How come, then," he was asked, "that you find it all right if the soup bucket is stopped up with a rag? And why didn't you report that the quartermaster company of your regiment attempted collectively to refuse to participate in the daily routine?"

The regiment commander returned to his unit, and upon inquiry discovered that the previous night a tiny hole had been found in the soup bucket and had been temporarily stopped up with a rag, and further that at the time of assembly for the daily routine two or three soldiers had remarked, in view of a heavy downpour of rain, "How nice it would be if there were no routine today." An overzealous informer had blown these items up into a secret report of inefficiency and rebelliousness.

Another story, this one taken from an official report of a wartime case in the Supreme Court of the USSR,[101] also casts ironic light on the way in which political and military matters may overlap in the life of the Soviet soldier. The case involved an army sergeant who was court-martialed for having "systematically uttered anti-Soviet opinions." It seems that the sergeant, whose military and political record was otherwise unassailable, had, in performing his military duties, expressed certain unfavorable opinions regarding the Constitution.

In sustaining an acquittal the Supreme Court stated: "Although these opinions were often clothed in rough unworthy form and contain politically incorrect formulations . . . it is clear that all these opinions were directed toward the strengthening of military discipline." It appeared from the evidence, the court said, that the accused "was a demanding person in connection with discipline." Apparently someone had provoked the sergeant by relying on his constitutional rights. Very likely the Deputy Commander for Political Affairs had pressed charges. Whether in peacetime the sergeant would have fared so well in the courts is open to question.

III

SOVIET MILITARY CRIMES
AND PUNISHMENTS

More serious offenses against Soviet military order and discipline are subject to criminal prosecution in military courts and, in general, to heavier punishments than those which may be imposed by administrative acts of superior noncommissioned or commissioned officers.

The present chapter is devoted to an examination of the substantive law of military crimes and punishments; in the following chapter we shall consider the system of military courts and procedure. However, certain distinctive features of Soviet military courts bear strongly on the scope of the substantive law and are therefore stated briefly at the outset of this chapter.

First, Soviet military courts, in contrast to military courts of Western countries generally, have jurisdiction over certain classes of political crimes whether committed by military personnel or by civilians. By treating these political crimes as military crimes, the Soviet system has reverted to a practice which was generally abolished in the late eighteenth or early nineteenth century by countries which came under the influence of the French Revolution, and which was abolished in prerevolutionary Russia by the liberal reforms of the 1860's.

Second, Soviet railroad and water-transport workers are under the jurisdiction of military railroad and water-transport courts, and service offenses committed by them are considered equivalent to analogous military crimes. Civil defense personnel are also under the jurisdiction of military courts. During the war, workers in war-industry enterprises and certain other classes of civilians were under the jurisdiction of military courts, and in certain localities the entire population was under military law. Thus the class of persons subject to Soviet military law is far wider than in most other countries.

Third, Soviet military criminal law is distinctive in the degree of its integration with Soviet nonmilitary criminal law; the military courts are subordinate to the Supreme Court of the USSR and are bound by the general body of criminal law and procedure, of which the military law is considered a part. At the same time, the military courts are entirely separate from the so-called Special Board of the Ministry of Internal Affairs, which in a secret administrative process tries many if not most of the persons who are considered to be serious political enemies of the regime.

In examining the Soviet law of military crimes and punishments, we shall therefore consider certain political crimes as well as certain other crimes committed by various classes of civilians who are under military law; we shall also consider the general criminal law of which Soviet military criminal law is a part.

1. GENERAL PRINCIPLES OF SOVIET CRIMINAL LAW

The fact that the definitions and sanctions of military crimes are contained in the general criminal code signifies a degree of fusion of military and nonmilitary law which is unusual if not unique in Europe and America.[1] Article 193, Sections 1–31, of the RSFSR Criminal Code and corresponding articles of the criminal codes of the other constituent republics,[2] dealing with military crimes and punishments, are in the Special Part of the code, in which particular crimes and punishments are specified. Like the other provisions of the Special Part, Article 193 is interpreted in the light of the General Part, which deals with the elements of a crime, criminal intent and negligence, insanity, complicity, the period of limitations, and similar matters. Thus Soviet military justice is explicitly and directly grounded in the general system of criminal justice. This unity of military and general criminal law is implemented by many provisions of a procedural nature, such as the provision for ultimate review of decisions in military courts by the Supreme Court of the

USSR, the provision for trial of civilians by military courts in certain types of cases, and the union of administration of military and nonmilitary courts in the Ministry of Justice, and of military and nonmilitary prosecutors and investigators in the procuracy of the USSR.

An exhaustive study of Soviet military criminal law would therefore involve an analysis of Soviet criminal law in general. Such an analysis is not attempted here. However, it may be profitable briefly to discuss certain important features of Soviet criminal law which form a necessary background for consideration of the military provisions.

(a) *Objective and Subjective Standards of Guilt.* It was the notion of the leading Soviet jurists in the twenties and early thirties, including the framers of the 1926 RSFSR Criminal Code, that criminal liability should be based solely on the socially dangerous character of the act and of the actor, and that all consideration of fault or guilt in the subjective sense (*culpa*; in Russian, *vinovnost'*) should be eliminated. Such was the significance, in their view, of Article 6 of the code, which states:

> Every act or omission shall be considered socially dangerous which is directed against the Soviet system [*stroi*] or which violates the legal order established by the Workers' and Peasants' power during the period of transition to a communist system.

Similarly, Article 7 authorizes the application of "measures of social defense" to persons "who have committed socially dangerous acts or who constitute a danger by reason of their connection with criminal elements or by reason of their past activity." On the other hand, Article 8 states:

> If a particular act was at the time of its commission a crime according to Article 6 of the present code, but at the time of investigation or trial has lost its socially dangerous character in consequence of a change in the criminal law or by virtue of the mere fact of a changed social-political situation, or if the person who committed it cannot, in the opinion of the court, then be considered socially dangerous, the act shall not render the person who committed it liable to measures of social defense.

Article 9, stating the purposes for which "measures of social defense" shall be applied, lists prevention of further crimes by the same persons, deterrence of other "unstable" members of society, and "adaptation of those who have committed criminal acts to the conditions of community life of the toilers' state." They shall not have as their purpose, Article 9 concludes, "the causing of physical suffering or the lowering of human dignity, and questions of retaliation and penalization (*kara*) do not arise."

The effect of these provisions in the first twenty years of Soviet legal development was to minimize the factors of personal will and personal responsibility — or, in legal terms, the requirements of criminal intent or criminal negligence. Although these latter requirements found expression in Article 10, which states that "measures of social defense of a judicial-correctional character" may be applied only to persons who acted intentionally (that is, with foresight of the socially dangerous consequences of their acts) or negligently (that is, under circumstances under which they ought to have foreseen such consequences) — nevertheless many provisions of the Special Part of the code defined crimes without reference to intent or negligence, and Article 10 of the General Part was ignored in the interpretation of those provisions.

For example, Section 24 of Article 193, on military espionage, imposes deprivation of freedom for not less than five years, with or without confiscation of property, for "communication to any foreign government . . . of any information concerning the armed forces or the defensive strength of the USSR," "but in instances in which the espionage had or could have had a particular harmful effect on the interests of the USSR, it [shall be punished by] the highest measure of social defense [i.e., death by shooting] with confiscation of property." Similarly, the 1934 statute on crimes against the state, which supplanted the above quoted Section 24 (together with various other sections) of Article 193, speaks simply of "acts committed by citizens of the USSR to the injury of" the military might, political independence or geographical integrity of the USSR — without reference to the intent, negligence, or other state of mind of the person charged.

In 1936 and 1937 the refusal of Soviet jurists to recognize the importance of personal will and responsibility, and of intent, fault, and guilt (culpa) was denounced as a "left deviation." Article 10 was given new importance. Many provisions of the code were reinterpreted to require not only negligence (foreseeability of the consequences) or a general intent to commit a wrongful act, but also a specific intent or even a desire to bring about the particular prohibited consequences. Thus the definition of a military crime is now stated not only in terms of the objective violation of the military legal order, as Section 1 of Article 193 defines it, but also in terms of subjective "culpability." Military treason, likewise, was interpreted by the Supreme Court in 1938 as requiring a specific treasonable intent, that is, a specific intent to injure Soviet military might, political independence, or geographical integrity.[3]

A 1950 textbook on criminal law states that criminal intent — that is, actual foresight by the actor of the consequences of his conduct — is required for such military crimes as absence without leave, unlawful disposition of military property, and marauding; that with respect to unlawful disposition of military property, "direct intent" — that is, in addition to foresight, a desire to bring about the consequences — is required; that with respect to crimes such as retreat from battle dispositions for the purpose of aiding the enemy, a specific purpose is required; but that with respect to certain other crimes, such as nonfulfillment of orders and breach of sentry rules, criminal negligence — that is, failure by the actor to foresee consequences which under the circumstances he ought to have foreseen — and not criminal intent, is sufficient.[4] These are judge-made rules based upon construction of the code provisions.

Nevertheless, the language of social danger and social defense remains on the books and may still be invoked when the immediate interests of the state override its long-run interest in "stability of laws." "The mere fact of a changed social-political situation" (Article 8) was apparently a sufficient ground for the courts during the war to exonerate persons called to the colors from punishment for minor crimes committed previously, especially if such punishment would interfere with the performance of their military service. Similarly, Article 8 provides a basis for a ruling of the USSR Supreme Court on January 7, 1943, that persons sentenced to loss of civil rights in addition to other penalties may be permitted to serve the basic part of their sentence and be released from loss of civil rights, if such loss would interfere with their military service.[5]

Far more serious, however, is the provision that innocent members of a serviceman's family may be punished if he flees across the frontier. Section 1, *c*, Part 2, of Article 58 states with reference to the crime of flight across the frontier by a serviceman:

> Adult members of the traitor's family who lived with him or were supported by him at the time the crime was committed shall be subject to deprivation of electoral rights and to deportation to remote regions of Siberia for five years.

"The political sense of this norm," wrote Colonel V. M. Chkhikvadze, director of the Military Law School, in 1948, "consists in the strengthening of the general preventive effect of the criminal law relating to such a very grievous crime as flight across the frontier, as a result of which the guilty person himself cannot be brought to punishment. The threat of application of repression to members of the family may impel the criminal to refrain from committing the treasonable act."[6]

Chkhikvadze adds that "Part 2 of Article 58, Section 1, *c* is an exceptional norm, since as a general rule (Article 10 of the RSFSR Criminal Code) criminal responsibility exists only in those instances when the person acted intentionally or negligently. Therefore Part 2 of Article 58, Section 1, *c* is not subject to extensive interpretation and should be applied only in instances directly stated in the law."[7]

(b) *The Doctrine of Analogy.* One of the most notorious provisions of Soviet criminal law is the doctrine of analogy, which permits a person to be punished for a socially dangerous act which is not directly prohibited by law, but which is analogous to a prohibited act.[8] This doctrine was designed to give the greatest possible leeway to prosecutors and judges to apply the spirit of the code as distinguished from its letter. It was hailed by Soviet jurists as the opposite of the "bourgeois" doctrine of "no crime, no punishment without a law."

The attack upon legal nihilism in the mid-1930's, and the emphasis then upon juridical form and upon legal stability, led to the limitation of the doctrine of analogy.[9] Soviet courts began to insist that analogy may only be applied if there is no provision of the Special Part of the Criminal Code directly covering the act in question (that is, it may not be applied to increase the penalty for a prohibited act), if the act falls within some provision of the General Part, and if the act is similar both in kind and in importance to the act to which it is analogized. The effect of these limitations was to make the doctrine of analogy merely a method of liberal interpretation of a criminal statute. Leading Soviet jurists proposed that it be abolished altogether.

During the war, however, the rapid changes in social conditions sometimes left legislation far behind, while the need for repressive measures was felt by the law-enforcing bodies to be greater than before. In these circumstances the courts returned to a somewhat broader application of the doctrine of analogy than that of the late 1930's, though not to the wilder interpretations of the preceding period. In 1946 a Soviet textbook on criminal law asserted that the doctrine of "no crime without a law" is carried even farther in Soviet law than in bourgeois law, and stated as the Soviet version of the doctrine: "No crime, no punishment without a law, without fault, without cause"; in 1954 a Soviet writer proposed that the doctrine of analogy be eliminated in the draft of a new criminal code.[10]

The 1948 Soviet textbook on military criminal law lists three requirements for the application of analogy in military law, similar to those mentioned above: the criminal act must correspond generally to the definition of a military crime — that is, it must be an infringement of the military order by a person subject to military criminal law; the code must contain no provision directly applicable to the act; and the act must be similar to a particular crime defined in the code.[11] Several examples are given, both negative and positive. Stealing from dead or wounded on the battlefield by a civilian may not be punished under the military criminal law by analogy, since a civilian is not a person ordinarily subject to military criminal law. However, stealing by a serviceman from a wounded man who is being transported to the rear may be punished by analogy under the provision concerning stealing from the dead or wounded on the battlefield. Similarly, the USSR Supreme Court ruled in 1945 that servicemen exercising functions usually assigned to officers may be punished for abuse of authority, excess of authority, neglect of authority, or negligent attitude toward duties, under Section 17 of Article 193, even though that section expressly applies only to officers.[12]

(c) *Disclosure of Intent to Commit a Crime.* In Soviet general criminal law, mere disclosure of intent to commit a crime is not in itself punishable. But under military law such disclosure is considered very harmful and constitutes at least a serious breach of discipline. It is considered especially serious if done by a commander in the presence of his subordinates.

The disclosure of intent may also be punished by court-martial, however, when it constitutes an independent crime. Thus a disclosure of intent to commit treason or some other counterrevolutionary crime is treated as the spreading of counterrevolutionary propaganda. Chkhikvadze quotes as other examples of disclosure of intent punishable as a military crime: disclosing to other servicemen the intention to desert to the enemy or to give oneself up as a prisoner, and negligent attitude toward service duties by a commander who incites his subordinates to a crime by divulging his criminal intent.[13] A disclosure of intent to leave without permission or to sell military equipment does not constitute a crime in itself and is punishable only as a disciplinary transgression.

Chkhikvadze points out as an especially dangerous type of disclosure of intent the threat of a subordinate against his commander, especially if the subordinate threatens to use force or firearms. Whether court-martial proceedings should be initiated depends on the character of the threat, on the general behavior of the subordinate, on the origin and reason for the threat, and so forth. If the reason is an anti-Soviet attitude, such a threat constitutes a counterrevolutionary crime.[14]

(d) *Complicity.* According to Article 17 of the Criminal Code of the RSFSR, punishment is "equally applicable both to persons executing the crime — the executors — and to their accomplices — the instigators and abettors. Instigators are persons who induce the commitment of a crime. Abettors are persons who assist in the performance of a crime by advice, instruction, furnishing means, overcoming obstacles for or concealing the criminal, or covering up traces of the crime."

An unusual feature of Soviet military criminal law is that mutiny, one of the most serious crimes in other systems of military criminal law, does not constitute a special, independent crime in the Soviet system. Mutineers are accomplices in the general crime of insubordination, such as failure to execute an order or resisting a person who is performing a service duty.

In military crimes, complicity of a group of servicemen is regarded as an aggravating circumstance, and if such complicity is a consequence of a premeditated agreement, it calls for a still heavier penalty. Article 47, paragraph *c* of the Criminal Code of the RSFSR includes as an aggravating circumstance "that the crime was committed by a group or band of persons."

If a commander participates in a crime as an accomplice he is subjected to a heavier penalty even though his participation may be only a passive one, as his responsibility makes his crime socially more dangerous.[15] On the other hand, Soviet legislators considered it expedient in 1935 to submit civilians participating in military crimes to the same responsibility as their military accomplices. In explanation of this provision Chkhikvadze remarks that there is no basic difference in the committing of a military crime by a serviceman or by a civilian. The serviceman infringes his oath and his military duties. The civilian infringes his duty of the defense of the country in assisting a military person to perform a military crime.[16]

2. MILITARY CRIMES

The major military crimes in Soviet law are classified by Soviet jurists under the following heads: (a) military treason, (b) evasion of military service, (c) insubordination and breach of military honor, (d) crimes against military property, (e) breach of rules of sentry, convoy and guard duty, (f) military official crimes, (g) disclosure of military secrets, (h) battle crimes, (i) crimes in violation of international conventions.

(a) *Military Treason.* Treason is defined in Soviet criminal law as "any act committed by a citizen of the USSR to the damage of the military might of the USSR, of its political independence, or the inviolability of its territory, such as: espionage, giving out of a military or state secret, going over to the enemy, flight by air or otherwise across the border." [17] It is punishable ordinarily by death by shooting with total confiscation of the offender's property; under extenuating circumstances it is punishable by deprivation of freedom for ten years with total confiscation of property. It is listed in the Criminal Code as a counterrevolutionary crime, under Article 58.

The examples of treason specified in the above-cited definition are not exhaustive. Under the Soviet Constitution, any infringement of the military oath is an act of treason.[18] In fact, many military crimes, including failure to obey an order, surrender to the enemy, refusal to bear arms during combat, abandoning the field of battle, and others, constitute treason if committed with treasonable intent.[19]

A special provision of the Criminal Code, Section 1, *b* of Article 58, makes treason committed by a serviceman punishable by "the highest measure of social defense," that is, death by shooting, with total confiscation of property. If treason by a serviceman, or military treason, takes the form of flight across the frontier, any adult member of his family who assists him in preparations or who, having knowledge of the crime, fails to bring it to the attention of the authorities, is punishable by deprivation of freedom from five to ten years with total confiscation of property.[20] As mentioned previously, other adult members of his family are subject to deprivation of electoral rights and exile to remote regions of Siberia for a period of five years.[21]

(b) *Evasion of Military Service.* Servicemen may be tried under military law for (1) desertion and absence without leave, (2) failure to report punctually, (3) evasion of service duties by infliction of self-injury, feigning illness, presenting false papers, or some other deceit, and (4) evasion of service duties, particularly under the pretext of religious or other convictions.

1. Desertion and absence without leave are declared punishable by Article 193, Section 7 of the Criminal Code, as amended July 6, 1940 and May 31, 1952. The 1940 amendment introduced the word desertion (*dezertirstvo*) into Soviet military law for the first time. It also introduced several degrees of desertion and absence without leave, and increased the severity of the penalties imposed. However, the 1940 amendment applies as a whole only to privates and noncommissioned officers; the definitions (so-called dispositions) of the older version of Section 7 of Article 193 remain applicable to officers, but the sanctions are increased.[22]

The older version, still applicable to officers, imposes punishment for absence without leave for more than six days, or for more than two days during fleet cruise or maneuvers or special assemblies; and for "flight" (*pobeg*) with intent to evade service duties for a prolonged period or altogether. The earlier punishments were deprivation of freedom up to one year and up to three years, respectively. The 1940 amendment increases the sanctions for both forms of the crime to deprivation of freedom for not less than two years with or without confiscation of property, and in time of war "the highest measure of social defense with confiscation of property." "Systematic" commission of absence without leave by officers is equivalent to desertion under Section 8, *b* of Article 193.

The 1940 provisions applicable to privates and noncommissioned officers make absence without leave up to two hours, first offense, punishable by trial before a comrades' court or by disciplinary action; absence without leave up to two hours, second offense, or from two to twenty-four hours — punishable in time of peace by sentence to a disciplinary battalion from six months to two years (as of May 31, 1952, from two months to two years), in time of war by deprivation of freedom from three to seven years (as of May 31, 1952, from three to five years); absence without leave for more than twenty-four hours (desertion) punishable in time of peace by deprivation of freedom from five to ten years, in time of war by death by shooting with confiscation of property.

The distinction between the various degrees of absence without leave and desertion rests not merely on the differences in length of absence, but also on the intent of the serviceman to be absent for a shorter or longer time. A serviceman who without leave departs on a train for a distant destination, but is apprehended and returned to his post within an hour after departure, may be guilty of attempted desertion (and on general principles of Soviet law an attempt is punishable equally with the successful act). Similarly, it is open to a serviceman who voluntarily returns after two days to prove that he intended to be absent for less than twenty-four hours but was detained longer by forces beyond his control — and thereby to reduce his penalty from death (in time of war) to deprivation of freedom from three to five years. If there was not a direct intent to be absent without leave (if, for example, the serviceman erroneously believed he had permission to be absent), the crime of absence without leave was not committed.[23]

2. Failure to report punctually without adequate reasons is a separate crime in Soviet military law. Section 10 of Article 193 specifies report for duty after an assignment, transfer, mission, or furlough, but these occasions are taken to be merely exemplary, and other similar occasions, such as return to one's unit upon release from hospital or guardhouse, are included by implication.[24]

The penalties for absence without leave and desertion are applicable also to failure to report punctually; in addition, by implication the distinctions in time of absence (up to two hours, up to twenty-four hours, more than twenty-four hours), in military situation (on fleet cruise, maneuvers, or special assembly; in time of peace or time of war), and the like, are likewise applicable, as are the distinctions between officers and enlisted men. However, the proof is different, for in the cases of failure to report punctually it is not necessary to establish that the serviceman intended to be absent for a particular period of time but only that his absence or lateness was without adequate reasons. "The evaluation of the adequacy of the reasons," writes

Chkhikvadze, ". . . belongs first of all to the command. Ultimately the evaluation belongs to the court." [25] He cites the following case:

In 1940 Junior Commander P. returned from a seven-day furlough two days late. On trial under Section 10 of Article 193 it was established that in contradiction to existing regulations P. was not given a railway transportation request and hence in returning home from his furlough suffered a delay of two days in obtaining a railroad ticket. P's conviction, affirmed by the Military Collegium of the Supreme Court, was reversed by the Plenum of the Supreme Court, on the ground that P. had taken all steps open to him, that the delay was due to circumstances beyond his control, and that hence there were adequate reasons for his failure to report punctually.

Hypothetical cases are given by Chkhikvadze of the applicability of the doctrine of extreme necessity, under Article 13 of the criminal code. A serviceman who is called upon by local inhabitants or local police to fight a fire or to chase a criminal and who, responding to such call, is delayed in reporting for duty, would be excused if he could show that the danger (spread of the fire, escape of the criminal) required his intervention, and that the danger could have caused the state greater harm than that caused by his failure to report punctually. "In the evaluation of all these factors, there should be taken into consideration all factual circumstances of the case, the conditions in which the military unit was situated, where the serviceman was supposed to report (for example, the situation of the unit in military operations), and so forth." [26]

3. Evasion of service duties by infliction of self-injury, feigning illness, presenting false papers, or some other deceit, is punishable under Section 12 of Article 193 by death by shooting with confiscation of property, if committed in time of war or in combat; and in time of peace by deprivation of freedom up to five years, or, under aggravating circumstances by deprivation of freedom for not less than three years.

The crime consists not merely in the practice of a deceit, but in the practice of a deceit for the purpose of evading a service duty. For example, a serviceman who falsifies papers concerning the financial condition of his family in order to obtain extra allotments is not guilty of violation of Section 12 of Article 193, though he may be guilty of one or more kinds of forgery of documents under the nonmilitary Articles 72 and 170; if, however, the forgery is for the purpose of obtaining a special furlough to visit his family, Section 12 of Article 193 applies.[27] As in the case of absence without leave, a direct intent is a necessary element of the crime.

4. Evasion of service duties particularly under the pretext of religious or other convictions is punishable under Section 13 of Article 193 by disciplinary action, or deprivation of freedom up to three years, or for not less than three years, or death by shooting with confiscation of property, depending on the circumstances.

According to Chkhikvadze, it is only necessary under this provision for the actor to give as a reason for his act his religious or other convictions, and it makes no difference whether or not he actually holds them. "In the Soviet Union," Chkhikvadze writes, "where every honorable citizen considers it his sacred duty to defend his motherland with weapon in hand, where the huge growth of enlightenment and culture stands against religious and any other survivals, religious and other convictions may not serve as a basis for liberation from military service or from individual military duties. Therefore the Law on Universal Military Obligation does not provide for the possibility of liberation from military service on these grounds . . ." [28]

The law referred to is that of September 1, 1939.[29] Prior to its enactment there was provision for exemption from military service for religious reasons. It is possible that before the 1939 law Section 13 of Article 193 was interpreted to apply to pretended convictions not actually held. However, it should be noted that the provision relates to evasion of service duties by men already in service.

The peculiar wording of Section 13 of Article 193, that is, the use of the word "particularly," makes it available as a catch-all provision for evasion of military service not covered by Section 12 or by Section 2 (failure to obey an order). Thus, intentional systematic lateness for work or for military school activities, refusal to report for duty, and refusal to take the military oath may fall within Section 13. Chkhikvadze notes that in the practice of military tribunals "there are instances of the application of Section 13 for refusal of a serviceman to serve in one or another kind of regiment, service in which presents great hardship." [30]

(c) *Insubordination and Breach of Military Honor.* Sections 2, 3, 4, 5, and 6 of Article 193, respectively, make punishable as military crimes (1) failure to execute an order, (2) resisting a person who is performing a service duty, (3) coercing a person to violate a service duty, and (4) insulting a superior or a subordinate and insulting another serviceman.

1. Although Section 2 of Article 193 makes punishable failure to execute an order "given in the course of service," it is now interpreted to apply to any order. Chkhikvadze writes: "Any attempt to introduce a juridical line between service and nonservice relations of commanders and subordinates would be incorrect . . . For the subordinate, any order of a commander is given in the course of service and is therefore unconditionally binding." [31] Chkhikvadze also states that "the subordinate should not submit to an *obviously* criminal order." Indeed, if he knows it is criminal, he is guilty of a crime in executing it. The authors of this book have been unable to find examples which shed light on how the Soviet military courts interpret the word "obviously."

The serviceman is obliged under Section 2 of Article 193, as interpreted, to execute orders given by his actual commanders only, and not those given by any other higher-ranking serviceman or officer. In some instances the commander may be of lower rank than the person to whom the order is issued, who must nevertheless execute it.

When two orders conflict, the person receiving them is supposed to report the conflict to the commander giving the second order, but if the latter insists, the second order must be executed.

Section 2 does not refer to the subjective element of the crime indicated. Chkhikvadze states that both intentional and negligent failure to execute an order are punishable, and that the difference is generally reflected in the severity of the sentence; but that if the serviceman does not know that the person giving the order is his commander, he is excused from failure to execute it.[32]

The usual punishment for failure to execute an order is deprivation of freedom up to five years. Under extenuating circumstances, disciplinary action is applicable. If committed in a group, or by commanding personnel, or if it had or could have had especially serious consequences, it is punishable by deprivation of freedom for not less than three years. If committed in time of war or during military operations, it is punishable by death by shooting with total confiscation of property.

2. Section 3 of Article 193 makes the willful offering of resistance to another serviceman in the performance of his service duties punishable by deprivation of freedom up to three years; and if committed by a group or with force or arms or during military operations, not less than three years; and if under still more aggravating circumstances, by death by shooting. There is no provision for disciplinary action under extenuating circumstances.

3. Section 4 of Article 193 makes willful coercion of another serviceman to violate his service duties punishable by deprivation of freedom for not less than one year; and if committed by a group or with force or arms or during military operations, not less than five years; and if under still more aggravating circumstances, by death by shooting.

4. Soviet writers note frequently "the very close connection" between the requirements of obedience and the rules of military honor. The Disciplinary Code and other sets of regulations (such as the Code of Internal Service) establish affirmative duties and marks of respect of one serviceman to another. The military criminal law protects military honor in Sections 5 and 6 of Article 193, which make punishable an insult offered by one serviceman to another when either is engaged in the execution of a service duty. Punishments range from disciplinary action to deprivation of freedom for not less than six months. Distinctions are made between insult by violent act and insult by word or nonviolent act, between insult by a subordinate to

a superior, and insult by a superior to a subordinate, and insult by one serviceman to another where there is no relationship of superiority and subordination.

An insult (the Russian word is *oskorblenie*, which may also be translated as affront) is a crime in Soviet law generally. It is punishable under Article 159 of the RSFSR Criminal Code by a fine up to 300 rubles or by public censure, if offered orally or in writing; by corrective-labor tasks (deduction of a percentage of wages) up to two months, or a fine up to 300 rubles if offered by an act; and under Article 160 by corrective-labor tasks (i.e., a deduction from wages) up to six months, or a fine up to 300 rubles if offered in printed words or pictorial representation or widely or publicly distributed.

Chkhikvadze defines the military crime of insult as "the expression of a negative evaluation of the human and military dignity of a serviceman, given in a form which is considered improper (*neprilichnoi*), that is, contradictory to the requirements of Soviet military discipline and the rules of socialist community life." [33] An insult by violent act is distinguished from the inflicting of physical harm punishable under other articles of the criminal code and other sections of Article 193. It includes an insulting bodily movement toward another (*nepristoinyi zhest*). The qualification that the act, to be criminal, must be committed "when either is engaged in the execution of a service duty" is interpreted as superfluous in the case of an insult to a commander, since "commanders are always in the execution of service duties in relation to their subordinates." [34]

(d) *Crimes Against Military Property.* Soviet military property is a form of public, socialist ownership, of which Article 131 of the Soviet Constitution states: "Every citizen of the USSR shall be obliged to preserve and guard public, socialist ownership, as a sacred inviolable basis of the Soviet order, as a source of wealth and might of the motherland, as a source of the prosperity and culture of all toilers. Persons who infringe public, socialist ownership, are enemies of the people." Every Soviet serviceman, in taking the military oath, swears "in every way to safeguard military and national property." [35]

Laws of August 7, 1932 and June 4, 1947 impose heavy sanctions upon theft of socialist property.[36] The 1932 law made such theft punishable by deprivation of freedom for not less than ten years, with confiscation of property, and under certain aggravating circumstances by death by shooting. The 1947 law, passed nine days after the abolition of capital punishment (which was restored in 1950 for certain crimes but not for theft of state property) provides for internment in a corrective-labor camp for seven to ten years, with or without confiscation of property, for theft of state-owned property; and five to eight years, with or without confiscation, for theft of collective-farm or coöperative property. For a second offense, or for commission by an organized band or on a large scale, the maximum penalty is twenty-five years with confiscation of property. These provisions are applicable to theft of socialist property, including military property, by servicemen.

Servicemen may also be tried for a special type of military property crime defined in the military article of the code. Section 14 of Article 193 makes punishable the embezzlement, destruction, or abuse of uniform or equipment entrusted to a serviceman. The punishment in time of peace is deprivation of freedom up to one year, or, under extenuating circumstances, disciplinary action; in time of war, not less than one year; but if the act is committed in respect of weapons, cartridges, or means of transport, the punishment is deprivation of freedom up to three years, and in time of war and under aggravating circumstances death by shooting. One who receives an article covered in this section knowing it to have been embezzled is equally punishable as an accomplice.

(e) *Breach of Rules of Sentry, Convoy, and Guard Duty.* Sections 15 and 16 of Article 193 make breach of rules of sentry, convoy and guard duty punishable, under normal circumstances, by deprivation of freedom up to six months. Where there are extenuating circumstances, disciplinary punishment is applicable. Where the sentry duty relates to the guarding of an arms depot, ammunition or explosives, "or anything else of special state or military significance," or where violation of the rules of sentry or convoy duty is likely to have and does have harmful consequences, the penalties are increased, and if in such a case the crime is committed in wartime or during military operations, "the highest measure of social defense" (that is, death by shooting) may be applied. Breach of the rules of internal guard duty is also subject to varying degrees of punishment depending on the circumstances, with a maximum penalty, however, of deprivation of freedom for three years.

(f) *Military Official Crimes.* Abuse of authority, excess of authority, neglect of authority, or negligent attitude toward service duties, committed by commanding personnel, are crimes punishable under Section 17 of Article 193. They are the military analogues of official crimes punishable under Articles 109–121 of the code, and are interpreted in the light of those articles.

Article 109 defines abuse of authority or of official position as "any act of an official which he can commit solely by virtue of his official position and which, not being required by considerations of official necessity, results in a clear interference with the correct work of the institution or enterprise or causes it property damage or causes interference with public order or with legally protected rights or interests of individual citizens."

Chkhikvadze gives several hypothetical illustrations of military abuse of authority: the commander of a motor pool uses trucks entrusted to him for the carriage of private freight; the commander of a supply depot distributes products without observing required formalities and illegally supplies them to persons of his acquaintance; the commander of a military institution expends for current needs funds assigned for money reserves, counting on receiving in time assignments to cover the expenditures.[37]

Excess of authority is defined in Article 110 as "the commission of acts clearly going beyond the limits of rights and powers given by law to the person committing them." The corresponding part of Section 17 of Article 193 applies, for example, to the unjustified use of force by a superior officer on a subordinate, and was applied by the Supreme Court of the USSR in a ruling of June 7, 1946, to the killing of a subordinate by his commanding officer.[38] Neglect of authority is defined in Article 111 as "the nonperformance by an official of any act which under the obligations of his office he ought to have performed." Negligent attitude toward official duties is defined in Article 111 as "a careless or unconscientious attitude toward duties imposed by office, if it results in procrastination, retardation in the carrying on of affairs and of accounts." In all forms of official crimes, harmful consequences are a necessary element.

Section 17 of Article 193 is not applicable to all cases which are covered by Articles 109, 110, and 111. Under the military article, the offensive act must be committed systematically, or from mercenary or other personal interest, or must have had serious consequences such as the disorganization of forces or of a task entrusted to the person charged or the disclosure of military secrets, or must have been known to such a person to be likely to result in such serious consequences, or must have been committed in time of war or during military operations.

Servicemen who are not officers but who are executing official functions may be punished under Section 17.

The sanction provided for violation of Section 17 are: deprivation of freedom for not less than six months, or, under especially aggravating circumstances, death by shooting. Without the special circumstances listed in the provision, mere abuse, excess, or neglect of authority, or negligent attitude toward service duties, are punishable by disciplinary action.

Special types of military official crimes are defined in Sections 18 and 19 of Article 193. Section 18 provides for punishment of commanders who prevent subordinates or their families from receiving benefits or privileges to which they are entitled. Chkhikvadze states (without citing authority or giving reasons) that intent is a required element of this crime (that is, criminal negligence alone is not sufficient).[39] Section 19 makes punishable the illegal employment of a subordinate by a commander in the discharge of personal services to the commander or his family.[40]

(g) *Disclosure of Military Secrets.* Under the law of June 9, 1947, servicemen who disclose military information which is "a specially-to-be-guarded state secret" are punishable by imprisonment in a corrective-labor camp from ten to twenty years.[41] In an accompanying decree such protected military information was defined to include practically all conceivable types of information bearing not only upon military plans and operations but also upon the physical and economic reserves of the state (including "human reserves subject to mobilization"), war industry, and technical means of defense.[42] Disclosure of such information is punishable if committed either intentionally or negligently.

The 1947 law amends Section 25, *a* of Article 193, which made "the disclosure of information, specially to be guarded as a state secret, about the armed forces and defense capacity of the USSR" punishable by deprivation of freedom for not less than one year. However, Section 25, *b* of Article 193, providing for "the highest measure of social defense, with confiscation of property" if such disclosure causes, or to the knowledge of the offender might have caused, especially serious consequences — may still remain in force.

The disclosure of military information not intended for disclosure but not a "specially-to-be-guarded secret" remains punishable under paragraphs *c* and *d* of Section 25 — by deprivation of freedom for not more than one year, or, under extenuating circumstances, by disciplinary action.

(h) *Battle Crimes.* Sections 20, 21, 22, and 23 of Article 193 make punishable various forms of surrender or retreat by a commander or a serviceman.

If improper surrender or retreat by a commander is committed for the purpose of assisting the enemy, it is punishable as military treason. Otherwise it is punishable only if done "in violation of military rules." However, Chkhikvadze states that "surrender of military forces to the enemy is not permitted under any circumstances." [43] Likewise, he states that "not a single military rule permits or can permit unauthorized retreat from assigned combat dispositions." [44] "Unauthorized" (*samovol'no*) means without specific orders from superiors. "Only under those entirely exceptional circumstances when a suddenly and rapidly changing military situation dictates a decision contradicting the received disposition, and there is no possibility of receiving a new order, must the commander show initiative and take upon himself the responsibility for retreat from dis-

positions . . . In such exceptional circumstances the acts of
the commander . . . will be evaluated on the basis of a thorough study of the given situation, the correspondence of the
commander's decision to that situation, the results of the decision made . . . If as a result of such thorough evaluation it
is considered that the commander acted incorrectly . . then it
will be concluded that there was a breach of military rules imposing responsibility for unauthorized retreat from assigned
combat dispositions under paragraph *b* of Article 21 of the
Statute [Section 21, *b* of Article 193 of the RSFSR Criminal
Code]. If it is considered that the commander acted correctly
and the retreat from assigned battle dispositions was actually
called for by the suddenly changing situation, that will mean
that the military rules were not violated and criminal responsibility falls away." [45]

The punishments for such acts, assuming no treason, are deprivation of freedom for not less than three years and, under
aggravating circumstances, death by shooting with confiscation
of property.

Even being lightly wounded, losing the use of one's weapon,
or the lack of ammunition, does not justify a serviceman's
abandonment of the battlefield or surrender to the enemy or
refusal to fight in time of battle. Only "if a serviceman was
taken prisoner by force and did not have the possibility of
making resistance (for example, if he was seriously wounded),
this is not an unauthorized act of surrender and therefore cannot be viewed as a criminally punishable act." [46] The punishment for unauthorized retreat, surrender, or refusal to fight, if
committed by an individual serviceman (as distinguished from
a commander who orders his troops to retreat or surrender) is
in all cases death by shooting.

Abandonment of a sinking warship by a commander before
fulfilling to the last his service duties (organizing the rescue of
persons, freights, valuables, documents; or destroying freight,
valuables, and documents that might otherwise fall into enemy
hands), or by members of the crew except at the order of the
commander, is also punishable by death by shooting.

(i) *Crimes in Violation of International Conventions.* Under

Sections 29, 30, and 31 of Article 193, ill-treatment of prisoners of war and unauthorized use or abuse of Red Cross or Red Crescent emblems are made punishable as military crimes, in accordance with the Hague Convention of 1907 and the Geneva Convention of 1929. Apparently there have been no prosecutions under these provisions, judging from Chkhikvadze's cryptic statement that "in the Soviet army — a highly disciplined army serving lofty progressive aims" these crimes "in practice did not occur." [47]

3. SOVIET PRINCIPLES OF PUNISHMENT

(a) *Theory of Punishment.* The doctrine of punishment in Soviet military criminal law has undergone an evolution in which increasing stress has been placed on condemnation both of the crime and the criminal. [48]

Prior to the mid-1930's, Soviet jurists avoided the word "punishment" altogether and spoke of legal sanctions as "measures of social defense" rather than penalties for wrongdoing. Strong emphasis was placed, in theory at least, upon the protection of society and the reëducation of the delinquent. In 1943, however, a Soviet text writer stated: "The mark of punishment which distinguishes it from other measures of political compulsion is that it inevitably causes the criminal a *definite suffering* which is painful to him." "Punishment," it was said, "should correspond in its severity, i.e., in the measure of suffering it causes the criminal, to the degree of his guilt." It is by punishment that the state expresses its "negative evaluation of the crime and the criminal." "Condemnation, disapproval, as a component of punishment, acquire special significance in the socialist state." Hence the chief characteristics of punishment were said to be its compulsory nature, its publicity, its infliction by the court, the suffering it causes the criminal, and the condemnation by the state of both the crime and the criminal. [49] The educational element is also stressed; however, the punishment itself is considered to be the most effective educational instrument.

Chkhikvadze, the leading Soviet writer on military criminal

law, justifies the severity of Soviet military punishment on the ground that such severity has mass approval. "Application of strict penal measures against violators of military discipline," he writes, "always meets with the approval and support of the broad masses of soldiers and commanders. Therefore the Soviet government, more than any other government, must apply severe penalties against transgressors of strict military discipline." [50]

(b) *Aggravating and Extenuating Circumstances.* In stating the punishment applicable to particular crimes, the Criminal Code often states minimum and maximum penalties, leaving the choice to the discretion of the court; in addition, many code provisions distinguish between the penalty to be imposed when the crime was committed under circumstances which aggravate its seriousness and when it was committed under extenuating circumstances.

The code provides that a crime is "aggravated," and hence more severely punishable, if it was committed under any of the following circumstances: with the intent to restore the bourgeois form of government; under circumstances which create a possibility of harming the interests of the state or the toiling classes; by a group or band of persons; by a person previously convicted of a crime; from mercenary or other morally low motives; or with extraordinary brutality, use of force or shrewdness, or against persons subordinate to the actor or dependent upon him, or against persons defenseless because of their age or for other reasons. [51]

This list is not exhaustive. Chkhikvadze adds that a military crime is also "aggravated" if it was committed in time of war or in combat; in regions of field operations, on the battlefield, or in regions under martial law or siege law; by a commander, especially if in complicity with a subordinate; with the use of weapons; while performing a duty, especially if in formation; in the presence of subordinates; under circumstances serving as an enticing example to others; during service in a penal battalion; with intent to insult or abuse a superior; and while on special service duty, such as guard duty. [52]

It is noteworthy that under the general criminal law certain crimes — murder, for example — are punished more severely if committed by a serviceman.

The Criminal Code considers a crime to have been committed under extenuating circumstances, and therefore to be less severely punishable, if committed under these conditions: though beyond the limits of self-defense, nevertheless to prevent harm to the Soviet state, the revolutionary legal order, or to the rights of the defendant himself or of another person; for the first time; for no mercenary or other morally low reasons; under pressure of a threat, intimidation, or employment or financial dependency; under the influence of a strong psychic provocation; under the influence of hunger, want, or serious personal or family distress; out of ignorance, during unconsciousness, or under accidental circumstances; and by a minor or a pregnant woman.[53]

It is apparent that not all these circumstances could be taken into consideration in connection with military crimes. Chkhikvadze points out that in the case of desertion the fact that it was committed for the first time would not be an extenuating circumstance, and that there can be no excuse for divulging military secrets, relinquishing a guard post, or disobeying an order. It is interesting to note, however, that the pressure of a threat, intimidation, or service dependency may be considered as an extenuating circumstance, according to Chkhikvadze, if the crime was committed by a subordinate under the influence of his superior.

Chkhikvadze gives the following examples of extenuating circumstances specifically applicable to military law: well-disciplined behavior of the accused serviceman in his previous service; absence of serious consequences; recent induction into service; commission of a crime before taking the military oath; and reporting the crime and pleading guilty.[54]

If it finds that a crime was committed under extenuating circumstances, a military tribunal has two courses of action open to it. It may pronounce a milder penalty within the limits authorized in the article of the code defining the crime and declaring the sanctions applicable; or it may apply Article 51 of the Criminal Code, which authorizes Soviet courts under special circumstances to impose a milder penalty than that authorized in the article of the code applicable to the particular crimes. The use of Article 51 was encouraged in the latter part of the war, especially in cases of capital crimes in which, as Chkhikvadze writes, "the military tribunals did not see in [the death penalty] a useful purpose." [55] In many cases of minor military crimes committed under extenuating circumstances, the code provides that disciplinary action, rather than a criminal penalty, is applicable.[56]

4. TYPES OF PUNISHMENTS

The Criminal Code lists the types of punishment applicable to crimes generally, without distinguishing between military and nonmilitary crimes. These types of punishment include some, however, which in their nature are not applicable to military personnel (e.g., expulsion from the territory of the USSR, and expulsion to another region of the USSR). Also, the code specifically excludes the imposition of so-called "corrective-labor tasks," which amount in practice to a money fine, upon military personnel below certain ranks, substituting therefor the penalty of so-called "disciplinary confinement" up to two months.[57]

The penalties generally applicable to both servicemen and nonservicemen are the death penalty, deprivation of freedom, deprivation of civil rights, confiscation of part or all of the convicted person's property, and money compensation for harm caused by a criminal act. In addition, penalties applicable only to servicemen are forfeiture of rank and transfer to disciplinary or penal battalions.

(a) *The Death Penalty.* Prior to the decree of May 26, 1947, abolishing the death penalty,[58] Article 193 made the death sentence mandatory for sixteen types of military crimes. Only five of these, however, were affected by the 1947 decree, since the remaining eleven are punishable by death if committed in time of war only, and the preamble of the 1947 decree specified the existence of peaceful international relations as a condition of its enactment. Of the five types of crime affected by the decree, three were punishable by death if committed under certain circumstances in time of peace *or* if committed in time of war; presumably the death penalty remained — and remains — applicable to those three types in time of war. Thus, fourteen types of military crime have been punishable by death both before and after May 26, 1947.

A decree of January 12, 1950, modifying but not repealing the decree of May 26, 1947, states that the abolition of capital punishment shall not be applicable to "traitors, spies, and saboteurs." [59] This apparently means that the death penalty is reintroduced for acts which fall in the category of counterrevolutionary crimes, punishable under Article 58. Thus military treason, punishable by death before May 26, 1947, is once again so punishable, whether committed in war or peace, bringing to sixteen the number of capital military crimes. The sixteen are listed below.

In time of war or peace:

1. Military treason; [60]

In time of war:

2. Failure to execute an order, under aggravating circumstances; [61]

3. Offering resistance to a person executing a service duty, under aggravating circumstances; [62]

4. Coercing a person to violate a service duty, under aggravating circumstances; [63]

5. Desertion by privates and noncommissioned officers (absence without leave for more than twenty-four hours); [64]

6. "Flight" (*pobeg*) by officers (absence without leave for more than six days, or on certain occasions for more than two days, or with intent entirely to evade military service); [65]

7. Absence without leave during combat; [66]

8. Failure to report punctually without adequate reason after transfer, assignment, mission, or furlough; [67]

9. Evasion of induction, under especially aggravating circumstances; [68]

10. Evasion of service duties by infliction of self-injury,

feigning illness, presenting false papers, or some other deceit; [69]

11. Evasion of service duties under pretext of religious or other convictions; [70]

12. Embezzlement, intentional destruction or injury, or breach of regulations concerning the protection of uniform or equipment; [71]

13. Breach of guard duties at arms or other important depots or with serious consequences, during military operations and under aggravating circumstances; [72]

14. Abuse, excess, or neglect of authority, or negligent attitude toward authority by commanding personnel, under especially aggravating circumstances; [73]

15. Stealing from the dead or wounded on the battlefield, under aggravating circumstances; [74]

16. Robbery, pillage, or violence committed against the civilian population in an area of military operations and under aggravating circumstances.[75]

Before May 26, 1947, the following military crimes were also punishable by death *in time of peace*:

1. Offering resistance to a person executing a service duty, if committed by a group of persons, or with force or arms, or under aggravating circumstances; [76]

2. Coercing a person to violate a service duty, if committed by a group of persons, or with force or arms, or under aggravating circumstances; [77]

3. Abuse, excess, or neglect of authority, or negligent attitude toward authority by commanding personnel, if committed systematically, or from mercenary considerations or other personal interest, or if it had or to the knowledge of the actor could have had serious consequences; [78]

4. Disclosure of military information "specially to be guarded as a state secret," if such disclosure had or to the knowledge of the actor could have had especially serious consequences.[79]

In 1954 the Supreme Soviet introduced the death penalty for murder committed under especially aggravating circumstances.* This is the first time in Russian history since 1754 that capital punishment has been made applicable to a crime which is neither political nor military. The 1954 law thus adds one non-military crime to the sixteen military and political crimes for which a Soviet soldier may be executed.

It is the duty of the president of a military tribunal to wire a report of every death sentence to the President of the Military Division of the Supreme Court and to the Chief Procurator of the Army or Navy. If no reply comes within seventy-two hours after receipt of the wire, the sentence must be executed, with the exception that in time of war military councils or commanders of army groups, armies, fleets, and military districts may postpone execution of the sentence.

The death penalty is executed ordinarily by shooting. However, by an edict of the Presidium of the Supreme Soviet of April 19, 1943, death by hanging was introduced for crimes by "German-Fascist war criminals and their abettors" against the population or against prisoners of war, and also for Soviet espionage and treason.[80]

(b) *Deprivation of Freedom.* The punishment most frequently applied by Soviet courts in general is deprivation of freedom. The maximum sentence is twenty-five years. Sentences up to three years are served in "general places of imprisonment," which include local jails and labor and agricultural colonies. Sentences above three years are served in corrective labor camps or, in the case of "the most dangerous crimes," in prison.[81]

In time of war, military courts are authorized by the Criminal Code to postpone execution of sentences of deprivation of freedom until the end of the war, with the condition that the convicted persons must be ordered immediately to the front, but with the further provision that upon recommendation of their military commanders the postponed penalties may later be annulled or reduced if the servicemen prove themselves "staunch defenders of the USSR in the ranks of the fighting forces." [82]

* *Pravda*, May 7, 1954.

Deprivation of freedom in the case of military personnel is usually accompanied by forfeiture of rank and by discharge from the service. It is sometimes accompanied by deprivation of civil rights and by partial or total confiscation of property. Postponement of deprivation of freedom until the end of the war is not authorized when it is accompanied by deprivation of civil rights. If deprivation of freedom is accompanied by forfeiture of rank, such forfeiture cannot be postponed even though the deprivation of freedom may be postponed.[83]

(c) *Deprivation of Civil Rights.* A Soviet court may pass sentence depriving the convicted person of any or all of the following rights: the right to vote or be elected to public office, the right to hold an elective office in social organizations (such as trade unions), the right to hold certain public offices, the right to hold honorary titles (such as Hero of Soviet Labor), parental rights, and the rights to social security benefits.[84] As an independent penalty, these rights may be taken away for a period up to five years.[85] According to Soviet writers, judicial practice has established a customary minimum of two years.[86] If imposed as a supplementary penalty, they are taken away for the duration of the deprivation of freedom, and, in the discretion of the court, for an additional period up to five years.[87] The loss of electoral (i.e., civil) rights by a serviceman involves discharge from the service and loss of all orders and medals.[88]

In January 1943 the Plenum of the Supreme Court of the USSR authorized lower courts to suspend previously imposed sentences of deprivation of civil rights — except in cases of persons convicted of "counterrevolutionary crimes (other than failure to inform) and banditism" — in order to permit ex-convicts to be called up for military service.[89]

The loss of the right to a pension may be imposed as a supplementary penalty in time of peace for most, and in time of war for all, of the military crimes listed in Article 193 of the Criminal Code.[90]

(d) *Confiscation of Property.* Confiscation of property may be pronounced by a Soviet court only as a supplementary penalty in cases specifically provided by law.[91] These include most capital military crimes. Confiscation of property supplements deprivation of freedom in cases of absence without leave during war operations, failure to report punctually without adequate reason after transfer, assignment, mission, or furlough under extenuating circumstances, and evasion of military duty in case of mobilization in time of war.

When confiscation of property is applied as a supplementary penalty to deprivation of freedom, the confiscation may be either total or partial; in cases of capital crimes the confiscation is total. However, even in cases of total confiscation, household belongings indispensable to the convicted person and to members of his family, and also tools used for handicrafts, artisan manufacture, and farming, are exempt. Instruments for professional activities may only be confiscated in cases in which the court forbade the convicted person to continue the pursuit of his profession. Also the convicted person and his family must be left with money and provisions sufficient, in terms of average local income, to maintain them for a period of three months.[92]

(e) *Compensation for Injury.* A Soviet criminal court may award damages, as a civil remedy to persons who suffered loss as a result of a criminal act, at the same time that it imposes the criminal sentence. By a law of 1943 military tribunals were authorized to decide, together with the criminal proceedings, civil claims in cases of destruction, embezzlement, or loss of public property.[93] Thus state agencies may recover compensation for losses suffered, but apparently private persons must bring separate actions in the civil courts.

In April 1945 the military tribunals were declared to have civil jurisdiction, in criminal cases, only with respect to suits brought by military units.[94]

The 1943 law was directed to the acute problem of waste and illegal sale of military equipment. Demonstration trials were held before the troops in order to combat these widespread crimes. In granting money compensation, tables for the appraisal of the value of military equipment by the courts were frequently changed in order to bring the damages imposed by the court up and beyond the level of black-market prices.[95]

(f) *Forfeiture of Rank.* Of this punishment Chkhikvadze writes:

According to the Statute on the Service of Commanding Personnel of the Soviet Army issued by decree of the Central Executive Committee and Council of People's Commissars of the USSR of September 22, 1935, the court has the right to apply deprivation of military rank in the case of commanding personnel convicted of crimes. This measure should be considered as a special form of deprivation of rights and should be applied as a measure supplementary to the basic punishment chosen by the court.

The deprivation of military rank is appropriate only in those cases when the military tribunal establishes that because of the character of the crime or other basic reasons, the convicted person cannot be worthy to bear military rank. Deprivation of officers' rank involves the removal of the serviceman from his official position in the army. In imposing a sentence of deprivation of military rank upon an officer, the military tribunal is obliged to send a copy of the sentence and also a notice concerning its issuance or its entrance into legal effect to the Ministry of Armed Forces of the USSR, for issuance and promulgation by order of the Ministry of Armed Forces of the USSR, and in any case of a person who has acquired military rank by decree of the government for presentation to the government.[96]

(g) *Disciplinary and Penal Battalions.* By a law of July 13, 1940,[97] the ancient Russian institution of special battalions for military offenders was reintroduced by the Soviet government. Called disciplinary battalions in time of peace, and penal battalions in time of war, these units serve as a means of utilizing for military purposes the services of persons who because of their crimes would otherwise be lost to military service.

Chkhikvadze writes: "The basic purpose of the disciplinary battalion consists in the compulsory education in the hard habits of those enlisted men and noncommissioned officers of the armed forces who have committed socially dangerous violations of the military or the general legal order. The entire internal life of the disciplinary battalion is subordinated to this goal." [98]

According to Chkhikvadze, only enlisted men and noncommissioned officers may be sentenced to a disciplinary battalion, and only as a substitute for the penalty of deprivation of freedom for a period from six months to two years for any crimes except counterrevolutionary ones. In fact, however, officers may be reduced to enlisted rank by verdict of a military tribunal or by disciplinary action and then sentenced to a disciplinary battalion. Another Soviet writer on military criminal law states that commanders may send enlisted personnel to penal companies as a matter of disciplinary action, and that officers may be sent to penal battalions (apparently by verdict of a military tribunal).*

The time spent in a disciplinary battalion does not count as time spent in military service; however, it is considered that persons serving in disciplinary battalions are still in the armed forces and they are retained on the lists of the units. Servicemen sentenced to deprivation of electoral rights and consequently to discharge from military service cannot be sent to disciplinary battalions. Men whose conduct is exemplary may be sent back to their units after the completion of one-third of their sentence at the discretion of the commanding officer of the battalion. After a serviceman is returned to his unit, he regains his previous status and the sentence of penal servitude in the disciplinary battalion is not counted as a criminal record.

The discipline is, of course, much stricter than in regular units; for example, any unauthorized departure, regardless of the length of the absence, is considered to be desertion. In addition, the sentenced man and his family lose all their allowances for the period of service in the disciplinary battalion.

It is striking that Chkhikvadze refers only once, and that in passing, to the use of these battalions in time of war. In fact, it is well known that sentence to penal battalions was common during the last war and was perhaps the penalty most frequently imposed. It was imposed not only on enlisted men and noncommissioned officers but also on officers (together with reduction to enlisted rank). These battalions were often given the most dangerous assignments, and those who survived several months of service in them certainly deserved rehabilitation into the ranks of their units.[99]

A former Soviet military procurator has given the following

* M. A. Chel'tsov, *Sovetskii ugolovnyi protsess* (Soviet Criminal Procedure; Moscow, 1951), p. 413. The passage is quoted below, p. 116.

description of the practice in regard to sentence in penal battalion during World War II.

First, there was a statement in the text of the sentence of the military tribunal that the convicted person deserved for his act the severest penalty — death by shooting. Then reference was made to Article 51 of the Criminal Code of the RSFSR, which provides that in exceptional circumstances the court may impose a less severe punishment than the minimum prescribed in the relevant article of the code. Having found some extenuating circumstances, the military tribunal then pronounced a penalty of deprivation of freedom for a considerable length of time. After that, a reference was made to Article 28, note 2 of the Criminal Code, permitting the execution of a sentence passed in war time, inflicting deprivation of liberty without loss of rights on a serviceman, to be postponed until the conclusion of military operations. Finally, the court granted to the convicted man the right to save his life by self-sacrifice and heroism — in a penal battalion. . .

The regime in the penal battalions was not much different from the regime in the corrective labor camps. Order in these battalions was upheld by special military details of the Ministry of State Security which were subordinated to the MVD Special Section of the Army.[100]

It is believed that special impetus to the institution of penal battalions was given by an order of July 1942, reportedly signed by Stalin, known as *Ni shagu nazad* ("Not a step backwards"). This order has not been published in any official Soviet materials, but is described by several former Soviet officers as instructing military courts to deal mercilessly with military personnel who retreated without instructions by their commanders, "breaking generals to privates, sentencing the guilty to penal units, etc., up to death by shooting." [101]

5. SUSPENSION AND COMMUTATION OF SENTENCES; REHABILITATION; AMNESTIES

(a) *Suspension and Commutation of Sentences.* Suspension of the execution of a sentence may be applied in military criminal law as in general criminal law "if the court considers that the degree of danger which the convicted person constitutes does not call for his compulsory isolation or the necessity to employ him on forced labor." The release of the criminal is conditional upon his not committing a "fresh crime of an equally serious character" for a period of probation from one year to ten years as fixed by the court. If the period of probation is survived successfully, the convicted person is "considered as not having been indicted." [102]

Under Article 28, note 2, as previously mentioned, the execution of a sentence in wartime may be postponed until the conclusion of military operations. It is further provided in Article 28, note 2, that a serviceman who "has shown himself to be a staunch defender of the USSR shall either be freed from the previously assigned measure of social defense on application of the proper military commander or have it replaced by order of the court which handed down the sentence." [103]

(b) *Rehabilitation*. It is a feature of Soviet criminal law, as of the criminal law of many countries of continental Europe, that a convicted person may be rehabilitated, in the sense that his conviction may be removed from his record. Indeed, Article 55 of the RSFSR Criminal Code states that any person found not guilty by the court and any person who has been given a conditional sentence and who during the period of probation has not committed a fresh crime equally serious in character — "shall be considered as not having been indicted." The same applies automatically to a person sentenced to deprivation of liberty for not more than six months and who has not committed a fresh crime equally serious in character within three years thereafter, and any person sentenced to deprivation of liberty for more than six months but not more than three years who during a period of six years has not committed a fresh crime equally serious in character.

(c) *Amnesties*. The Soviet Constitution gives the Presidium of the Supreme Soviet of the USSR or of a constituent republic the power to grant an amnesty to convicted criminals. The two most recent general amnesties were in 1945, after the victory over Germany, and in 1953, after the accession of the Malenkov government.[104]

By an edict of July 7, 1945, the Presidium of the Supreme Soviet of the USSR granted an amnesty to all servicemen whose sentences had been suspended under Article 28, note 2, as well as to persons convicted of military crimes under Sections 2, 5, 6, 7, 9, 10, 10*a*, 14, 15, and 16 of Article 193 of the Criminal Code, persons convicted of absence without leave from enterprises of war industry, and all persons sentenced to deprivation of freedom for not more than three years or to lighter punishments.

In addition the 1945 amnesty reduced by half the remaining terms of persons sentenced to deprivation of freedom for more than three years, except those sentenced for counterrevolutionary crimes, theft of socialist property, banditism, counterfeiting, intentional homicide, and robbery. The edict also annulled the conviction of certain classes of persons amnestied, and discontinued the investigations and trials of pending cases of crimes to which the amnesty would apply if the accused had already been convicted. In pending cases in which the court had discretion to impose a sentence of more than three years' deprivation of freedom, the sentences were to be reduced by half, except for the crimes listed above. Administrative fines not yet exacted were to be rescinded. Expressly excluded from the 1945 amnesty, however, were persons who had been repeatedly convicted of squandering, theft, and so-called hooliganism (a crime roughly equivalent to breach of the peace).

The 1953 amnesty went even farther than the 1945 amnesty, liberating all persons sentenced for five years or less, all persons convicted of official and economic crimes, and all persons convicted of military crimes under Sections 4, *a*; 7, 8, 10, 10*a*, 14, 15, 16, and 17, *a*, of Article 193 of the Criminal Code, as well as all women with children up to ten years of age, all pregnant women, minors up to eighteen, men over fifty-five, women over fifty, and persons with serious incurable ailments. Provisions for reducing sentences over five years by half, and for discontinuing pending cases, similar to those in the 1945 edict, were also included in the 1953 edict.

The 1953 amnesty was expressly inapplicable to persons

condemned for more than five years for counterrevolutionary crimes, large-scale plunder of socialist property, banditism, or intentional homicide.

An important provision of the 1953 amnesty annulled the conviction of, and restored civil rights to, not only those amnestied under the edict but all persons previously convicted who had served their sentences.

Although detailed information concerning the implementation of the 1953 amnesty is not available, there is reliable evidence that it was carried out at least to a large extent if not entirely.

IV

SOVIET MILITARY COURTS
AND PROCEDURE

1. ORGANIZATION OF MILITARY COURTS

Each of the sixteen Soviet constituent republics has a separate hierarchy of courts for the trial and appeal of criminal and civil cases, starting with local People's Courts and culminating with the Supreme Court of the republic. At each level beyond that of the People's Courts there are separate criminal and civil divisions (*collegia*). Over the republican courts is a single federal court, the Supreme Court of the USSR, which also has a criminal and a civil division.[1]

In addition to criminal and civil courts, the Soviet judicial system contains so-called "special courts," of which there are four types: military, rail-transport, water-transport, and camp courts.[2] These are permanent courts established at military headquarters, railway centers, waterway centers, and corrective-labor camps, respectively. Appeals taken from the lower courts go up through separate judicial hierarchies, independent of the regular republican courts, but culminate also in the Supreme Court of the USSR, which has a Military Division, a Rail-Transport Division, a Water-Transport Division, and a so-called "Judicial Division for the Affairs of Camp Courts." Representatives of all the divisions of the Supreme Court (which comprises some seventy-five members in all) sit as a Plenum, with jurisdiction to review cases decided in a particular collegium.[3]

On January 1, 1942, the rail- and water-transport courts were reorganized as military courts.[4] This change reflected a general militarization of the transportation system, which in 1943 was declared to be under martial law.[5] The transport courts continued to have jurisdiction over crimes connected with transportation, whether committed by railroad workers or others, but their organization and procedure was now governed by military criminal law. They remained subordinate to the Rail-Transport and Water-Transport Divisions of the Supreme Court. Apparently there has been no "demilitarization" of the transport courts since the war.

A separate system of military courts exists for troops of the Ministry of Internal Affairs (MVD). MVD troops are not immediately subordinate to the Ministry of Defense but are under the Chief Administration of Border and Internal Guards of the MVD. However, MVD military courts are, like the regular military courts, subordinate to the Military Division of the Supreme Court. The MVD military courts also have jurisdiction over service offenses by persons employed by the MVD.

An intricate network of relations exists between the military courts, other organs connected with the administration of justice, and other organs connected with military administration.

(a) *Relations Between Military Courts and Other Organs of Justice.* Supervision over the military courts is exercised by (1) the Supreme Court of the USSR, (2) the Ministry of Justice of the USSR, and (3) the Office of the Procurator-General of the USSR.

1. The Statute on Military Tribunals states: "General direction of the activities of military tribunals belongs to the All-Union Supreme Court of the Soviet Union. Immediate direction of the activities and administration is performed by the Military Division of the All-Union Supreme Court." [6]

The Military Division consists of a president, a vice-president and four other judges. Like the members of the other divisions of the Supreme Court, they are chosen by the Supreme Soviet of the USSR for a term of five years. The Military Division has original jurisdiction over cases of special political importance (for example, it sat on the great purge trials of 1937 and 1938), and it is a court of review for cases tried by subordinate military courts.

Thus the military courts form an independent hierarchy, with reviewing authority in the higher courts rather than in the commanders of the units to which they are attached.

2. The Ministry of Justice exercises supervision over military courts through its Chief Administration for Army Military Tribunals, Chief Administration for Navy Military Tribunals, Chief Administration for MVD Military Tribunals, and Chief Administration for Transport Military Tribunals; it also has a Chief Administration for Camp Courts. The chief administrations are concerned with organizational problems of the military courts, the efficiency with which they conduct their activities, the training of their personnel, and similar matters. Although they have no jurisdiction to reverse decisions of military courts, they may receive complaints about such decisions and have the right to ask the president of a higher court to protest decisions which they believe to be wrong. According to N. Semenov, a former Soviet military procurator, the chief administrations for military courts of the Ministry of Justice are in fact, however, "sections of cadres for the Military Division of the Supreme Court which operate according to its instructions." [7]

3. The Office of the Procurator-General of the USSR is not only in charge of criminal investigations and prosecutions but also exercises a general supervision over all official bodies, whether legislative, administrative, or judicial. It has the power to "protest" any action of an official body to the superior authorities; in the case of judicial organs, it has the power to "protest" the decision of any court to the next higher court.

Separate offices of the Procurator-General of the USSR, headed by his deputies, exist for the army, the navy, rail-transport, and water-transport; in addition the military procuracy of the army has a special division of military procurators for MVD troops. There is a military procurator for each military court. The military procurator exercises functions similar to those of civilian procurators: he supervises the investigation of criminal cases, conducts the prosecution, and "protests" decisions of lower courts.

(b) *Relations Between Military Courts and Other Organs of Military Administration.* In the light of their relations with the Military Division of the Supreme Court, the Ministry of Justice, and the Procuracy, it is apparent that the military courts are in most respects independent of the commanders of army, navy, transport, and MVD units. There are, however, some connecting links between military courts and military command which deserve to be mentioned.

The military courts are attached to headquarters of higher military units. Military courts of first instance are found at the level of division, corps, garrison, subarea, fortified region, and army, and at corresponding levels of the navy. Higher military tribunals, with both original and appellate jurisdiction, are found at the level of army group, independent army, and military district, and at corresponding levels of the navy. The particular headquarters provides the administrative requirements of the court, including such necessary personnel as the clerk of court, court reporter, statistician, librarian, typists, orderlies, and an officer who administers the affairs of the court and gives it military protection.[8] All these except typists and orderlies are military personnel. The professional military judges, too, are military personnel of officer rank, with particular ranks attached to particular judicial offices.[9] They are therefore subject to military regulations.

In addition, while the permanent professional judges of military courts are appointed by the Military Division of the Supreme Court (or by other higher military courts), two temporary lay judges who normally sit on the three-judge military trial court are chosen from the military unit. Theoretically at least, each of these lay judges (called people's assessors) has an equal voice with the permanent judge. (Actually, from all indications, they usually subordinate themselves to him.) The assessors are chosen from a list (by whom prepared is not certain) and serve a certain number of days each year, during which time they are relieved from their normal military duties.[10]

Another connection between the military courts and the military units at which they are located is the fact that the preliminary investigation and inquiry, which play such an important part in Soviet criminal justice, may be conducted in less serious cases by investigators appointed by the military commander. The commander has a special responsibility in regard to military crimes committed by his subordinates, and apparently it has been thought undesirable to remove investigation and inquiry entirely from his control. The military procurators, although independent of unit commanders and subordinate only to higher officials of the procuracy, are nevertheless supposed to coöperate with unit commanders and to help them carry out their policies.

Perhaps the most important link between the military courts and army command is through the military councils. Formally, the military councils have only two connections with the military courts. The president of a military court is supposed periodically to inform the appropriate military council of the army group, district, or independent army, or the commanding officer of the appropriate lower unit such as corps or division, of the work of the courts and of their fight against criminality in the particular unit concerned. Secondly, in localities under martial law and in regions of war operations the military councils have the right to stay execution of a capital sentence. Informally, however, the military councils influence the courts through their declarations of policy. "The successful execution of military tasks," it was stated in 1946, ". . . demands the concerted action of command, of political organs, of military justice and of the military procuracy under one common leadership — the leadership of the military councils of armies and army groups." [11]

(c) *Military Courts in Localities Under Martial Law and in Regions of Military Operations.* During the war certain changes were made in the organization and jurisdiction of military tribunals in localities under martial law and in regions of military operations. A statute of June 22, 1941,[12] established military tribunals at headquarters of army corps and other military organizations and militarized institutions, and at headquarters of military districts, army groups, and naval fleets. These are permanent tribunals, composed of three members. The three members may all be permanent judges, or two of them may be assessors nominated by the particular army command. Joint control over the tribunals is exercised, under the statute, by the

Ministry of Justice and the Ministry of Defense, which decide upon the composition of particular tribunals, appoint new judges, and transfer chairmen and vice-chairmen of tribunal or military areas, army groups, and armies. (The chairmen of courts below these. levels are transferred by the chairmen of military tribunals of army groups and naval fleets.)

2. JURISDICTION OF MILITARY COURTS

(a) *Jurisdiction of Person and Subject Matter.* Soviet military courts have jurisdiction over these crimes: (1) all crimes committed by servicemen, members of the reserve during training period, and enemy prisoners-of-war, (2) service crimes committed by certain classes of persons serving under the Ministry of Internal Affairs and Committee (formerly Ministry) of State Security, (3) service crimes committed by rail- and water-transport workers, (4) service crimes committed by civil defense personnel, and (5) certain crimes no matter by whom committed.

1. Prior to the law of December 13, 1940, military courts had jurisdiction over certain types of crimes committed by servicemen, namely, military crimes as defined in Sections 1–31 of Article 193 of the RSFSR Criminal Code, counterrevolutionary crimes as defined in Article 58, and especially dangerous crimes against the administrative order as defined in Article 59. For other crimes, particularly those not connected with service duties, servicemen were triable in the ordinary criminal courts. The 1940 law has enlarged the jurisdiction of military courts over servicemen to include all crimes committed by them.[13]

2. Military courts of the Ministry of Internal Affairs have jurisdiction over service offenses of the following classes of persons: officers of the Ministry of Internal Affairs and the state security organs, operative ("line") personnel and economic-administrative personnel of the police, personnel of the military guard of corrective-labor camps and colonies and supervisory personnel of prisons of the Ministry of Internal

Affairs, and personnel of the military guard of enterprises and the military fire guard.[14]

3. Similarly, the military courts of rail- and water-transport have jurisdiction over service offenses of transport workers. Respecting rail-transport, these offenses were defined by a law of November 27, 1930,[15] before the militarization of the transport courts, as follows: malicious breach of labor discipline by transport workers; breach or nonfulfillment of traffic regulations causing damage or destruction of railroad rolling stock and installations or causing accidents to persons; breach or nonfulfillment of traffic regulations representing an immediate threat to the correctness or security of traffic; crimes causing an accumulation of empty cars at unloading places as well as stoppage of freight cars and keeping superfluous freight cars in pools; poor quality repair work and releasing for use poorly repaired freight cars, locomotives, tank cars, or other transport equipment; other crimes committed against transport in breach of the normal work of transport; and all cases of counterrevolutionary crimes connected with the work of rail-transport, with the exception of those which are under the jurisdiction of military tribunals.

A similar list of offenses for water transport was promulgated by a law of June 7, 1934.[16] These offenses may also be committed by others than transport workers, unless otherwise specified in the definition of the offense.

In addition to the above offenses, military crimes as defined in Article 193 of the Criminal Code may be committed by railroad workers, who are apparently still under martial law. In 1948 transport workers were subject to the same punishment for desertion as servicemen.[17]

4. Some sixteen million Soviet citizens, mostly youth, are enrolled in the civil defense organization called *Dosaaf*. (See Chapter I.) This organization is civilian, in the sense that its members are not in the armed forces and its work is directed primarily to air-raid protection, organization of the population in besieged places, clearing of mines, and similar civil defense work, as well as military sports. However it also serves the armed forces more directly and is considered as an auxiliary

volunteer force. Its branches are under the jurisdiction of the military councils. The Plenum of the Supreme Court of the USSR ruled on February 18, 1943, that service offenses committed by local civil defense personnel are punishable according to military criminal.law and are under the jurisdiction of military tribunals.[18]

Also, persons conscripted through military commissariats into units of local antiaircraft defense (MPVO) were declared by the Supreme Court to be subject to the Statute on Military Crimes and under the jurisdiction of military tribunals for crimes committed against the order established for the performance of such service.[19]

5. Civilians are tried in Soviet military courts for the following crimes:

i. Counterrevolutionary crimes of treason, espionage, terror, sabotage, arson, "and other types of subversive acts," under Sections 6, 8, and 9 of Article 58 of the Criminal Code;

ii. All counterrevolutionary crimes in which military information is involved;

iii. Violation of the Edict on State Secrets of 1947;

iv. Theft of firearms or ammunition, or purchase or possession or sale of stolen firearms or ammunition, under Article 59 (3a) of the Criminal Code;*

v. Spreading false rumors which create alarm among the population in time of war;

vi. Unauthorized quitting of enterprises of war industry by workers or employees; [20]

vii. Evasion of call-up during mobilization or breach of military registration in time of war;

viii. "Other crimes which threaten the strength and might of the Workers' and Peasants' Red Army, jurisdiction over which may be assigned to military tribunals in the established procedure." [21]

ix. In addition, crimes against rail- and water-transport, no matter by whom committed, are tried in the military transport courts.

* This provision was enacted originally in 1934 as Article 17 of the Statute on State Crimes. It is translated in Berman and Kerner, *Documents*, no. 28.

x. Civilians are tried in military courts for complicity in any military crime. If a particular case falls within the jurisdiction of both the civilian and the military courts (as, for example, where several crimes are committed by one person, or one crime is committed by several accomplices of whom some are subject to military jurisdiction), the military court has exclusive jurisdiction.[22]

xi. In localities under martial law and in regions of war operations the jurisdiction of military courts was enlarged by a law of June 22, 1941, to include practically all serious crimes no matter by whom committed, and indeed, if deemed necessary by the military authorities, all crimes whatsoever. This law was repealed on September 21, 1945, and July 4, 1946.[23]

xii. By a law of February 27, 1934, which has remained in force, military tribunals have jurisdiction over crimes committed in localities "where by force of exceptional circumstances general courts are not functioning." [24]

(b) *Division of Business Among Military Courts.* In general, the army military courts have jurisdiction over crimes committed by army personnel, the navy military courts over crimes committed by navy personnel, the MVD military courts over crimes committed by MVD troops (as well as service crimes by other classes of MVD personnel), the military courts of transport over crimes committed by transport troops (as well as service crimes committed by transport workers).

Jurisdiction over counterrevolutionary and allied political or semipolitical crimes is divided chiefly between the army and MVD military courts, with power left to the military transport courts to try counterrevolutionary crimes associated with transport. The lines of division are far from clear-cut. The army military courts are said to have jurisdiction over crimes of treason, espionage, terrorist acts, and sabotage. The MVD military courts are said to have jurisdiction over the following: arson of houses of rural leaders ("activists") and public buildings (schools, rural soviets, collective-farm buildings, etc.) in rural localities, and terroristic acts and terroristic agitation relating to the rural leadership; spreading false rumors which create alarm among the population in time of war; unauthorized quitting of war enterprises by workers or employees; evasion of call-up during mobilization and breach of regulations of military registration; and disclosure of state secrets and loss of especially important documents.[25]

In addition, MVD military courts were given wartime jurisdiction over all important crimes committed by nonservicemen in localities under martial law, except for crimes committed on railroads and waterways which remained under the jurisdiction of the military transport courts. Further, in areas adjoining the regions of military operations, MVD military courts were organized as special courts for the protection of the rear. These courts had jurisdiction over cases of desertion from military service, as well as the usual jurisdiction of MVD military courts.

The political character of MVD military courts is corroborated by the statement of the authors of a leading Soviet treatise on judicial procedure that "the military tribunals of troops of the Ministry of Internal Affairs carry out all their activities in concurrence with the political organs of the corresponding districts." [26]

Within a particular hierarchy of military courts, original jurisdiction is divided according to the rank of the accused, insofar as high-ranking officers are subject to trial by courts of the next higher unit. Thus military tribunals of a division have original jurisdiction over members of the division of the rank of battalion commander and below; corps military tribunals have original jurisdiction over members of the corps of the rank of deputy regimental commander and below; tribunals of military districts (army groups, independent armies, and fleets) have original jurisdiction over all above the rank of deputy regimental commander, with the exception of those who are subject to the original jurisdiction of the Military Division of the Supreme Court of the USSR.

The Military Division of the Supreme Court of the USSR has original jurisdiction over military crimes committed by the following classes of persons: heads of the Chief Administrations of the Ministry of Defense; heads of the Chief Administration of the Border and Internal Guards of the Ministry of Internal Affairs; commanders and members of military councils of army groups, independent armies, fleets, and military districts; heads of Chief Administrations of military districts; commanders of armies, corps, divisions, and independent brigades; and deputies and assistants of all the above named persons. The Military Division also tries all cases of chairmen and members of military tribunals and of military procurators and their assistants. Also, it has original jurisdiction over all serious cases of espionage, treason, terrorist acts, and sabotage, as well as over any individual case assigned to it by decision of the Presidium of the Supreme Soviet of the USSR. Further, it may on its own motion take any case from any military tribunal by reason of its complexity or its political or social importance.

3. PROCEDURE IN MILITARY COURTS

(a) *Principles of Soviet Criminal Procedure.* Just as the general principles of Soviet criminal law (contained chiefly in the Criminal Code) are applicable to military crimes, so the general principles of Soviet criminal procedure (contained chiefly in the Code of Criminal Procedure) are applicable to the procedure of military courts. The Code of Criminal Procedure also defines certain special features of military criminal procedure. However, a more comprehensive guide to those special features is found in the Statute on Military Tribunals and the Military Procuracy.[27] In addition, the special needs of wartime procedure were met by the Statute on Military Tribunals in Localities under Martial Law and in Regions of War Operations, enacted on June 22, 1941.[28]

In general, Soviet criminal procedure, though far more informal and "inquisitorial" than that of the United States, rests on certain basic principles of due process which are characteristic of Western law. The trial is public; the accused is presumed to be innocent until proved guilty; both sides are heard; witnesses are examined in open court; the accused has a right to be represented by legal counsel; an appeal may be taken to a higher court. However, three important qualifications must be made to these basic principles of Soviet criminal procedure.

First, they are inapplicable to cases of persons suspected by the MVD of being "socially dangerous" and tried by the "Special Board" of the MVD: the procedure of the Special Board is secret, summary, and arbitrary, with no provision for legal representation of the accused (who may in fact be tried in absentia) and with no right of appeal.[29]

Second, in cases of espionage, terrorist acts, wrecking, and other subversive acts, which under the Code of Criminal Procedure are within the exclusive jurisdiction of the military courts, the procedure is likewise summary and arbitrary, with explicit provision for trial "without the participation of the accused" and with no right of appeal.[30]

Third, even in nonpolitical cases tried by the ordinary criminal courts, the Soviet judge plays a "parental" role, treating the accused with less objectivity and dispassionateness than is traditional in Western legal systems.[31] In general, the Soviet judge is less concerned with the particular criminal act charged and more concerned with the accused's whole personality than is his American counterpart. Further, the Soviet judge is supposed to bring to bear on each case the entire weight of state policy. The results of this parental attitude of the Soviet judge would probably strike most Americans as praiseworthy in some cases, outrageous in others.

In addition, it should be mentioned that Soviet criminal procedure differs from that of the United States but resembles that of most countries of continental Europe in placing great stress on a preliminary investigation, conducted by an examining magistrate, prior to the issuance of an indictment.[32]

Finally, an important and distinctive feature of the Soviet system of criminal procedure consists in the broad authority of the procuracy to "protest" court decisions to higher judicial bodies.[33] Although the procuracy is also the prosecuting arm of the state, its protest functions seem to be entirely separate from its prosecuting functions, and many cases are reported in which the procuracy has protested convictions.

(b) *Special Features of Soviet Military Procedure.* The

chief distinction between the usual Soviet military preliminary procedure in peacetime and the preliminary procedure of the ordinary Soviet criminal courts is that the period allowed for the preliminary investigation in cases of ordinary military crimes is limited to two weeks, whereas in the nonmilitary criminal procedure it is limited to two months but may be extended indefinitely with permission of the procuracy.[34]

In respect to trial of persons accused of terrorist acts, referred to above, the Code of Criminal Procedure provides that the preliminary investigation must be completed within a period of ten days, that the indictment shall be delivered to the accused within twenty-four hours before trial, and that the case shall be decided without the presence of the accused; and also that no appeal or petition for pardon shall be allowed and that the death sentence must be executed immediately upon pronouncement of the sentence.[35] In cases of espionage, treason, sabotage, and certain other counterrevolutionary activities, which are also triable by military courts, the normal criminal procedure is modified in that the indictment is delivered to the accused within twenty-four hours before trial, no appeal is allowed, and the death sentence must be executed immediately upon the rejection of a petition for pardon.[36]

During World War II Soviet military procedure had the following features distinguishing it from the ordinary criminal procedure and from the peacetime military procedure in nonpolitical cases:[37]

1. The military courts could try cases twenty-four hours after the indictment was delivered to the accused.

2. Trials in military courts could be (and were generally) conducted in the absence of both the prosecutor and defense counsel.

3. Trials in military courts could be conducted, at the discretion of the president of the court, by three professional military judges, without the participation of people's assessors.

4. There was no right of appeal, though decisions were reviewed by higher courts under the usual "protest" procedure.

5. The power to protest decisions of lower courts was extended to the President of the Military Division of the Supreme

Court of the USSR and military courts of army groups.

6. It was provided that notice of any death sentence be cabled to the President of the Military Division of the Supreme Court of the USSR and the Chief Procurator of the Army or Navy, and that unless one of these authorities ordered the sentence to be suspended it would go into effect within seventy-two hours after receipt of the cable.

7. The number of persons exercising the right to suspend execution of death sentence was broadened to include commanding generals of army groups, independent armies, fleets, and military districts, who were required to notify the President of the Military Division of the Supreme Court of the USSR and the Chief Procurator of the Army or Navy in case of such suspension, and to recommend further procedure.

(c) *The Preliminary Investigation.* Soviet criminal procedure, like that of continental European countries generally, places great stress upon a pretrial investigation, in which an investigator interrogates the suspect and the witnesses and examines evidence. It is the investigator who, if he finds sufficient grounds, draws the indictment, which states in detail both the charges and the evidence against the accused. At the trial, the burden of proof of the facts alleged in the indictment is on the prosecutor.

The preliminary investigation, like the prosecution and the protesting of decisions to higher courts, is a function of the procuracy. The Soviets have undone the reform introduced in Russian law in 1864 which removed control over preliminary investigation from the procuracy to the courts.

In addition to the investigating organs of the procuracy, there are other investigating organs which may carry out preliminary investigations, such as the investigating organs of the MVD, of the state security apparatus and of the police (*militia*). Further, a so-called "inquiry" may be carried on, in a particular case, by organs of various departmental inspectorates, government institutions and enterprises, and in the armed forces by organs of commanding officers.

In the armed forces there are military investigators at the headquarters of the Chief Procurator of the Army, at the headquarters of the procurators of military districts, army groups, armies, corps, divisions, garrisons, and MVD units.[38] A corresponding organization exists for the navy. Officers may be specially assigned to conduct inquiries for a period of time by commanders of military units. There are five to six such officers assigned in a regiment.

A Soviet treatise gives the following description of the rules governing the inquiry in cases of military crimes.

The inquiry, as a rule, should be assigned and begun on the day of discovery of the crime and should continue not more than two to three days. Only in cases of great complexity may the commander of the unit receive the consent of the procurator of the particular military command for prolongation of the inquiry for a period up to fourteen days.

The completed inquiry is presented to the commander of the unit, who decides the question of the further disposition of the case.

According to Article 19 of the Disciplinary Code of the Armed Forces of the USSR: "In those instances when military criminal laws prescribe for an offense various punishments according to the degree of guilt, some of which punishments are imposed by a court and others in the disciplinary procedure — it shall depend on the commander whether to present the evidence against the guilty person to the organs of military investigation or to confine himself to a disciplinary penalty."

The commander of the unit and the military procurator supervise the conduct of the inquiry.

The inquisitor has the right to carry out all investigative acts. . . .

In the event that the criminal is apprehended at the place of the crime or with the corpus delicti, the organ of inquiry has the right to detain him, immediately informing the military procurator thereof. Within forty-eight hours the procurator is obliged either to affirm or to reverse the detention. The commander of the unit bears full responsibility for the correct conduct of the detention.

After arraignment of the accused one of the following preventive measures may be applied to him:

1. Closest observation in the unit (in the case of privates, and sergeants and master sergeants in restricted service);

2. Signed promise not to leave the place of service and residence (in the case of sergeants and master sergeants in extraterm service, junior and senior officers, and also voluntary employees);

3. Arrest in the guardhouse or in prison.

The decision concerning the selection of the preventive measure is issued by the commander of the unit.

At the conclusion of the inquiry, it is reported to the commander of the unit, who (depending on the results of the inquiry) determines its further disposition.

He may decide:

1. To present the accused for trial by a military tribunal;

2. In wartime, to send to penal companies persons of private, sergeant, and master sergeant rank, who are convicted of breach of discipline through cowardice or irresoluteness, and in the case of junior or senior officers subject to be sent to penal battalions for such crimes to present the inquiry to the commander of the command;

3. To decide the case in the disciplinary procedure;

4. To discontinue the inquiry in the event of the absence of the elements of a crime in the acts of the accused;

5. To send the inquiry to the military procurator for preliminary investigation.

The military procurator exercises supervision over the conduct of the inquiry and has the right to give instructions binding upon the organs of inquiry. In the event of disagreement with an instruction of the military procurator, the commander of the unit has the right to appeal it to the superior procurator, but without suspending execution of it.

The military procurator has the right also to remove from the commander of the unit an inquiry discontinued by him and to review the correctness of the discontinuance.

A preliminary investigation is not obligatory in cases of crimes covered in Articles 2–4, 6–8, 10, 11, 14, 17, and 19 of the Statute on Military Crimes [i.e., Article 193 of the Criminal Code]; in remaining cases under the jurisdiction of military tribunals, a preliminary investigation is obligatory (Article 25 of the Statute on Military Tribunals and the Military Procuracy).[39]

The rules governing the conduct of the inquiry are essentially the same as those governing the conduct of the preliminary investigation carried out by the professional military investigator. The Code of Criminal Procedure does not provide any punishment for the accused for failing to coöperate at the preliminary examination, and enjoins the investigator from using "violence, threats, or similar methods"; [40] the investigator, it is stated, "shall not have the right to refuse the request of the accused or of the complaining witness to interrogate witnesses or examine experts and to collect other evidence if the facts or circumstances sought to be established may have significance for the case"; [41] the accused must be asked questions the answers to which would tend to exonerate him as well as questions directed toward proving his guilt,[42] and he must be informed of his right to examine any part of the record.[43] In the trial proper the prosecutor cannot introduce evidence not previously known to the defendant.[44] On the other hand, appeals from abuses of pretrial procedure may be taken only to the procuracy, not to the courts.[45]

A conviction based upon an improper pretrial investigation may be reversed on appeal only if the impropriety consisted in failure to clarify circumstances whose clarification would have a necessary bearing upon the verdict and only if those circumstances were not clarified in the trial;[46] in other words, abuses in the investigation are not in themselves grounds for reversal.

These rules are equally applicable to military and non-military procedure.

The following description of the pretrial procedure in cases of military crimes is presented by N. Semenov, Soviet *émigré* with broad experience in military law:

Authorized investigators of the MGB conduct the investigation in cases of counterrevolutionary crimes, and military investigators and inquisitors in cases of military crimes. In conducting a preliminary investigation, a military investigator is under the supervision of the military procurator, while an inquisitor, who is named by the commander of the unit from among his subordinate officers for investigation of crimes and extraordinary occurrences, is under the supervision of the commander of the unit and of the military procuracy, and the instructions of the military procuracy are binding. The organs of the special section of the MGB, called "Smersh," are only formally under the supervision of the procurator. . .

In more complicated cases the preliminary investigation is conducted, according to Article 108 of the Code of Criminal Procedure, not by inquisitors subordinate to the commander of the unit, but by organs of the military procuracy, which is independent of the command and not subordinate to it in its activities. The military investigator . . . can restrict himself to doing the following: taking the case, presenting the accusation, questioning the accused, deciding the question of preventive measures of confinement, acquainting the accused with the evidence in the case, and composing an indictment (Articles 109, 110, 128, 129, 143, 206 of the Code of Criminal Procedure). Such a simplified procedure of investigation is widespread. As a rule the investigator inclines toward an inadequate investigation of the case and frequently influences its outcome only negatively. There are frequent instances when the organs of preliminary investigation (the organs of the MGB and the military investigators) do not fulfill the requirements provided by Article 206 of the Code of Criminal Procedure [whereby the investigator is required at the conclusion of the investigation to acquaint the accused with all the evidence, to give him the right to request further investigation of any concrete circumstances, with notation of the request in the record, to state in the record his reasons for refusing such a request, and to submit the record for the accused's signature] — and instead of acquainting the accused with *all the evidence* of the investigation, he restricts himself merely to a declaration that the preliminary investigation is concluded. At trial it is difficult for the accused to show violations committed by the investigator, since the record of the conclusion of the preliminary investigation is signed by him and no objections are mentioned in it. Not always does the military tribunal return such a case for a new investigation.

The character of the indictment has considerable significance. Cases to be tried by military tribunals, according to Article 27 of the Judiciary Law and Article 237 of the Code of Criminal Procedure, first pass through a preparatory stage, called a dispositional session. This is conducted by the military tribunal in plenary session, with the participation of the military procurator. The latter reports the case and proposes the issuance of the indictment and the presentation of the accused to trial. As a rule, the military tribunal consents to the request of the procurator. The return of a case for new examination is exceptional.

In this dispositional session attention is paid only *formally* to the fulfillment of criminal procedural norms by the organs of the preliminary investigation . . . If the accused is presented for trial . . . the military tribunal assigns the case for hearing and hands the accused a copy of the indictment within three days prior to the hearing. At the same time the military tribunal has the right, according to Article 391 of the Code of Criminal Procedure, to order that the case may be tried without calling the witnesses questioned in the preliminary investigation. [Actually, Article 391 permits the court to dispense with the calling of "those witnesses questioned at the preliminary investigation whose testimony does not raise a doubt as to its trustworthiness." — H.J.B. and M.K.]

In cases subject to trial under the law of July 10, 1934 and of December 1, 1934 [involving counterrevolutionary crimes] the indictment is not handed to the accused, but instead one day prior to the hearing of the case a short excerpt of the indictment is read to him (this procedure is not applied in cases subject to be tried in a demonstration trial).[47]

An unusual feature of the military criminal procedure is the control exercised by the commander of the unit over the bringing of the accused to trial. The military procurator is obliged to obtain the consent of the commander of the division before presenting to the military tribunal an indictment of an enlisted man. Officers may be brought to trial, in peacetime, only with the consent of the commander of troops of the military district or of the Minister of Defense (or, formerly, of the Minister of the Navy); if the consent of the minister is needed, the request for it must be submitted by the Chief Military Procurator, and only after consent is obtained from the district commander of troops. M. A. Chel'tsov, in stating these requirements, explains them as "special forms" established "in view of the great significance, from the point of view of maintaining discipline, of the authority of commanding personnel of the army." [48]

(d) *The Trial.* In the Soviet criminal trial, whether military or nonmilitary, the judge plays an active part in interrogating the defendant and the witnesses on both sides, and in calling his own impartial experts when necessary. However, certain adversary features are also present: both the prosecutor and the defense counsel question the witnesses and argue their respective cases, and the defendant may also put questions personally at any time during the trial.[49] The prosecutor is treated as a party.[50]

In assessing the fairness of Soviet military trials, it is again necessary to draw a sharp distinction between nonpolitical and political crimes. The following statement by N. Semenov, corroborated not only by other unofficial sources but also by a careful reading of Soviet sources, is an apt description: "The distinctive procedural order of judicial deliberation applicable in military tribunals depends on the character of the cases subject to trial. In cases of general and military crimes, the military tribunals apply the general norms of criminal procedure according to the Code of Criminal Procedure, observing the principles of publicity, orality, and immediacy [i.e., the right of confrontation of witnesses]. The judicial process runs quite differently when the object of consideration in the military tribunal are cases of counterrevolutionary crime and particularly such cases as espionage, subversion, terrorist acts, and treason, classified in Soviet criminal legislation as especially dangerous crimes against the state." [51] In such cases, tried *in camera*, the courts, through application of Chapter 28, and particularly Articles 394–397 of the Code of Criminal Procedure, which permit wide judicial discretion in proceedings in regional and military courts, may refuse to call witnesses for the accused, may receive testimony of witnesses not present in court, may use unpublished evidence in reaching a verdict, may cut off argument for the accused. "The observance of procedural norms in these cases," the author states, "is considered desirable only in demonstration trials," where the fate of the accused is settled beforehand by political organs and where "the formal observance of procedure on the part of the military tribunal is exclusively for propaganda purposes and not at all for the help of the accused."

It is interesting to note how a recent Soviet writer treats the question of military criminal procedure in cases of counterrevolutionary crimes. A 1951 treatise on Soviet criminal procedure states the following:

The task of military tribunals — of securing the rapid and ruthless repression of traitors to the Soviet socialist motherland, spies, terrorists, and subversives — in some instances requires the acceleration and shortening of the scope of the judicial deliberation. But only the observance of the basic principles of procedure (with limitations upon them dictated by the situation of the court and the circumstances of the case) can secure the accuracy of the repression which [accuracy] is necessary for achieving the aims of justice.

In the Code of Criminal Procedure of the RSFSR there has been formally retained Chapter 28, establishing a series of special procedures in provincial (now area and regional) courts and military tribunals. In this chapter are contained Articles 394–397, which permit very significant limitations upon the orality and immediacy of the trial, upon the completeness of the investigation of the case and upon the right of the accused to defense. Entirely opportune in conditions of wartime, these limitations certainly are not appropriate to the usual type of work of the military tribunal and its tasks. In particular, Article 397 of the Code of Criminal Procedure, permitting the court not to allow the argument of the parties, clearly departs from the article of the Constitution of the USSR guaranteeing to the accused the right to defense (Article 111).

Therefore one must take as correct the position of the Code of Criminal Procedure of the Ukrainian SSR, from which this entire chapter is excluded. Consequently, in the Ukrainian SSR the judicial deliberations in a military tribunal proceed according to general procedural rules. This fully corresponds with Article 5 of the Judiciary Law, which speaks of the principle of a uniform court equal for all citizens.[52]

The Constitution of the USSR provides that, "In all courts of the USSR . . . the accused is guaranteed the right to defense" (Article 111). The meaning of the Russian word for "defense" includes the idea of defense by counsel, and the Soviet courts have so interpreted it.[53] In theory, at least, the Soviet lawyer is supposed to defend his client. As one Soviet treatise states: "The role of an attorney in the trial has special features. It cannot be equalized to the role of a representative of the defendant who would be obligated to accede to all of his demands nor to the role of an assistant to the court who would not depend at all on the accused and would be only concerned with the discovery of an objective truth. In the activities of the Soviet attorney both these sides are combined. The basic duty of the attorney is to defend his client." [54]

The Code of Criminal Procedure provides that the participation of defense counsel is obligatory in cases in which there is an "accuser" and in cases in which the accused is dumb, deaf, or under some similar disability.[55]

It has already been noted that the right to legal counsel is specifically denied in cases of espionage, treason, sabotage, and terrorist acts. Furthermore, in cases before military courts the right to legal counsel was in fact denied during the war. This was justified on the ground that under war conditions it was practically impossible to assign lawyers to the defense of persons accused before military tribunals; a legal justification was also found in Article 381, of the RSFSR Code of Criminal Procedure relating to trial in regional courts but applicable also to military tribunals, which states that the court has discretion to admit or not to admit the "accuser" *and* the defense counsel, depending upon "the complexities of the case, the conclusiveness of the evidence, or the special political or social significance of the case." A note to this article in the code calls attention to the fact that the RSFSR Constitution guarantees to the accused the right to defense counsel [56] — the clear implication being that the later provision of the Constitution governs the application of the article of the code. The code provision in question then goes on to state that the regional [or the military] court is obliged to admit or to assign defense counsel if it admits the "accuser."

It was this code provision which was relied upon by the military courts during the war as authority for dispensing with the presence of both the procurator and defense counsel. Thus one writer states: "In normal times the privilege of legal defense is also attributed to defendants before a military court, both formally and in practice. But in war conditions a situation may arise in which the formal right of the defendant to appoint a defense counsel may prove to be impossible in practice. It would not be permissible to postpone the handling of these cases until a time when it would be possible to have a defense counsel participate in the proceedings. Therefore the criminal procedural law of the constituent republics (e.g., Article 381 of the Code of Criminal Procedure of the RSFSR) entitles the military courts to proceed without the presence of the parties, i.e., without a procurator and a defense counsel." [57]

(e) *Review of Decisions*.[58] In general, except as noted before in cases of "especially dangerous crimes against the state,"

Soviet law permits appeals by the parties from sentences, rulings, and decisions of a trial court to the next higher court, with the exception that there may be no appeal from a Division of the Supreme Court of the USSR or from the Supreme Court of a constituent republic. Thus a verdict of a divisional military tribunal may be appealed to the army group military tribunal, and a verdict of an army group military tribunal (sitting as a trial court) may be appealed to the Military Division of the Supreme Court of the USSR. A second appeal may not be brought by the parties. However, the decision of an appellate court may be "protested by way of supervision" to the next higher court either by the procuracy or by the President of the Supreme Court of a republic or the President of the Supreme Court of the USSR. A verdict of the Military Division of the Supreme Court of the USSR in cases of original jurisdiction, which may not otherwise be appealed, may be protested to the Plenum of the Supreme Court by the President of the Supreme Court or the Procurator General of the USSR. Similarly, decisions in cases of "especially dangerous crimes against the state," which may not be appealed, may be reviewed "by way of supervision," through the protest procedure. In a "supervisory" review, defense counsel is not present, nor, apparently, is the prosecutor. In an appeal as of right, both defense counsel and prosecutor may appear.[59]

Although decisions of the Plenum of the Supreme Court of the USSR are final and cannot be appealed or protested, the interpretation of a law by the Plenum may be "presented" by the Procurator General of the USSR to the Presidium of the Supreme Soviet, which is under the constitution the supreme authority for the interpretation of the law.[60]

Even after a decision has become final, it may be protested by the Procurator General of the USSR, the procurators of the constituent republics, the President of the Supreme Court of the USSR, or the President of the Supreme Courts of the constituent republics. Thus even a decision of the Presidium of the Supreme Soviet upon "presentation" of a case from the Plenum of the Supreme Court of the USSR could conceivably be followed by a subsequent reopening of the case in the Plenum upon further protest by the Procurator General or by the President of the Supreme Court of the USSR.

A verdict may be reversed on the following grounds: that the preliminary investigation was inadequate or incorrect *and* resulting "unclear circumstances" were not clarified at the trial, that there was a substantial violation of the trial procedure, that there was a breach of incorrect application of the law, or that the verdict or sentence was clearly unjust.[61]

4. THE MILITARY PROCURACY

(a) *Functions of the Procuracy.* The procuracy is the cornerstone of the Soviet legal system. The Soviet Constitution states that "supreme supervisory power over the strict execution of the laws by all ministries and institutions subordinated to them, as well as by public servants and citizens of the USSR, is vested in the Procurator General of the USSR." [62] According to the Constitution, the Procurator General is appointed by the Supreme Soviet for a term of seven years; [63] he, in turn, appoints procurators of republics, territories, and regions, and confirms the appointment by the republican procurator of area, district, and city procurators.[64] "The organs of the procuracy," states the Constitution, "perform their functions independently of any local organs whatsoever, being subordinate solely to the Procurator General of the USSR." [65]

The "supreme supervisory power" of the procuracy takes many diverse forms. The procurators keep watch over the entire system of administration, to see that executive and administrative bodies do not overstep their legal authority. They sit in as consultants on sessions of the local city councils and receive copies of orders and regulations issued by regional and republican and federal executive-administrative organs. When the procurator considers that an act is in violation of the Constitution or the decrees of the government, he may "protest" to the executive-administrative organ immediately superior to the body which has issued it. If a ministry has exceeded its authority, the procurator's protest is lodged with the Council of Ministers. The procurator also is supposed to supervise the legality and correctness of actions of the Ministry of Internal Affairs, the police, the organs of criminal investigation, and the corrective-labor institutions.

In respect to the judicial system, the procuracy's functions are still broader. It has the power to order the arrest of those suspected of crime, and it appoints the examining magistrates who conduct the pretrial investigations of criminal cases. It is the prosecuting arm in criminal trials. But beyond that, the procuracy watches all civil proceedings and may initiate or enter any lawsuit at any stage on either side. Further, it may appeal, by way of protest, any decision, civil or criminal, of any court below the level of the Supreme Court of the USSR. It may move to reopen any case after the decision has been handed down. Before an appellate court renders its opinion in any case, it must hear the opinion of the procurator.

According to Soviet authors, "the military procuracy in the USSR is inseparably connected with the general procuracy in the organization, in its principles of work, and in its general tasks." [66] During the war its "basic task . . . was to supervise and examine the punctual execution of all laws, orders, and instructions relating to martial law, to the fulfillment of all needs of the fighting forces, to the protection of the interests of the Red Army men's families." [67] Thus it performed supervisory functions over both administrative and judicial proceedings.

(b) *Organization of the Military Procuracy.* The office of the Procurator General of the USSR contains the chief administrations of the military procuracy of the army, the navy, and the rail- and water-transport systems. The heads of these chief administrations are called chief procurators and are deputies to the Procurator General of the USSR by whom they are appointed.

Local branches of the procuracy in the Soviet army are: military procuracies of divisions or independent brigades, of aviation regions, of corps, of fortified regions or garrisons, and of military areas, army groups, independent armies, and fleets. Procuracies of the armed troops of the Ministry of the Internal Affairs are subordinated to the army procuracies. Like organs of the procuracy in general, the organs of the mili-

tary procuracy are strictly centralized. "Every military procurator is subordinated to his superior and to no other local
authority." [68]

Coöperation between the Chief Administrator of the Military
Procuracy of the Soviet Army and the Ministry of Defense is
provided by a close liaison between the Chief Political Administration of the Ministry of Defense and the Procurator General
of the USSR.

(c) *Training of Procurators and of other Personnel for
Military Justice.*[69] In 1939 the Council of Ministers ordered the
establishment of a Military Law School of the Red Army, under
the Ministry of Defense, to train army and navy personnel to
be military judges, military procurators, military investigators,
and military advisers. The Military Law School was to give a
four-year course for this purpose and was also to be a scientific
institution for problems of military law. During the war the
course was shortened to one year, but as early as 1943 the four-
year course was reëstablished.

Applicants for admission to the Military Law School must
be officers of not more than thirty-five years of age, not less
than two years' experience in command or in political or judicial work, and with a general education of college level and
with military training equal to that of a military or military-
political college. Students are required to be physically fit for
combat service and to possess good combat qualifications. They
must have passed an examination in the Russian language,
history of the USSR, military topography, and rules of infantry
combat. The students are selected by the Chief Political Administration of the army through the military councils of army
groups or military districts.

The basic educational goals are to give general training in
law equal to that of a university law school, to give political
and military legal training, and to provide special training necessary for the work of a military judge, military procurator, or
military investigator.

The curriculum includes political science, history, logic,
psychology, and general military sciences, as well as law and,
in particular, military law. Students of the Navy Department

of the School are also taught principles of navy organization, shipbuilding, navigation, artillery, mines and torpedo warfare, chemical warfare, communications, naval tactics, naval history, naval geology, and naval administration. There are courses in the military law of other countries as well. The Military Law School also trains teachers of military law for military colleges and academies on the principle that "every officer of the Soviet army and navy needs to know the principles of legal institutions and of international law." The training of teachers is through a postgraduate course culminating in a dissertation. The school has a library of more than 70,000 volumes; it publishes its own textbooks as well as a law review;[70] its educational program is supervised by the Ministry of Higher Education.

Great emphasis is placed on practical training. Practice court sessions are arranged in which students act as judges, procurators, and lawyers. In addition, a special refresher course is given to military-legal personnel.

To coördinate the study of military law with that of other branches of law, there is a military legal division of the Law Institute of the Academy of Sciences of the USSR.

V

AN APPRAISAL OF THE SOVIET SYSTEM OF MILITARY LAW AND ADMINISTRATION

1. DIFFICULTIES OF APPRAISAL

Any appraisal of the Soviet system of military law and administration must suffer from the relative lack of available information regarding the unofficial, informal standards and procedures which, as in any military system, underlie the official, formal structure. Our impressions of day-to-day Soviet military life, and the day-to-day practices of Soviet military administrators, commanders, judges, prosecutors, and other law-enforcing personnel, are derived from the fragmentary personal experiences of a relatively few people, including one of the authors, Mr. Kerner, and from what can be read between the lines of Soviet case reports, treatises, newspaper articles, and similar published materials. There are no Soviet publications, so far as we know, which even attempt to evaluate systematically the Soviet system of military law and administration in the light of its actual day-to-day operation.

It is, of course, discouraging to have to report "this is what the Soviets say they do," without following up in as full detail with "this is what they actually do." However, it is important to note that what they say is often quite revealing of what they think and what they want. Witness the four Disciplinary Codes of 1918, 1926, 1940, and 1946 — each reflecting a different philosophy of military life. Moreover, there is no question that *much* of Soviet military legislation effectively symbolizes what is actually done in practice. The only question is, *how* much. There is no reason to doubt that Soviet Supreme

Court reports, for example, represent the way in which many actual cases have been treated in that court; what is primarily lacking is data on the treatment of cases which do not reach the Supreme Court and of cases which do not reach any court. We have, then, a fairly comprehensive body of legal materials (including commentaries) relating to the Soviet system of military administration, discipline, military crimes and punishments, and military courts and procedure — and scattered experiences of some people who have lived under that system. It has seemed to us best to devote our work *mainly* to interpretation of the official and semiofficial legal materials, drawing such inferences as can be derived from examination of those materials, with occasional checking of those references against the reports of ex-Soviet writers on Soviet military law and administration. We have done so in the belief that such an exegesis would be revealing in and of itself and is in any case a necessary foundation for analysis of the Soviet military system as a whole. Nevertheless, we also believe that the difficulties of an over-all appraisal in larger terms do not excuse us from making such an appraisal, however tentative it must be.

2. GENERAL SIMILARITIES BETWEEN THE SOVIET SYSTEM AND OTHER SYSTEMS OF MILITARY LAW AND ADMINISTRATION

The Soviet system of military law and administration is in many respects like the French, German, English, American, and other systems — more like the French or German than the English or American, because of historical factors which link both Russian military traditions and Russian legal traditions with those of the continent of Europe. The Soviet system of direct management of the armed forces by the Ministry of Defense, which is also the system of various European countries, reflects a greater interconnection of military and civil authority in the governmental structure than is traditional in England or the United States. The promulgation of a disciplinary code by the Ministry of Defense is in the tradition of some European countries, as is the subordination of military criminal law to the general system of criminal law as set forth in the criminal code. Likewise, the system of permanent military courts, staffed by professional military judges and prosecutors, has its parallels on the continent of Europe; the 1950 Uniform Code of Military Justice has reformed American military law in a similar direction by establishing "law officers" of American courts-martial and by setting up a civilian tribunal with authority to review decisions of courts-martial.

Basic to the general similarities between the Soviet system of military law and administration and that of other countries is the fact that an army is an army; it must have strict discipline, based on a hierarchy of commanders, and it must have the kind of efficiency for which a "bureaucratic" administration is indispensable. Military organization and administration, as well as military law, are inevitably conditioned by military needs. Certain basic military needs of the Soviet Union are not essentially different from basic military needs of other countries at comparable stages of military development.

However, the mere fact that the Soviet Union has military needs comparable with those of other countries — comparable in terms of military organization, requirements of military training, and so forth — does not in itself explain the similarities in administrative and legal structure and processes. These similarities are due also to the fact that the Soviet leadership has recognized a significant degree of autonomy of military needs and of the military system within the general social economic and political system; that is, it has constructed a body of law and administration in response, in significant part, to the requirements of military discipline and efficiency *as such* — rather than persisting in its original attempt to mold the military system absolutely to political and ideological requirements. In political terms this has meant some degree of separation of military and political authority — less separation, it should be stressed, than in the Western tradition, but enough to account for important similarities in structure.

Connected with the partial separation of military and civilian authority is the partial resurgence of the prerevolutionary Russian military tradition and the development of a class of officers whose primary devotion is to that tradition. The restoration of iron discipline and of sharp distinctions of rank has tended to bring both military administration and military law into line not only with the prerevolutionary Russian military system but also with Western military systems, since the Russian system and the Western systems exercised a mutual influence upon each other. Indeed, it is characteristic of military systems of hostile or potentially hostile countries that they tend, given time, to resemble each other.

It may come as a surprise to some that the Soviet military system, like that of other countries, establishes formal processes of law and concomitant elaboration of the rights of subordinates. To Soviet military leaders, no doubt, law seems secondary to efficiency and discipline; in this, too, however, they resemble military leaders of other countries. Nevertheless the very system of hierarchical command makes necessary the restriction of the powers of inferior commanders over their subordinates: a company commander who had absolute authority over his troops could defeat the system imposed on him by his superiors. By granting rights to subordinates the top leadership is better able to control the middle links in the chain of command.

At the same time, satisfaction of the soldier's sense of justice is itself an important element in maintaining discipline. The soldier's sense of justice is of course not constant; it varies in different countries and in different periods of time. But in Soviet Russia as in the West, the armed forces are comprised chiefly of people with civilian background who look forward to return to civilian life. They therefore inevitably carry with them standards of justice based upon their civilian experience. Soviet citizens, like citizens of other countries, resent arbitrary, unequal application of the law; they feel the need for a fair hearing and for impartial decision. The nature of such resentments and feelings will be considered later; the fact we wish to stress here is that to whatever extent military leaders — whether Soviet or non-Soviet — may be reluctant to establish rights which may be invoked by subordinates against superiors, they must recognize that a system of military regulation which neglected to meet the minimum requirements of justice of the men sought to be governed would incur their hostility and would, in the long run at least, threaten the system of military discipline itself.

Because law is conceived in most armies primarily as an adjunct of discipline and efficiency, it is often abused — more often, generally speaking, than in civilian life. The gap between the law in books and the law in action, familiar in all societies, is still more familiar in all armies. Thus the very fact of this gap is an element of similarity between Soviet and non-Soviet systems of military law; the size and nature of the gap, however, is an important matter, to which we shall return.

The similarities between Soviet and non-Soviet military systems may seem less interesting than the differences. We stress the similarities because it is important to realize that a military system has its own requirements; that if it is to work efficiently it must have a certain autonomy. By its nature, then, the military system limits the totalitarian character of the Soviet state, just as totalitarianism limits the military system. If the Soviet leadership wants military strength and efficiency, it must recognize and give effect to the inherent needs of military administration and military law. The history of Soviet military law and administration demonstrates that the Soviet leaders have learned many bitter lessons in this regard. They have learned, for example, that political commissars must be subordinated to military commanders for the sake of unity of command. They have learned — to take another example — that ideological considerations of equality must be sacrificed to the need for the kind of incentives and controls which are symbolized in distinctions of rank.

Many scholars have interpreted Soviet developments in terms of the "priority of power," and the struggle between various competing power structures. Among such scholars it is debated whether the military establishment is a threat to the power of the Party and the state security system, or whether the Party and secret police firmly control the military establishment. Our study suggests that this kind of analysis is too abstract and too impersonal. The leadership — which is a combined leadership of Party, police, military, industrial, agricultural, and other groups — is, like any other leadership, perpetually confronted with basic dilemmas which cut across power lines. If the leadership does not recognize the distinctive character of military life and the distinctive needs of the military system, and if Party and police controls upon the military establishment are drawn too tight, then the efficiency and morale of the armed forces will suffer. This is not a matter of simple choice between alternatives to which power priorities can be allocated. It is a characteristic dilemma of all societies in which military authority and civilian authority are both separate and interconnected. It is a dilemma which is not resolved in the Soviet Union despite fusion of military and civilian authority at the top levels.

3. GENERAL DIFFERENCES BETWEEN THE SOVIET SYSTEM AND OTHER SYSTEMS OF MILITARY LAW AND ADMINISTRATION

As the similarities between the Soviet system of military law and administration and non-Soviet systems are due in large part to the separation of Soviet military and civilian authority, so the most striking differences are due to the relatively high degree of fusion of those authorities. This fusion is, as we have seen, characteristic of Soviet politics and economics at the higher levels, where responsibility for all aspects of the Soviet social order is vested in a relatively small group of people. The fusion of military and civilian authority is also characteristic of Soviet administration at the level of the military district, insofar as the district commander, typically a prominent Communist Party official and a member or candidate member of the Central Committee of the Party, has administrative problems affecting civilian activities governed by local, regional, and republican administrative bodies whose leaders are also prominent Party officials. The military district council, under the chairmanship of the commander, has control over the system of conscription and over civil defense. The fusion of military and civil authority is seen again in the jurisdiction of military courts over political crimes, as well as in the militarization of the railroad and water-transport courts. Finally, it appears in the fusion of military and nonmilitary criminal law and in the ultimate control of the Supreme Court, the Procurator-General, and the Ministry of Justice over the military judiciary, the military procuracy, and the military section of the Ministry of Justice respectively.

Above all, the high degree of fusion of Soviet military and civilian authority is seen in the two institutions of political deputy and state security officer within the various units of the armed forces.

The political deputy, or zampolit, in addition to his political functions, combines functions exercised in the American army by the chaplain, the Information and Education Officer, the Special Services officer, and the censor, and in addition he exercises a supervisory role with respect to discipline, reporting infractions of discipline by subordinates as well as abuses of authority by superiors. His reports on expressions of political or ideological dissent have an important bearing upon promotions. Although he is subordinate to the military commander he is also part of the Chief Political Administration of the Ministry of Defense, which is at the same time the Military Section of the Central Committee of the Communist Party. The zampolit is thus loyalty officer, propaganda officer, and morale officer, and in the performance of these roles he is subordinate to political as well as to military authorities.

The Special Sections of the state security organization within the armed forces, on the other hand, are separate from military command; they are in the military units but not of them. While the zampolit is in the forefront of day-to-day military life, the Special Section is in the background. It keeps dossiers on all officers and on those enlisted men who are reported to it. It operates in secret. It is an unknown quantity, meant to be feared by all potential subversives. In many cases it acts as an agency for bringing to prosecution disciplinary offenses.

The interweaving of military, Party, and police controls makes it difficult to diagnose Soviet politics in terms of simple conflicts between the various organizations. Any basic conflict between the Party and the army, or the security police and the army, would also split the army internally.

Apart from politics and administration, and apart from

internal security, Soviet social life itself is characterized by a high degree of semimilitarization, which makes the contrast between military and civilian life less striking for the Soviet citizen than for his Western counterpart. It would be a mistake, therefore, to compare the rigors of Soviet military life with those of American military service. The Soviet military recruit has been prepared for military life by his experience of a mobilized social order. He is accustomed to restrictions upon travel, fines for lateness to work and absenteeism, and (until 1951, at least) two to four months' imprisonment for quitting a job without authorization. Many Soviet soldiers were drafted at the age of fourteen for the State Labor Reserves, sent to training schools for three years, and then assigned to factories. Above all, Soviet soldiers have been brought up in a revolution which has deliberately applied to peacetime pursuits a war philosophy — that is, a philosophy of discipline, self-sacrifice, unity, collective action, central planning. Even at nineteen, the Soviet recruit is accustomed to being recruited. All his life he has seen or heard or read about shock brigades on the collective farm front, Heroes of Socialist Labor, and many others who in their daily pursuits "storm bastions" of one kind or another.

To this experience is added several hundred hours of military training in school, starting in the seventh grade, and, for many millions, extensive premilitary training in civil defense organizations.

Thus the severity of Soviet military discipline and military criminal law undoubtedly comes as less of a shock to the Soviet soldier who experiences it than it does to the American observer who studies it. At the same time the American observer is apt to be surprised by some of its more lenient features, and its emphasis on incentives and rewards.

In terms of basic differences between Soviet military law and Western military law, the relative harshness of certain provisions of the Soviet system and relative leniency of other provisions is less significant than the higher degree of capriciousness of the Soviet system. Every system of military law is apt to be administered with less objectivity than its corresponding civilian legal system, due largely to the military necessity of strict subordination and the concomitant personal authority of superiors in the chain of command. In the Soviet system this inherent tendency of military law toward arbitrariness in administration is aggravated by the infiltration into the military hierarchy of Party and security hierarchies; the Soviet soldier who breaks a regulation, and the soldier who may be charged with breaking a regulation, must reckon not only with military men but also with ideologists and the secret police. Even more basic is the fact that the law-enforcement officers, judges, and lawmakers must also reckon with these authorities. As a result they tend to vacillate and to resort to protective ambiguity. This tendency gives evidence of being a conscious one. Thus the gap between law in books and law in action in the Soviet military system, is not merely an inevitable consequence of military life but also to a certain extent a deliberate policy of the Soviet authorities.

4. THE SOVIET SYSTEM OF MILITARY LAW AND DISCIPLINE IN ACTION

Any generalizations with respect to the harshness or leniency, objectivity or capriciousness, effectiveness or ineffectiveness of the Soviet system of military law and discipline *as it is actually applied*, are of necessity based upon rough impressions. Similarly, any generalizations with respect to the docile or rebellious character of the Soviet soldier, and his attitudes toward superiors and toward the system of military law and discipline, are inevitably the product of intuitive judgment founded on fragmentary evidence. Some inferences with respect to these matters may be drawn from the official legislation, the reported cases, and the semiofficial Soviet commentaries — as we shall attempt to demonstrate in subsequent sections of this chapter. However, the inferences drawn from the published materials are undoubtedly influenced by the authors' impressions gained from non-Soviet and ex-Soviet reports of personal experiences, and especially from the personal experiences of one of the authors, Mr. Kerner. We know of no better way of conveying to the reader our rough impressions of Soviet military law and discipline in action than to give Mr. Kerner's personal and informal account of his experiences gained while serving as a colonel with the Czechoslovak Army unit on the Eastern Front, that is, with the Red Army, from January 1, 1944 until the end of the war in May 1945.

At the time of my arrival the Czechoslovak unit had a strength of one independent brigade with a training center. The brigade was under the First Ukrainian Army Group, and operationally was a part of the Fortieth Army. It had been deployed a few miles southwest of Fastov, a large railway center near Kiev. The training center was in Buzuluk, near Kuibyshev.

Of our group of twenty-eight officers who were sent from Great Britain to the USSR one half went to the training center and the other half to the front.

We had in our brigade quite a large number of Red Army men, especially drivers, signal-men, tankists, and liaison officers. Also, the Special Section of the NKVD was entirely Russian.

Our first impression of the discipline was quite good. It corresponded to our expectation of an army in combat, with a much greater camaraderie than there usually is in the barracks. Pretty soon, however, I realized how much harder it was to discipline Red Army men than our own men. The driver of the jeep which was assigned to me was a Russian sergeant. Once we rode at night back to our headquarters when Misha spotted a hare. (Nobody drove with dimmed lights!) My orders to go ahead did not stop Misha from chasing the hare for some twenty minutes, and trying to shoot him with his pistol.

We had plenty of difficulties with the Russian drivers of our supply convoys. On almost every trip some of them stopped in a peasant's house, got drunk, and gave away part of the cargo in exchange for homemade vodka. These transgressions were very common and no action was taken against the transgressors. It was considered that their work was so hard that they deserved some liberties. This was, of course, true, since driving in the Ukrainian winter was a most strenuous task with a lot of digging, pulling, finding one's own way, et cetera.

It was also brought home to me pretty soon that getting normal rations was not a matter of routine but an exciting game of bargaining. The numerical strength of the individual units was a constant puzzle. Reports given through field channels and quartermaster channels never agreed. Consequently a good guess had to be made in requesting rations. But the first time I went to army headquarters to do so, I was given a very useful hint by the major who headed the food section. His advice was always to ask for twice as many rations as were needed, with the result that after some bargaining one usually received from 60 to 75 per cent of the actual requirement.

Our liaison officer for the quartermaster headquarters of the brigade was a Soviet major. In February 1944 we received a shipment of American cigarettes sent by Czechs and Slovaks in the United States. The general commanding the brigade decided that each man would get one package and each officer two packages. Our Soviet major vehemently protested because he thought it very inconsiderate that a major should get the same amount of cigarettes as a second lieutenant. When I tried to explain to him that according to our democratic concepts amenities like cigarettes should be distributed equally he said that "this is a funny kind of democracy." In his opinion true democracy should work on the principle "the higher the rank, the larger the rations" (*chem vyshe, tem bol'she*).

Living off the country was a general principle and nobody minded if the soldiers took things from the population. Generally it was done on a bargaining basis, mostly by exchanging German booty or even one's own equipment for peasants' goods. However, there were certain strict limits. First of all, school buildings had to be protected against any unnecessary damage. Second, livestock breeding had to be preserved. One of our officers ordered a purebred bull to be shot. Strictest proceedings were ordered by the Special Section, and the educational officers (corresponding to the Soviet zampolits) used the case in the daily news sheet, mimeographed for the brigade, as an example of irresponsible behavior toward Soviet economy. General comment was that if it had been a Soviet officer he would have been sent to a penal battalion.

The concern for the morale of the army was very great. There was to be no doubt that the Red Army is superior to any other army. We had been warned earlier by our military attaché in Moscow not to express any unfavorable opinion on the Red Army organization, equipment, discipline, and the like. Some of us who came from England did not heed the warning and by the end of February 1944 the Czechoslovak command was asked to send five officers back to England. Their main guilt was that they had told Soviet liaison officers that they thought British equipment to be generally superior to that of the Red Army.

Some ten days after my arrival at the front we were quartered in a Ukrainian village. Just as we were finishing our supper a Czechoslovak noncommissioned officer came quite calmly into our house and said that in the next house a Soviet officer had shot a Soviet soldier. I wondered that the news did not excite anybody. The comment was that such cases happened quite often.

Mutual relationships between officers and men and between various grades of officers were sharply split into three categories. Privates, noncommissioned officers, and company officers formed one group, whose members easily mingled together, were on very comradely terms, shared quarters, hardships, and were molded into a very compact combat unit. Officers of field rank, starting with the rank of major, formed a distinctively separate group. They addressed each other by their ranks and with quite a lot of respect. Subordination was strictly preserved and orders by a colonel were fully respected by a lieutenant colonel. The behavior of a senior toward a junior was that of an elderly comrade who expects to be regarded as the wiser one; but if advice or a general hint was not sufficient to command obedience, a strict order followed and had to be executed without further objections. Field officers were ready to use regulations, and I witnessed several cases in which a major or a colonel quoted them to a junior officer to prove his point. If members of this group wanted to show that they were good friends they did it in the old traditional Russian way by calling each other by the first name and patronymic.

An entirely different story applied to generals. It is at this level that all privileges of rank came out most conspicuously. They had their own orderlies and special dining rooms, and got the best of everything available. Their uniforms were spotless, and usually their quarters were equipped with a mobile electricity power station out of American lend-lease supplies. Their headquarters were strictly guarded, and at the top echelon one could only gain access if accompanied by a member of the guard detachment. Privates and noncommissioned officers stood in immense awe of generals, and officers showed them unconditional subordination. Their cars were given absolute priority on the roads. The undisputed authority of the generals was also apparent in the lack of remarks about "top brass" or "the old men" so usual in other armies. Soviet generals were, of course, mostly not old men, as their average age was forty-five. The careers of many of them were popularized in the military press as stories of heroes.

In the spring of 1944 the Czechoslovak Independent Brigade was reorganized into a corps. Corps headquarters had been set up in the city of Efremov, some seventy miles south of Moscow. A second brigade was organized as a parachutists' unit. I was transferred to Efremov at the beginning of March. There I had my first opportunity to observe court proceedings. Our field tribunal enjoyed autonomy and conducted its business according to the Czechoslovak law. The two most frequent crimes handled by the tribunal were embezzlement of military property and insubordination. Soldiers were selling blankets and other parts of their clothing to the civilian population at black market prices. Russian NKVD liaison officers pressed for strict penalties. In order to comply, the Czechoslovak Field Tribunal computed values of the embezzled material on the Soviet scale, which equaled the black market prices.

Insubordination cases included instances in which our soldiers refused to jump from the plane during parachutists' training. Our medical experts expressed a view that men may be overcome with such a degree of fear as to be deprived of control over their own actions and that therefore these men should not be criminally responsible. But the Soviets insisted that an order is an order, and all accused were, under Soviet pressure, court-martialed for insubordination. All of them, on the other hand, appealed from the field tribunal's decision, being kept in prison in the meantime. The general agreement within our Czechoslovak command was that nobody should be forced to serve in a parachute unit and that those who were not suitable for such combat duty should be transferred to other field units. The whole matter was referred to President Benes, who commuted the sentences by way of clemency, and the men were transferred to other units. Soviet soldiers would have been, without any doubt, transferred to penal battalions or in some cases perhaps even shot.

At the same time, in Efremov, while many enlisted men were being tried for embezzlement of army property, large amounts of officers' rations were being sold on the "bazaar." Officers were sending their orderlies to the bazaar to sell mainly bread, butter, and sugar and to buy eggs, milk, and cheese. Although this was against regulations it was generally tolerated. We knew that in cities with Red Army garrisons it was done on a much larger scale, and therefore nobody was afraid of doing it.

In May 1944 the whole corps, including the training depot, which had been earlier transferred from Buzuluk to Efremov, was moved to the vicinity of Chernovitsy, the capital of Bukovina. We went by train from Efremov to Kamenets Podolsk, and then by truck. The distance from Efremov to Kamenets Podolsk, some 500 miles, was covered in three weeks.

When we arrived in Kamenets Podolsk I realized how strictly the discipline on railways was enforced there. We had several trains of material coming in and each had to be unloaded within six hours. Once we did not finish unloading in time, as our trucks were delayed. The railway commander immediately called to his office our Soviet liaison officer, threatening that the responsible officers would be handed over for court-martial. With great difficulty, and the promise of British material for a uniform, we got two additional hours to unload. But our liaison officer was scared to death by the threat of a court-martial, and I realized that apparently no arguing would help in court-martial proceedings.

At that time, in June, the first show trial on the Soviet pattern was held in our corps. In March 1943, when the first Independent Czechoslovak Battalion participated in the battle for Kharkov, its quartermaster officer had been accused of leaving the battle line and of cowardice in front of the enemy. The charges hinged mainly on the testimony of his deputy, a noncommissioned officer of questionable character. The proceedings were long drawn out, as our prosecutor was not too keen on prosecuting. But later, when the corps was being readied to go into action after a third brigade had been organized, the chief educational officer decided, with the support of the NKVD liaison officers, to press for a public court-martial trial. Each brigade sent deputations; education officers of all units were present; demands for capital punishment were uttered from the audience; and the corps daily sheet published at the beginning of the trial an article demanding "most severe penalties" for cowards. The sentence was, of course, the death penalty. The sentenced officer appealed and the sentence was committed to reduction to the rank of a private. This was intolerable to the Soviets, and as in the meantime we were fighting again in the Carpathian Mountains and a penal battalion had been organized, the sentenced man was transferred into its ranks, where he was killed in action the second day after his transfer.

Probably the most efficient disciplinary action used by the Red Army command was an indiscriminate and large-scale removal of commanding officers in case of a miscarried operation. Such an operation happened at the beginning of the attack on the Carpathian passes in the first days of September 1944 in the vicinity of the Polish city of Krosno. The German command anticipated exactly the day of the attack and at dawn of the D-day withdrew its forces for some five miles into a second, well-prepared line of defense. The tremendously powerful and concentrated Russian artillery barrage went into a vacuum, and when the infantry units started to advance, anticipating only a slight German resistance, they were met with a devastating German fire and suffered terrific losses. Marshal Konev accused the Soviet command of poor counterintelligence, bad camouflage, and negligence in attacking. More than sixty high-ranking officers were removed, including three generals, one being General Kratochvil, commander of the Czechoslovak Corps.

At that time I realized for the second time the enormous endurance of the Russian soldier. First, I saw it in the rugged Ukrainian winter in January and February 1944. Now, in the mountains, it was even more conspicuous. The soldiers endured more than machines and animals; and we Czechs and Slovaks questioned the necessity for the often-changing orders requiring a lot of shifting from one part of the front to another, under most difficult conditions and almost constant rain. It seemed incredible not to cease operations for a while but the Soviet command kept pressing and Russian officers and men kept going. Losses were amazingly high and all the more serious since the wounded could not be transported fast enough to get efficient medical care.

As I consider, even today, the main reasons for the astonishingly high fighting morale of the Russian soldier, I think that there are two principal explanations. First, in his daily struggle for survival a Russian is used to the most rugged conditions. Second, the tradition of the glorious Russian armies is very strong and effective. It divulged itself in such utterances of common soldiers as "the Russians did this before," and "we are many and we shall survive."

On the other hand, there is no doubt that Soviet law plays an important role. Its harshness is a handy instrument whenever it is applied. Also, it seems to me that the restriction of its application to exceptional conditions makes it work; otherwise it would be impossible for anybody to carry on.

In Soviet Russia (and apparently this was so in Tsarist Russia, too, though to a lesser degree) the citizen and the law-enforcing authorities play a never-ending game of who catches up with whom. Everybody knows that most severe penalties await him if he is caught in illegal activities, but nevertheless he goes on with them.

Is this due to a traditional disregard for law? I do not think so. It is caused by the impossibility of meeting the requirements of the law and the regulations.

When we were stationed in Efremov we were told as quartermaster officers how strict Soviet requirements were for preservation of cleanliness and hygiene in the military kitchens. Our liaison officers often used to point out that we should have more cleaning utensils, more garbage bins, washing basins, soap, and towels for kitchen personnel. Our replies always were, "but you know that we cannot get them" — to which they would react with a stereotyped answer, "somebody will pay for it." Then suddenly there was an inspection, and certainly plenty of people were reported as infringing regulations. Our Czechoslovak command dismissed the charges when we proved that they were not our fault, but in the Red Army, we were always told, strict penalties would have followed.

The chief medical officer of our corps was an ardent Communist and pressed me, when I became quartermaster of the corps, to issue more washing basins, more linen, and more cleaning material to our field hospitals, according to the Soviet regulations. When he pressed too much I put him off by pointing out that all the regulations were of no use if we did not get the supplies, and by telling him that when we got pure alcohol, the Russian medical officers drank it instead of using it for medical care. His answer again was, "they will pay for it some day." And some did.

Another case of the working of Soviet justice was told to me by a quartermaster general of the army named Dergachov, who was stationed in the summer of 1945 in Prague. There were plenty of cases in 1943 when Russian soldiers died after drinking or eating supplies captured from Germans. Strict instructions were issued that such supplies had to be handed over to higher commands, from division up, and that only after a professional inspection could they be issued for consumption. In the fall of 1943, when Dergachov was the quartermaster officer of a division, some twenty men died in one of the division's regiments. The procurator investigated and brought charges against the quartermaster officer of the division because he found out that the men died after drinking vodka rations issued from divisional supplies. Dergachov told me that he was sure that he would be sentenced to be shot unless he could himself prove that the unit in which the incident occurred had some German booty of its own. He therefore asked the commander of the division to allow him to investigate on his own. He went to the place where the regiment kept its food supplies and after a very thorough inspection found one vessel of German origin. Starting there, he got some soldiers to admit that they had taken some German supplies and had handed them over to their regimental quartermaster, who kept them for the regiment, mixing them into supplies issued by the division. The regimental quartermaster was then shot, instead of my friend. But the interesting thing about his story was that he was not annoyed at all that a grave miscarriage of justice almost occurred in his case. He was proud of the story because he showed the procurator what a tough guy he was.

By virtue of his drill and training, the Russian soldier is accustomed to respect orders and take them literally. If he is given an order to stand guard somewhere, he will stay there as long as he is not relieved. If he is told not to admit anyone, he will not admit anyone — and he will shoot whoever disregards his warnings. In the spring of 1945 in Slovakia, I often drove into the operational zone of the Second Ukrainian Front (ours was the Fourth Front). Traffic guards had orders to let through only persons with specific orders. I had my orders in Czech, which the guards could not understand, but I had "a paper (*bumazhka*)" and that was enough. Without a written order there was nothing doing. Similarly, if there was an order that only two persons might ride in the driver's cabin, all vehicles which disregarded the order were stopped and the third person had to get out.

The camouflage orders on the front were strictly respected, and if anyone disregarded them he was immediately reprimanded by others.

On the other hand, traffic discipline was always very poor. Drivers behaved in the most selfish way and this is probably due to the fact that a Russian driver considers himself as "master" of the road on which he is driving, as if it were something exceptional to drive a car or another vehicle. If Russian tanks were coming along a road nobody else was safe, as they would push anybody off the road without the slightest concern.

Basically a Russian is not apt to be a disciplined citizen, and never was. The Communists fight survivals of the Russian *nichevo* attitude — the traditional inclination to nihilism. For example, the Soviet government during the war encouraged joyous, manly, patriotic songs, suitable for military drill. Nevertheless, the most popular songs were rather romantic and sentimental. Russian spleen, fatalism, and devotion were expressed in these songs in a way which corresponded to the mood of the fighting Russian *muzhik* — which the Soviet soldier still basically is.

Two extremes were conspicuous: thorough drill, as in the attitude of a Soviet guard where a simple command was followed without any thinking or devotion; and, on the other hand, willingness to suffer or even to die, stemming from the traditional devotion to "our Motherland." In between was a very large field of daily actions and attitudes which I would characterize as "next to the law." We used to describe in Europe actions which were "according to the law," actions which were "against the law," and actions which were "next to the law." The last category comprises most acts of Soviet citizens. They are not done with the intention of infringing the law, nor with the intention of staying within the legal limits. The Soviet citizen knows perfectly well that he is acting "next to the law," just outside the law, but he is also well aware of the fact that most of his actions have to be in this sphere. He knows that if the authorities decide that he should be punished for such behavior, he will have to pay, and the penalty will be very harsh.

In cases where the government decides to be strict, nobody can help the violator. But there are many instances in which grievances can be settled through a channel which is lacking in other armies. The Soviet zampolit is not only the organ of political indoctrination and the political watchdog. He is also a peacemaker who intervenes in the unnecessary tensions between commanders and subordinates. He sometimes sides with the command, at other times with the men. Like a chaplain, he listens to the soldiers' private problems. He often sees to it, especially when so directed by party campaigns, that the men get all their allowances. Also, very often, he is the exemplary soldier, or on the battlefield, the most courageous fighter. He is the cream of the Communist youth and Communist leadership. His duties are numerous and his responsibilities enormous.

The foregoing account of personal experiences of Soviet military law and discipline in action, if taken alone, would suggest the following conclusions:

1. Soviet enlisted men blatantly disregard some kinds of disciplinary regulations and get away with it. (Thus military drivers did not dim their lights as required; Colonel Kerner ordered the driver Misha to go ahead but Misha nevertheless chased a hare for twenty minutes; drivers habitually stopped to drink and exchanged military supplies for homemade vodka; such offenses went unpunished; traffic discipline was always very poor.)

2. Other kinds of regulations are obeyed unconditionally and literally. (Thus a guard would not leave his post until relieved, no matter how long he had to wait, and would shoot anyone who disregarded his warnings. Likewise, strict discipline was enforced with respect to damage and seizure of civilian property *in the Soviet Union* and the severest sanctions were applicable to violations.)

3. During the war it was not considered extraordinary for a Soviet officer to shoot a Soviet enlisted man as a matter of "company punishment."

4. There are sharp differentiations of rank, and it is accepted that "the higher the rank, the larger the rations."

5. Privates, noncommissioned officers, and company officers are on comradely terms within the company.

6. Field grade officers are formal and respectful to each other; there is a good spirit among them, but if a suggestion from a superior to a subordinate does not suffice the superior can give an order which has to be executed unconditionally.

7. Generals are held in awe by all and have extremely great privileges.

8. Explicit reliance is often placed on military regulations in giving and enforcing orders.

9. Soviet liaison officers sometimes press for strict penalties for insubordination. (Thus no mercy was shown for Czech parachutists who refused to jump from the plane during training or for a Czech quartermaster officer charged with leaving the battle line and cowardice before the enemy.)

10. In case of a miscarried operation, Soviet military authorities might, as a disciplinary measure, remove a large number of commanding officers. (In one such case, more than sixty high-ranking officers were removed, including three generals.)

11. Soviet personal endurance and will-power is enormous; this seems to be due in part to the fact that in his daily struggle for survival a Russian is used to the most rugged conditions, in part to the fact that the Soviet troops have great pride in the glorious Russian military tradition, and in part to the harshness of Soviet military law.

12. Soviet military law is in some respects so harsh that it can only be effectively applied in exceptional circumstances; that is, it is often impossible for Soviet soldiers to perform necessary tasks without breaking the law, and it is understood that not all violations will be punished. However, whether or not a violation will be punished apparently depends on circumstances extraneous to the particular violation. If the offender

is caught he must pay, and little mercy is shown him; whether or not he is caught depends on what offenses the authorities happen to uncover and want to prosecute at the particular moment.

13. The Soviet zampolit often intervenes as a peacemaker in unnecessary tensions between superiors and subordinates, perhaps taking the side of the superior, perhaps that of the subordinate. Thus the rigors of the disciplinary system are mitigated in practice by the existence of an official of high authority, one of whose main concerns is morale.

5. AN APPRAISAL OF THE SOVIET DISCIPLINARY CODE

Analysis of the Disciplinary Code confirms many of the conclusions derived from Mr. Kerner's experiences and suggests other insights into the nature of Soviet military discipline.

The Disciplinary Code demands unconditional obedience to orders. The 1940 code, in operation throughout the war, permitted a commander to shoot a subordinate in case of disobedience and even in case of "malicious breach of discipline." It stated that the commander who exercised such right "shall not be held responsible for the consequences." The 1946 code limits the right of a commander to use violence to "an extreme case which does not permit delay" and requires the commander to report his action immediately.

The Disciplinary Code imposes sharp distinctions of rank. Its distinctions between company officers, field grade officers, and general officers correspond to Mr. Kerner's personal impressions. At the same time, the code establishes a system in which each rank, from corporal up, has important powers over subordinates. Thus noncommissioned officers may, under the code, impose company punishment on subordinates. Company commanders may place junior officers under arrest with confinement in the guardhouse, as a matter of company punishment; commanders on the company level and above may, in turn, be confined in the guardhouse by commanders one grade higher than their immediate commanders. Officers may be relieved of official duties by their commanders, and officers may be reduced in rank as a matter of nonjudicial punishment, though only on very high authority. Noncommissioned officers may be reduced to privates by disciplinary action.

Together with the large disciplinary powers of commanders over subordinates there are limitations upon abuse of such powers. The limitations are in part defined in general substantive terms — that is, it is provided that the punishment should fit the offense and should not exceed certain limits set for each rank. The limitations upon abuse of powers are also expressed in procedures for complaint against excessive or arbitrary action by a commander and for punishment of such abuses. These substantive and procedural limitations provided by the code and the military legal system can only be effective, however, if there is, first, an underlying respect for discipline and law among officers and men of all ranks, and, second, if there is an effective system of enforcement of discipline and law.

The code itself can tell us something about the spirit of discipline and legality in the Soviet armed forces. The elaborate provisions for an Officers' Court of Honor, for example, are evidence of some pride in matters of discipline. The elaborate system of rewards shows that respect, not only fear, is considered basic to discipline. The distinctions of rank are evidence of belief in the efficacy of such distinctions for maintaining correct behavior. The code as a whole appears to be intended as realistic and effective law. It gives the impression of objectivity and impartiality and is free of political considerations. The Soviet soldier who reads it — and all are strongly encouraged to do so — must gain a vivid impression of the strict discipline which is expected not only of him, but also of his superiors all the way up the line.

However, the code itself tells us nothing about the extent of violations of its provisions or the system of their enforcement. It gives no inkling of the *nichevo* (or "so what?") attitude of the Russian soldier in some circumstances, or of his capacity for absolute obedience in other circumstances. It sets up no special system for enforcement. Its practical efficacy must therefore be judged on the basis of other data, such as the data which we have presented on the role of the zampolit and the Special Sections, and on the role of the military procuracy and the military courts.

6. AN APPRAISAL OF THE SOVIET SYSTEM OF MILITARY CRIMES AND PUNISHMENTS

There is a necessary relationship in any army between non-judicial enforcement of discipline ("company punishment") and judicial enforcement of military criminal law. In the Soviet system, the standards and procedures of disciplinary action are rigorous, even merciless, in their insistence upon absolute obedience to the orders of superiors; the standards and procedures of military criminal law applicable in the military courts, on the other hand, place stress on safeguards to the accused and on discretionary leniency in various situations. The commander has a wider range of nonjudicial punishments available to him than the American commander; but if these do not suffice his purpose, and he prefers charges with the military prosecutor, the soldier will be tried by professional judges, independent of command, under a system of law which is far more elaborate than the American system in its protection of the accused.

The fact that the military courts are staffed by permanent professional military judges makes it possible to incorporate much of the general criminal law into the military criminal law. Thus problems relating to criminal intent, insanity, complicity, extenuating and aggravating circumstances, and other basic aspects of criminal law, are governed by the same norms in the military courts as in the civilian courts. Also the procedure of the military courts is similar in its basic elements to the procedure of the civilian courts — with some notable exceptions.

A system which leaves large disciplinary powers in commanders but removes jurisdiction of military crimes to permanent professional military courts operating upon the same general principles as civilian courts, has the distinct advantage of safeguarding both discipline and justice within separate spheres. The soldier cannot easily avoid discipline in the name of justice; on the other hand the commander cannot easily pervert the system of justice in the name of discipline.

Within the system of justice, the military courts are governed by a Code of Military Criminal Law, which is noteworthy for its adaptability to the varying circumstances in which criminal acts may be committed. Under Section 2 of Article 193, for example, failure to carry out an order is punishable by deprivations of freedom up to five years, if it is committed in peacetime; by deprivation for not less than five years (that is, from five to eight years), if it is committed in wartime; by death, if it is committed in combat. The punishment may be further varied depending on whether there were extenuating or aggravating circumstances, whether serious consequences were foreseeable, and whether the crime was committed by an individual alone or by a group.

Similarly, under Sections 7, 8, and 9 of Article 193, absence without leave is treated differently in peacetime and in wartime; it is one thing if committed with intent to evade execution of military duties and another if it is not; again, it is one thing if committed during military operations, and another if it is not.

This high degree of adaptability of Soviet military criminal law makes it an effective instrument for carrying out varying policies of the Soviet military leadership. The distinctions between wartime and peacetime crimes, and in wartime between combat and noncombat crimes, enables the law more effectively to symbolize the responsibility of a serviceman to his unit; for example, his failure to carry out an order or his absence without leave is a more serious offense when his unit is in danger than when it is not. (It should be noted also that Section 2 of Article 193 is interpreted to mean that a serviceman is obliged to execute orders given by his actual commanders only, and not those given by any other higher-ranking serviceman or officer.)

The many distinctions based on the intent with which an act is committed enables the law more effectively to educate and mold the hearts and minds of servicemen, by punishing them when their hearts and minds are guilty, and exonerating them when their hearts and minds are innocent. Thus a serviceman who is absent from his unit under the mistaken belief that his absence was permitted is not guilty of absence without leave; on the other hand, if he intended to desert, though he be absent but for an hour and is then apprehended and returned to his post, he is guilty of attempted desertion, which is punishable equally with desertion itself.

In types of cases in which this educational policy of the military criminal law appears to the Soviet leadership to be inadequate to accomplish its purpose, the emphasis on intent is lessened. In some cases intent is disregarded entirely. Thus we find the ruthless provision that close relatives of one who flees across the frontier are subject to absolute criminal liability; they are guilty and punishable though they had no connection whatsoever with the flight. The extremes of ruthlessness and leniency characteristic of Soviet military criminal law are to be explained not as manifestations of humanitarian or inhumanitarian motives, but as manifestations of an explicit and conscious effort to use the law to accomplish specific social policies. Since these specific policies vary, the code spells out the varying means which may be used to accomplish them. The wide variety of punishments available to Soviet military courts is a mark of this flexibility: loss of civil rights, money fines, partial or total confiscation of property, sentence to disciplinary or penal battalion, deprivation of freedom ranging from one to twenty-five years, death by shooting, death by hanging.

It is *not* one of the policies of the Soviet leadership to supplement the many privileges that go with increased rank by a greater leniency toward officers guilty of abusing those privileges. In most cases Soviet military criminal law is no less severe, and in many cases it is more severe, upon officers than upon enlisted men. Failure to carry out an order if committed by an officer is more severely punishable than if committed by an enlisted man. Unauthorized retreat by a commander is punishable by death. Abuse of authority or a "negligent attitude toward service duties" on the part of an officer is punishable under certain circumstances as a military crime under Section 17 of Article 193. If there are aggravating circumstances it is punishable by death. We would like to know more about the practical application of these provisions. Even without such knowledge, we may conclude that Soviet legislation, in and of itself, presents to Soviet officers and enlisted men an impression that the higher the rank the greater the responsibility for misdeeds. An exception to this is the provision that the 1940 law increasing the penalties for absence without leave is applicable to enlisted men only.

Even without the specific provisions of the Criminal Code it would be possible, conceivably, for Soviet military courts independently to make the various distinctions between wartime and peacetime crimes, between combat and noncombat crimes, between aggravating and extenuating circumstances, between offenses which have serious consequences and those which do not, between individual and group crimes, between various types of specific intent, and so forth. The virtue of incorporating these distinctions in the Criminal Code is that thereby the Soviet military courts may adapt the legal system to specific cases and to specific governmental policies without departing from the letter of the law. The legislation itself is adaptable; its varying provisions are there for all to read; the military court which applies them may do so with objectivity.

Where there is a gap in Soviet military legislation, the courts may use the doctrine of analogy to supply the necessary adaptability. An example is furnished by the Case of Zatyk.[1] Zatyk, a port stevedore, was absent without leave for seven hours, on January 19, 1946. Under a 1943 law railroad and water-transport workers were placed under military law with responsibility for crimes equal to that of servicemen. Absence without leave for more than two hours on the part of a serviceman had previously been made punishable by transfer to a disciplinary battalion. Nothing was said in the 1943 legislation about the sanctions applicable to transport workers for absence without leave. They could not be sent to disciplinary battalions, since these were military units to which only servicemen were "eligible." The issue in Zatyk's case was whether deprivation of freedom was an analogous penalty which might be imposed. The Plenum of the Supreme Court, reversing the Military Water-Transport Division of the Supreme Court, held that deprivation of freedom was not analogous to sentence to a disciplinary battalion. It stated that deprivation of freedom was a more severe penalty than sentence to a disciplinary battalion

— a statement which would surely be incorrect in wartime. It stated further that the purpose of the disciplinary battalion is to inculcate in its members "firm habits of military discipline," and that an analogous punishment for workers convicted of military crimes would be corrective-labor tasks (that is, a fine paid by monthly deductions from wages), whose purpose is "education in labor discipline."

The Case of Zatyk, in addition to illustrating the adaptability of Soviet military legislation, as interpreted by the courts, to specific conditions and to varying wartime and peacetime policies, also points up the difficulties involved in the application of military law to civilian work discipline. These difficulties also appear in two other cases, the Case of Golubeva [2] and and the Case of Chadaeva.[3]

In the Case of Golubeva, a woman who in 1943 was mobilized for war work registered at the place of mobilization but then failed to appear at the war-industry enterprise to which she was assigned. She was tried by a military tribunal of the NKVD under the edict of December 26, 1941, which made absence without leave from a war-industry enterprise punishable by imprisonment from five to eight years. The edict denominated such absence as desertion and gave jurisdiction to the military tribunals. In July 1944, Golubeva was sentenced to six years' imprisonment. On March 30, 1945, the Military Division of the Supreme Court reversed the decision on the ground that Golubeva's offense was not absence without leave but rather evasion of mobilization, which was punishable under an edict of February 13, 1942, by corrective-labor tasks up to one year. On May 4, 1945, the Plenum of the Supreme Court reversed the Military Division and reinstated the orignal sentence. The legal issue involved was whether Golubeva, by registering for mobilization and receiving an assignment, had become a worker at the enterprise to which she was assigned even though she had not appeared for work there. Logical arguments can be made on both sides with at least almost equal force. The Plenum of the Supreme Court finally resolved these arguments against the accused and in favor of the harsher policy. Its opinion states conclusions but does not give the premises on which those conclusions are based. The Military Division, which had taken the opposite position, may have had in mind the distinction made by Soviet military law between absence without leave and failure to report for duty. In peacetime this view might well have prevailed.

In the Case of Chadaeva a woman locksmith in a water-transport enterprise was absent from work on October 8 and over the weekend of October 13–15, 1945. Chadaeva's absence was unauthorized and she was tried by a military tribunal. The only issue was whether her absence from work on October 14, a rest-day, should be included in the period of absence without leave. If October 14 were included, her absence from October 13–15 would amount to seventy-two consecutive hours of absence, and hence desertion; if it were not included, her absence would amount to two separate absences of less than twenty-four hours each, and hence not desertion. The Military Tribunal of the Upper-Volga Basin, in a decision of October 29, 1945, and the Military Water-Transport Division of the Supreme Court, in a decision of November 23, 1945, took the view that she was guilty of two separate absences of less than 24 hours each. The Plenum of the Supreme Court, in a decision of May 17, 1945, took the other view. The Plenum stated that the duration of absence without leave is measured by the time elapsing between the beginning and end of the absence, and that the end of the absence occurs when the absent person appears for work or is apprehended. The court further reasoned that if the absence was considered to be cut off by an intervening rest period, it would be impossible for a worker to desert, since there is an intervening rest period after every eight hours of work. However, the Plenum dismissed the case on the ground that Chadaeva no longer "represented a social danger"; that is, the Court was content to establish a principle for future cases which it would not apply to the case before it — perhaps on the unexpressed ground that the principle, having never before been announced, should not be applied retroactively.

The Golubeva and Chadaeva cases make clear some of the problems inherent in the Soviet application of military law to transport workers. The soldier is under military discipline twenty-four hours a day for the duration of his term of service. The worker, on the other hand, is under work discipline only during the time he is in the factory. Having made unauthorized absence from certain types of work a military crime, the Soviet lawmakers refused to recognize that such unauthorized absence may be quite different from a soldier's unauthorized absence from a military unit. The reasoning of the Plenum of the Supreme Court in the Chadaeva case is questionable, since Chadaeva, as a transport worker, was not subject to military law during the time she was not required to be at work. Being under no duty to work on her rest-day, her absence on that day was not unauthorized, and the period of unauthorized absence was therefore interrupted. The analogy which the court made between Chadaeva's weekend absence and an absence from work for a day, which would be unpermitted only during a part of the day (eight hours), is illuminating. The court apparently recognized that to treat Chadaeva's weekend absence as two separate unpermitted absences of Saturday and Monday would reduce to absurdity the application to factory work of the military laws regarding absence without leave and desertion. In addition, it might well encourage unauthorized weekend absences.

In general, the military provisions of the Criminal Code contained in Article 193, like the provisions of the Disciplinary Code, give the appearance of objectivity and impartiality. The decisions of the Supreme Court indicate that they are taken seriously. The fact that decisions of lower courts are reversed on appeal is evidence of judicial independence on at least one of those levels. Whether or not we approve of the severity of Soviet rules and decisions with respect to failure to carry out an order, absence without leave, embezzlement of military property, abuse of authority by an officer, unauthorized surrender to the enemy, and the other crimes defined in Article 193, we cannot deny that these rules and decisions show a concern for both legality and justice and that they comprise a workable and effective military code.

With respect to counterrevolutionary crimes, the picture is entirely different. The looseness of the language defining such crimes testifies to the arbitrary quality of "political justice" administered by the military courts. Under Section 1 of Article 58 of the Criminal Code, an act is considered counterrevolutionary if it is "directed toward the . . . weakening of the authority" of the Soviet Government, or indeed "of the basic economic, political, and national [i.e., ethnic] conquests of the proletarian revolution." Treason is defined under Section 1, *a*, as any act which "damages the military might of the USSR." Under Section 10, "propaganda or agitation" which "appeals" to a "weakening" of the Soviet authority is a counterrevolutionary crime. Under Section 11, "any kind of organizational activity" "directed" toward the preparation of a counterrevolutionary crime, or "participation" in an organization "formed for" the preparation or commission of a counterrevolutionary crime, is made punishable. The quoted language is so imprecise as to give no guide to the courts and to enable them to reach any result they choose.

The interpretation in 1938 by the Supreme Court of the USSR that in order to be convicted of a counterrevolutionary crime the accused must be found to have had a specific counterrevolutionary intent was an improvement in the original legislation, and an indication that the excesses of the earlier period from 1934 to 1938 were to be curbed. The new requirement mitigates, for example, the harshness of Section 12 of Article 58, which makes punishable "failure to report authentic news of the preparation or commission of a counterrevolutionary crime." However, the word "counterrevolutionary" remains vague, and is definable only in terms of the attitudes and thoughts of the accused.

Thus in the case of K.,[4] though a noncommissioned officer who valued military discipline more highly than the Constitution was acquitted of the charge of "counterrevolutionary utterances" on the ground of absence of counterrevolutionary intent, nevertheless the fact that he could be indicted and his case tried and appealed through the entire hierarchy of military courts is evidence of a lack of objective and general standards which is inherent in the nature of the crime. His guilt or innocence depended not on the character of his act or of his words but on the character of his subjective and particular intent; further, whether or not his intent was "counterrevolutionary" depended on the official policy with respect to the relative importance of military discipline and political orthodoxy — a policy which was indeterminable in advance and which has fluctuated from time to time.

The proof of the instability of Soviet law respecting political crimes may be found in the fact that a later edition of the Supreme Court opinion in the Case of K. edits out certain crucial sentences.[5] The original report of the case states that K. was charged under Section 10 of Article 58 with "systematically uttering anti-Soviet opinions." The case as reported in a later collection of 1944 decisions of the Soviet Supreme Court, published in 1948, states that K. was charged with "systematically uttering slanderous opinions," and omits any reference to Section 10 of Article 58. The "anti-Soviet" features of the case are also omitted from the description of K.'s activities. The original report refers at one point to "one of the most odious episodes of the accusation, concerning an evaluation of the Constitution of the USSR." The 1948 edition excises the words "concerning an evaluation of the Constitution of the USSR," and gives no indication of any excision. Further, the 1948 edition substitutes "criminal orientation" for the original "orientation against Soviet authority," and omits any reference to the conditions necessary to a finding of a "counterrevolutionary" crime.

These changes in the official report of the case are significant. As the case was originally reported in 1944, the Supreme Court held that one who made odious statements about the Constitution is not guilty of violation of Section 10 of Article 58 of the Criminal Code unless a specific counterrevolutionary intent is proved, and that the fact that the statements were directed toward the strengthening of military discipline is a circumstance negating such intent. In the case as reported in 1948, the holding is that *slanderous* statements are not punishable if they are "not evoked by a *criminal* orientation." In 1948 the Soviet editors were unwilling to let the original holding stand. The policy with respect to what is and what is not counterrevolutionary had changed. Still more significant is the fact that the Soviet authorities were willing to distort a previously recorded judicial opinion. Stalin's famous call for "stability of laws" was evidently considered inapplicable to the law of counterrevolutionary crimes.

7. AN APPRAISAL OF THE SOVIET SYSTEM OF MILITARY COURTS AND PROCEDURE

There are two basic questions which must be asked by anyone who attempts to determine the quality of a judicial system: are the judges independent, that is, are they free from outside influence upon their decisions? and are they honest, intelligent, and able? No matter how excellent the framework of the judicial system, it cannot be an effective instrument either of legality in a narrow sense or of justice in a broader sense if the men who sit as judges are subject to political or administrative pressures, or if they are corrupt or incompetent.

In evaluating the Soviet system of military courts, it is impossible to give a definitive answer, and difficult even to give an approximate answer, to these two questions. On the one hand, the framework of the Soviet system of military courts encourages a high degree both of judicial independence and of judicial competence. On the other hand, we do not know what lies behind that framework, and this very lack of knowledge, in so far as it is attributable to Soviet secrecy, produces a natural skepticism as to what we would find out if the veil of secrecy were lifted — if, for example, we were permitted access to the Soviet Union, or even if Soviet writers themselves published comprehensive factual data relating to the administration of justice, or if at the very least the Soviet regime permitted the export of all the Soviet law books which are published.

However, some important inferences concerning the quality of the Soviet military courts may be drawn from a close reading of Soviet cases and other Soviet literature. It is clear that there are Soviet military courts, that they are staffed by professional judges, that there are appeals or protests from lower military courts to higher ones and ultimately to the Plenum of the

Supreme Court of the USSR, that the decisions of lower military courts are sometimes reversed on appeal or protest and sometimes reinstated on further appeal or protest, and that the opinions of the Supreme Court of the USSR (which is the only court in the Soviet Union whose decisions are reported) are reasoned opinions — in many cases, well-reasoned opinions. Of the quality of the lower military courts we have little indication, except that a training in law (including military law) is apparently a prerequisite for becoming a military judge and that military law schools exist for the purpose of providing such training. However, the decisions of lower military tribunals in cases which reach the Supreme Court of the USSR reveal, in general, a rather mediocre judiciary on the lower levels. Emigrés accounts, even allowing for bias, corroborate the view that the lower military courts are not of a very high quality.

Are the military judges independent? Our answer is, not entirely — in other words, no. The system of appointment of military judges by the Ministry of Justice, and of subordination of lower military courts to higher ones, is some evidence that there is freedom from external pressure by military commanders. The separation of the military judiciary from the military procuracy, and the fact that procurators' appeals or protests to higher military courts are sometimes denied, are some evidence that the military judges are free from external pressure by military procurators. As to pressure by security agencies and by Communist Party authorities, however, there is no reliable evidence of a general character, and the authors can only state a rough impression. Our impression is that there is such pressure in some cases, though probably such cases are a relatively small proportion of the total number of cases, and that where the pressure is applied it is generally effective. In other words, although in general the military judges are supposed to be independent, nevertheless a high Party or security official may occasionally tell a military judge what to do; such intervention by Party or security officials is at their discretion and only the most courageous of military judges would defy them; further, the only effective means of resistance open to such courageous military judges would be a personal appeal to still higher Party or security authorities.

It seems to us that the Soviet system — both the political and the legal system — is designed to minimize political and administrative pressures upon the judiciary at the lower levels, and to maximize such pressures at the higher levels where political or administrative interests are seriously involved. This view corresponds to our view of the nature of Soviet autocracy, which fuses authority in a small group of persons at the top, but diffuses authority on the intermediate and lower planes.

In the armed forces as well as in civilian life, the Soviet leadership attempts to run law and terror in double harness. To deal with serious political opposition there is no need to resort to the judicial process at all, under the Soviet system: secret administrative trial by the Special Board of the MVD is available. If the regime considers it desirable to give a somewhat stronger flavor of legality to the proceedings, it may have the political opponent tried — secretly — in the military division of the Supreme Court of the USSR under Sections 6, 8, or 9 of Article 58 of the Criminal Code and under Articles 466–470 of the Code of Criminal Procedure; in such cases the accused is not allowed to participate in the trial, and the death sentence is executed immediately, with no right of appeal or of petition for mercy. In 1953 Lavrenti Beria was tried and executed under that procedure. However, the leadership may for political purposes decide upon a "demonstration trial," as in the famous purge trials of the late thirties and several similar trials of Poles and other satellite or enemy groups during and immediately after the war; such trials proceed *formally* according to the general system of Soviet court procedure, but actually the testimony is carefully prepared in advance so that the trial will "demonstrate" whatever the regime wishes to have demonstrated.

The famous demonstration trials have led many to believe that *all* justice in the Soviet Union is a farce, and that the forms of law are in *all* trials merely a disguise for political terror. It is undeniable that these trials have tended to obscure the distinction between Soviet law and Soviet terror. Yet it is foolish to believe that this distinction has no validity. The provisions of Articles 466–470 of the Code of Criminal Procedure, by their explicit denial to the accused of the basic elements of due process of law, show that the Soviet leadership knows perfectly well what due process of law is and chooses in certain cases not to permit it. Similarly the system of administrative trials by the Special Board of the MVD is itself evidence that those trials are intended to have a different significance from that of ordinary judicial trials.

How well the Plenum of the Supreme Court of the USSR understands the meaning of due process of law — when it wants to — is demonstrated in the Case of Muzykin *et al.*,[6] in which the Plenum revised a conviction of five servicemen on the grounds, first, that they had been deprived of their right to counsel and second, that the trial court had erroneously denied a petition to appoint an expert to examine and verify an important document in the case. The trial court had divided the five defendants into two groups, and had appointed two defense counsels, one for each group. However, there was a conflict of interests between several of the accused who were represented by the same lawyer. The Military Division stated that the trial court had violated the Code of Criminal Procedure in not appointing an additional lawyer, but held that the trial had nevertheless been just and therefore sustained the conviction. The Plenum, in reversing the Military Division's decision, stated:

[V]iolation of the law guaranteeing the most important right of an accused, the right of defense counsel, belongs by its very nature to those essential procedural violations which cannot fail to affect the rendering of a just verdict: moreover, the views of the [Military] Division are in direct conflict with the law which includes such violation among the unconditional grounds for reversal of a verdict. Under Article 415 of the Code of Criminal Procedure of the RSFSR a verdict is unconditionally subject to reversal if the case was tried without participation of defense counsel when such participation is obligatory. It is perfectly clear that a case in which one counsel is appointed for defense of two or more accused who have conflicting interests must belong to the category of cases tried without participation of defense counsel, since such organization of defense is equivalent to leaving one or another or all of the accused without defense counsel.

In addition, the trial court's refusal to appoint an accountant to verify an audit of the regiment's food supply (the defendants were charged with abuse of authority resulting in a large deficiency in their regiment's food supply) was held to be erroneous. The trial court had first denied the petition of one of the accused to have an expert appointed, on the ground that the case was "clear." The Plenum said that a refusal on that ground is in itself unjustified, and further the offer of such a justification "testifies to the prejudiced attitude of the court toward the case." A second petition for expert examination was made by both defense counsels, and was denied in part on the ground that an audit had once been made in the presence of the accused and they had expressed no objections. The Plenum stated that this ruling was erroneous in that it "prejudges the evaluation of the evidence"; the court must evaluate the evidence "on the basis of examination of all the circumstances of the case in their aggregate" — and not, in other words, on the basis merely of what the accused said or failed to say with respect to an audit made before he was even indicted.

If we consider only nonpolitical military crimes, and if we accept as a hypothesis the nonintervention of political or police authorities in the trial of such crimes, do we find any distinctive features in the Soviet system of military courts and procedure as it applies to servicemen (as distinguished from railroad and water-transport workers and, during the war, workers in war-industry enterprises)?

One such feature is the existence of a permanent professional military judiciary, a permanent professional military procuracy, and a military section of the Ministry of Justice, subordinate to the Supreme Court of the USSR, the Procurator-General of the USSR, and the Minister of Justice of the USSR, respectively. By establishing an integrated system of professional military-legal cadres, and by linking that system to the general system of administration of justice, the Soviet regime has assured to the serviceman charged with a military crime more objective and more systematic legal protection than he would have if the administration of military law were left largely to military commanders (as under the American system). At the same time, the Soviet system enables the leadership more objectively and more systematically to enforce its military-legal policies.

A second distinctive feature of the Soviet system of military courts and procedure is the crucial role of the military procuracy, which investigates military crimes, prosecutes them, and may protest decisions of lower courts to higher courts. The investigating, prosecuting, and protesting functions of the military procuracy (as of the Soviet civilian procuracy) are supposed to be distinct from each other, and are handled by distinct branches of the procuracy. The preliminary investigation is supposed to be impartial. The supervisory branch of the procuracy may, and sometimes does, protest convictions obtained by the prosecuting branch. However, the centralization of these three functions in the hands of one organization is a threat to justice. Even apart from the question of Communist Party intervention, it is doubtful that the procuracy can avoid confusing its three functions in many cases. If the procurator of a military district, for example, wishes to make a victim or a scapegoat of a particular serviceman, it would be easy for him to "rig" the preliminary investigation; if the serviceman were acquitted by the trial court, the procurator could have another crack at him by protesting the acquittal to the next higher court (and again, if necessary, step by step, to the Plenum of the Supreme Court).

These powers of the procuracy are especially significant in view of the sweeping prohibitions of Soviet legislation and the consequent inevitability of widespread violations. It is the procuracy, primarily, that determines which of the guilty "deserve" to be prosecuted. On the other hand, the broad powers of the military procuracy may be exercised in favor of subordinates against their commanders. The military procuracy, like the military judiciary, is thus an equalizing force which tends to curb arbitrary power at the higher levels of military command.

A third distinctive feature of the Soviet system of military courts and procedure is the conscious use of the judicial process to instill in Soviet military personnel a strong sense of their legal, political, and military responsibilities. The inquisitorial features of pretrial investigation and of the trial itself are directed, in part, to that end. The flexibility of the substantive law provides the court with an opportunity to adapt its decision to that end. During the war, when the trial court proceeded without defense counsel or procurator, merely on the basis of the indictment, calling its own witnesses and interrogating them and the accused, the adversary features of the trial dropped out of sight almost entirely; but even in peacetime the Soviet military judge — like his civilian counterpart — is lord of the trial, and the accused, though represented by counsel, is like a little boy or a youth charged with being naughty.

Of course there is in all criminal trials, in whatever system of law, a "parental" element. The judge is like the father — whether he be stern or lenient; the accused is meek — whether he be innocent or guilty. It is not merely a question of two sides, the prosecution and the defense, doing legal battle before a referee. In military courts, in whatever system, the authority of the court is still further heightened by the superiority in military rank — generally — of the judge over the accused.

In the Soviet system of military criminal procedure the "parental," or "educational," or "disciplinary" features of the trial are especially striking. Indeed the whole system both of procedure and substantive law is geared to inculcating attitudes of obedience, self-sacrifice and loyalty into the minds and hearts of servicemen — the accused who is before the court as well as his comrades who are not.

Elsewhere, one of the authors has developed the idea that Soviet law in its entirety is based on the concept of a "parental" relationship between the official representatives of the state, on the one hand, and the citizen on the other.[7] In all his legal relationships, whether as a worker seeking workmen's compensation, a husband seeking a divorce, a state business manager making a contract with another manager for delivery of goods,

or a person charged with theft, murder, or embezzlement —
the Soviet citizen is treated by the courts and by other official
agencies less as an independent possessor of rights and duties
than as a dependent member of society, a ward, a youth, who
needs training and guidance. (The fact that punishment is considered one of the most important instruments of such training
does not contradict the theory.) The Soviet citizen's relationship to officialdom is thus assumed to be more personal, more
intimate, than the relationship of the individual to the state in
modern Western society. It is more like the feudal relationship
of man to lord and lord to overlord. (The very word for state
in Russian, *gosudarstvo*, means "lordship.") The Soviet "state"
is father, mother, leader, master, teacher; the Soviet "individual" is son or daughter, follower, servant, pupil. Law does not
merely define and delimit rights and interests; it educates and
disciplines a people conceived to be essentially immature and
undisciplined, though capable of becoming more mature and
better disciplined.

The authors believe that the use of law by the Soviet regime
to mold and develop the attitudes and habits of the people is due
in part to "power" considerations, but that it is also in part a
response to the fact that the people governed by Soviet law
are themselves indeed more childlike, more spontaneous and
impulsive in their actions, and less amenable to legal controls
in their daily lives, than Western peoples. This is a generalization which cannot be proved and which needs numerous qualifications. We risk it nevertheless. We risk another beside it:
that Soviet officials at all levels are inclined to be less objective
and formal, less respectful of law, and less legalistic than their
Western counterparts.

If these two generalizations are true, one may wonder why
the Soviet regime places as much emphasis as it does upon law,
as contrasted with other less formal and less indirect means of
training and discipline. To explain this we must risk a third
generalization: the Soviet leaders have learned that a complex
urbanized and industrialized society cannot operate efficiently
without an objective, formal, rational-legal structure. They

therefore seek to use law to inculcate rationality into the economy, the administration, and the social order generally, including the military system.

On these hypotheses, we are confronted with a system of law which in itself has characteristics similar to Western legal systems, but which has been incorporated into a social order in which there is marked hostility to certain aspects of law both in the people as a whole and in the leadership. The leadership seeks to remake the people, to overcome their hostility to law, to transform them into an efficient, disciplined, law-conscious, law-abiding people. The leadership is not willing, however, to take the risk of treating its subjects as though they were already disciplined, law-abiding people; especially in the political sphere, it is not willing to take the risk of treating its subjects as though they were loyal. Instead of giving law to the people, it uses law to transform the people. The transforming power of the law which it uses is seriously diminished, however, by the fact that the leadership remains the master, rather than the servant, of the legal order.

Our study shows that the Soviet leadership has been resourceful and imaginative in creating a system of military law designed on the one hand to encourage a sense of discipline and responsibility among Soviet military personnel on all intermediate levels, and on the other hand to preserve the autocratic authority of the rulers at the top.

APPENDIX I

List of Documents Referred to in this Volume and Translated in Harold J. Berman and Miroslav Kerner, Documents on Soviet Military Law and Administration

I. MILITARY ADMINISTRATION

1. Provisions of the Constitution of the USSR relating to the armed forces, Articles 14,*b*, *g*; 18a, 18b; 30–32; 48; 49; 60,*f*, 64–68; 70; 74–78; 102–104; 112–115; 117; 130; 132; 133
2. Statute on the People's Commissariat of Defense of the USSR (1934)
3. Statute on the Military Council of the People's Commissar of Defense of the USSR (1934)
4. Statute on the Military Council of the District (Fleet, Army) of the Worker-Peasant Red Army (1937)
5. Amendment of the Statute on the Military Council of the District (Fleet, Army) of the Worker-Peasant Red Army (1937)
6. Statute on Military Commissars of the Worker-Peasant Red Army (1937)
7. Edict on the Abolition of Military Commissars (1940)
8. Edict on the Reintroduction of Military Commissars (1941)
9. Edict on the Abolition of Military Commissars (1942)
10. Charter of the Communist Party, Chapter X (1952)
11. Law on Universal Military Obligation (1939, as amended to 1941)
12. Decree on Universal Military Training of Citizens of the USSR (1941)

II. MILITARY DISCIPLINE

13. Text of the Military Oath (1918)
14. Text of the Military Oath (1939, 1947)
15. Edict on the Procedure for Taking the Military Oath (1939)

16. Edict on the Establishment of Military Ranks of Higher Commanding Personnel of the Red Army (1940)
17. Edict on the Introduction of Guard Ranks for Servicemen of Guard Units and Commands of the Red Army and Navy (1942)
18. Edict on the Establishment of Additional Military Ranks for Higher Commanding Personnel of Aviation, Artillery, and Armored Tank Troops (1943)
19. Edict on the Procedure for Conferring Military Ranks on Servicemen of the Red Army (1943)
20. Edict on the Division of Servicemen of the Navy into Rank and File, Petty Officers, and Officers (1943)
21. Edict on the Establishment of Additional Military Ranks for Higher Commanding Personnel of the Red Army (1943)
22. Edict on the Introduction of New Insignia of Rank for Personnel of the Red Army (1943)
23. Disciplinary Code of the Armed Forces of the USSR (1946)

III. MILITARY CRIMES AND PUNISHMENTS

24. Military Crimes (RSFSR Criminal Code, 1952 ed., Chapter Nine)
25. Counterrevolutionary Crimes (RSFSR Criminal Code, 1952 ed., Article 58(1)–(14))
26. Edict on Responsibility for Disclosure of State Secrets and for Loss of Documents Containing State Secrets (1947)
27. Decree on the Establishment of a List of Information Comprising State Secrets, Disclosure of Which Shall be Punished by Law (1947)
28. Theft of Firearms (RSFSR Criminal Code, 1952 ed., Article 59 (3, *a*))
29. Property Crimes Subject to Jurisdiction of Military Tribunals (RSFSR Criminal Code, Articles 164*a*, 166*a*)
30. The Case of Golubeva (1945)
31. The Case of Chadaeva (1946)
32. The Case of Poliakov (1948)
33. The Case of K. (1944)
34. Deprivation of Freedom (RSFSR Criminal Code, Article 28)

35. Directive Instruction of the Plenum of the Supreme Court of the USSR on the Possibility and Procedure of Applicacation of Note 2 to Article 28 of the Criminal Code of the RSFSR and Corresponding Articles of the Criminal Codes of Other Constituent Republics in Cases of Desertion in Wartime (1942)

36. Directive Instruction of the Plenum of the Supreme Court of the USSR on the Procedure for Serving of Punishment by Privates and Noncommissioned Officers Condemned to Deprivation of Freedom up to Two Years (1946)

37. Directive Instruction of the Plenum of the Supreme Court of the USSR on the Procedure for Deciding the Question of Compensation for Harm in Cases Tried by Military Tribunals (1945)

38. The Case of Zatyk (1946)

39. The Case of Il'in (1946)

40. Edict on Amnesty in Connection with the Victory Over Hitlerite Germany (1945)

41. Edict on Amnesty, March 27, 1953

IV. MILITARY COURTS AND PROCEDURE

42. Provisions of the Law on the Judicial System of the USSR relating to military courts (1938)

43. Statute on the Formation of the All-Union People's Commissariat of Internal Affairs (1934)

44. Statute on the Trial of Crimes Investigated by the People's Commissariat of Internal Affairs and Its Local Organs (1940)

45. Edict on Martial Law (1941)

46. Edict on Military Tribunals in Localities Under Martial Law and in Districts of Military Operations (1941)

47. Edict on the Introduction of Martial Law to All Railroads (1943)

48. Edict on the Introduction of Martial Law to Marine and River Transport (1943)

49. Edict on the Repeal of Martial Law (1945)

50. Edict on the Repeal of Martial Law (1946)

51. Statute on Military Tribunals and the Military Procuracy (1926, as amended through 1940)

APPENDIX II

The Evolution of the Ministry of Defense Prior to 1934

When the Bolshevik regime came to power on November 7, 1917, the Russian army was in a state of disorganization, although the war with the Central Powers was still in progress. The new government (the Council of People's Commissars) included a People's Commissariat of Military and Naval Affairs,[1] which dealt chiefly with matters "pertaining to the old army, its rapidly dissolving personnel, and its still vast important materiel."[2] The Commissariat was headed by a three-man committee,[3] which was replaced on December 20, 1917, by a seven-man All-Russian Collegium for the Organization of the Workers' and Peasants' Red Army.[4] On December 29, 1917, there were organized in Petrograd, on the basis of the plans and proposals of the All-Russian Collegium, the first units of the new Red Army.[5] On February 23, 1918, subsequently celebrated annually as Red Army Day, regular Red Army units engaged German troops in combat for the first time.

The first stages of development of Soviet military administration were characterized by a series of reorganizations at the top, although actual control remained in the hands of a relatively few men, Party leaders, aided by military leaders inherited from prerevolutionary times.

On January 28, 1918, the Council of People's Commissars enacted a basic decree on the organization of the Red Army. The decree stated that "the supreme controlling organ of the Workers' and Peasants' Red Army shall be the Council of People's Commissars. Immediate control and administration of the armies shall be concentrated in the Commissariat of Military Affairs, in its special All-Russian Collegium."[6] (A separate subordinate People's Commissariat of Naval Affairs was established later.) By a decree of the same date "On the Institution of the All-Russian Collegium for the Formation of the Workers' and Peasants' Red Army,"[7] the composition and powers of that body were defined. It consisted of two representatives of the Commissariat of Military Affairs and two representatives of the Chief of Staff of the Red Guard.[8] The functions of the All-Russian Collegium were declared to be "the direction and coördination of the activities of local, regional, and district organizations for the formation of the armies, the enrolling of newly formed military units, control of (their) formation and training, securing to the new army weapons and supplies, sanitary and medical aid, financial administration, preparation of new codes, instructions, etc." The Collegium was instructed to organize divisions for organization-agitation, formation and training, mobilization, ordnance, supply, transport, sanitation, and finance.

"At present," stated Leon Trotsky on April 23, 1918, "we are merging . . . the departments of the All-Russian Collegium for the Organization of the Workers' and Peasants' Army with the respective departments of the Commissariat of War, the latter still reflecting the old army which no longer exists." [9]

In March 1918, a Supreme Military Council was formed, consisting of the People's Commissar of Military Affairs as chairman, the People's Commissar of Naval Affairs, and two "military specialists." This body — or perhaps its successor, the All-Russian Supreme Staff, formed on May 8, 1918 — seems to have replaced the All-Russian Collegium. However, the administrative changes within the Commissariat — from three-man committee to seven-man All-Russian Collegium to four-man Supreme Military Council to five-man All-Russian Supreme Staff — seem not to have affected seriously the actual functioning of the Commissariat. Indeed some of the leading personnel remained on all three organizations.[10]

On September 2, 1918, a Revolutionary Military Council of the Republic was established to coördinate all operations, administration, and supply of the armed forces both at the front and in the county at large. (Although the war with the Central Powers ended on March 3, 1918, new campaigns against interventionist forces were fought thereafter, and the Civil War continued until 1921.) The chairman of the Revolutionary Military Council was at the same time the People's Commissar of Military and Naval Affairs — Trotsky; and the Collegium of the People's Commissariat of Military and Naval Affairs (united again on August 19, 1918) was included in the membership of the Council. It was headed by a three-man bureau — Trotsky, Vatsetis (the Commander-in-Chief), and Aralov.

On November 30, 1918, a Council of Workers' and Peasants' Defense was established, headed by Lenin, with Trotsky, Nevsky, Briukhanov, Krasin, and Stalin as members. The Council of Defense was given supreme power in military affairs. However, direct control of the army and navy was left in the hands of the Revolutionary Military Council of the Republic.[11]

Meanwhile, the administration of military affairs on the lower levels was highly disorganized. On March 31, 1918, European Russia was divided into six military districts.[12] The supreme military-administrative authority in each district was vested in a Military District Council, consisting of the military leader of the district and two political commissars.[13] Aided by a large Military District Committee,[14] the Military District Council was under the control of the People's Commissariat of Military Affairs.[15] Its tasks included registering persons and material resource for military purposes, forming military units, and furnishing military units with needed supplies.[16]

Eight days later, the Council of People's Commissars established local commissariats for military affairs on the levels of small rural district, county, province, and (large) district, with even broader functions than those of the Military District Councils. The local commissariats were in charge of registration for military service, formation of military forces, military training of all workers and those peasants "not engaged in exploitation of the labor of another," and "satisfaction of the material requirements of military supply." [17] The relationship between the new local commissariats and the Military District Councils was not stated.

At the same time the local governing organs, the councils (*Soviets*), organized Red Army units independently, under instructions of the army headquarters itself. Thus the army headquarters duplicated the work of the People's Commissariat of Military Affairs, and the local councils duplicated the work of the Military District Councils and the local commissariats for military affairs. Fedotoff White reports that one local soviet decided to organize a whole army, with an infantry regiment, a cavalry regiment, a battery of field artillery, an armored car detachment, and an automobile column.[18]

With the settling down of the Soviet regime after the Civil War, the competence of the People's Commissariat of Military and Naval Affairs was more clearly defined in law.

The 1923 statute on the People's Commissariat of Military and Naval Affairs of the USSR was enacted on the basis of the first Constitution of the USSR effective from January 21, 1924, which gave unity to the Russian, Ukrainian, Belorussian, and Transcaucasian Republics. Articles 37 and 49 of the 1924 Constitution established the Council of People's Commissars as the executive and administrative organ of the legislature (which was then called the Central Executive Committee), naming ten commissariats, including the People's Commissariat of Military and Naval Affairs. Article 51 listed the Commissariat as one of the five centralized All-Union Commissariats. Article 56 established in each People's Commissariat a Collegium, under the chairmanship of the People's Commissariat, whose members were to be named by the Council of People's Commissar. Article 57 states that the People's Commissar "shall have the right personally to make decisions on all questions within the competence of the corresponding commissariat, reporting on them to the Collegium. In case of disagreement with a decision of the People's Commissar, the Collegium or individual members thereof, without suspension of the execution of the decision, may appeal it to the Council of People's Commissars of the USSR." Thus a "collegiate" system of control was established for each People's Commissariat.

The statute on the People's Commissariat of Military and Naval Affairs gave that body the functions of planning, organizing, and administering the military and naval defense of the USSR. It was empowered to call up the population for military service, to form units of the army and navy, including territorial troops, to organize military preparation and military sports for age groups not within the army and navy, to conduct the political education of servicemen, to secure to the army and navy all forms of supplies for war or peace, and so forth. Its legislative powers were defined as follows (Article 3):

1. To present for confirmation by the supreme organs of the USSR drafts, prepared by the People's Commissariat, of decrees on questions relating to its sphere of competence;

2. To issue for the Red Army and Navy orders, regulations, statutes, instructions, etc., binding upon organs of the Military and Naval Department and all servicemen throughout the USSR;

3. To establish and to change, within the limits of existing legislation, the organization of subordinate organs of military and naval administration and command;

4. To issue, under existing laws, regulations binding upon all citizens of the USSR in regard to (1) registration and conscription of the population for military preparation and military service, and (2) registration of horses, vehicles, harnesses, and other objects subject to be supplied to the Worker-Peasant Army [sic] and Navy in the event of war;

5. Upon proclamation of mobilization to issue regulations binding upon all citizens and the whole population of the Union concerning the method of conscripting citizens into the Worker-Peasant Red Army and Navy and the method of supplying objects necessary for the Worker-Peasant Red Army and Navy;

6. To establish the method and form of military and naval registration.

The Revolutionary Military Council of the USSR, which replaced the Revolutionary Military Council of the Republic, was the supreme governing organ of the Commissariat. Article 5 of the Statute stated that in extraordinary circumstances the People's Commissar could act independently, but under Article 6 the general regulations of the Commissar were required to be issued through orders of the Revolutionary Military Council. The Council was declared to be the Collegium of the Commissariat (Article 7) and its membership included the People's Commissar as chairman, the Vice-Commissar as vice-chairman, the Commander-in-Chief of all the armed forces of the USSR, and the members named by the Council of People's Commissars (Article 8). The executive and administrative organs of the army, navy, and air force were declared to be immediately subordinate to the Revolutionary Military Council; this included the Political Administration (PUR), which was in charge of political activities and political education in the armed forces (Articles 9, 28). At the head of the Political Administration was a commander named by the Revolutionary Military Council (Article 29).

Article 41 stated that all local organs of military and naval administration were controlled by orders of the Commissariat. Article 42 stated that districts shall be administered by commanders of troops who shall be named by the Revolutionary Military Council, and that "in necessary cases the Revolutionary Military Council of the USSR may form Revolutionary Military Councils in the districts."

The 1923 statute was designed for the administration of a large standing army, which had been retained from the period of the Civil War without significant changes in its structure. This army, under the leadership of Trotsky as People's Commissar of Military and Naval Affairs, was kept on a war footing — a fact which was later attributed to Trotsky's conviction that world revolution was imminent.

In 1924, however, Trotsky ceased to control the Commissariat, and the so-called Military Reform of 1924–1925, undertaken under the leadership of Frunze and Voroshilov,[19] established a mixed system of permanent standing army, on the one hand, and temporary territorial units on the other. (Actually, territorial units were introduced as early as August 1923.[20]) However, there were permanent cadres in the territorial units as well, comprising from one-tenth to one-sixth of their personnel, and technical troops, air and naval forces, and most cavalry units consisted entirely of permanent cadres.[21] Nevertheless the period between 1924 and 1928 was marked by the creation of a new territorial army, with the service spread intermittently over a five-year period,[22] and by a large reduction in size of the standing army.

Following upon these changes in the organization of the army, on January 30, 1929, a new statute on the People's Commissariat of Military and Naval Affairs was enacted. The new statute did not alter in any essentials the powers of the Commissariat as established in the 1923 statute, but it omitted the detailed description of military and naval administrative organs. Also the powers of the Revolutionary Council are stated in the 1929 law much more briefly and generally. Article 4 states: "At the head of the People's Commissariat of Military and Naval Affairs shall stand the People's Commissar of Military and Naval Affairs. He shall also stand at the head of all the armed forces of the USSR, comprising the Workers' and Peasants' Red Army, and shall be the chairman of the Revolutionary Military Council of the USSR." Article 5 states: "The Revolutionary Military Council of the USSR shall be the Collegium of the People's Commissariat of Military and Naval Affairs. Its membership shall include, in addition to the People's Commissar of Military and Naval Affairs, the Deputy People's Commissars of Military and Naval Affairs (who shall be vice-chairmen of the Revolutionary Military Council of the USSR), confirmed by the Presidium of the Central Executive Committee of the USSR, and members personally named by the Council of People's Commissars of the USSR." No specific powers of the Revolutionary Military Council are mentioned. The reduction in the power of the Revolutionary Military Council was consonant with a general reorganization of commissariats in 1928–1929, toward greater "one-man control." [23]

The development of local military administration in the period following the Civil War was marked, first, by the transformation of certain military commissariats into military sections of the local soviets. This was done in the case of county (*volost*) military commissariats by a decree of the Council of People's Commissars of March 21, 1921, which transferred to the executive committees of the county councils the function of registering and mobilizing persons liable to military service.[24]

With the organization of a territorial army, the remaining military commissariats were transformed into territorial administrations; each corps, division, and other military unit administered the military affairs, including the registration and mobilization of citizens for military service, of the territory in which it was located. The decree of January 9, 1925, "On the Reorganization of the Local Organs of the

People's Commissariat of Military and Naval Affairs," imposed on the territorial administrations "the execution of the functions of the military sections of corresponding [local] executive committees." [25] Thus the local commissariats and the military sections of the local governing organs were reunited into the system of the military commands. The 1929 statute on the People's Commissariat of Military and Naval Affairs retained this feature, as did the 1934 statute on the People's Commissariat of Defense.

APPENDIX III

*Chronology of Changes in the Formal Organization of the
Ministry of Defense Since 1917*

On November 8, 1917, a People's Commissariat of Military and
Naval Affairs was established.

On January 28, 1918, this was divided into a People's Commissariat of Military Affairs and a subordinate People's Commissariat of
Naval Affairs (the exact date of the formal creation of the latter
Commissariat is not clear, but it was in existence by March 1918).

On August 19, 1918, the two Commissariats were reunited into the
People's Commissariat of Military and Naval Affairs.

On June 20, 1934, a People's Commissariat of Defense was established to replace the People's Commissariat of Military and Naval
Affairs.

On July 30, 1937, a People's Commissariat of the Navy was
established.

On February 1, 1944, the People's Commissariat of Defense was
transferred from an all-union to a constituent republican status.

On February 25, 1946, the People's Commissariat of Defense and
the People's Commissariat of the Navy were again merged under
the new name of the People's Commissariat of the Armed Forces.

On March 15, 1946, all the People's Commissariats were renamed
Ministries.

On February 24, 1950, the Ministry of Armed Forces was divided
into a Ministry of War and a Ministry of the Navy.

On March 19, 1953, the Ministry of War and the Ministry of the
Navy were reunited into a Ministry of Defense.

APPENDIX IV

List of Ministers (former People's Commissars) of Defense
(former Military and Naval Affairs, Military Affairs,
Armed Forces, War) Since 1918

Leon Trotsky — March 17, 1918 to January 26, 1925.
Mikhail Vasil'evich Frunze — January 26, 1925 to October 31, 1925.
Kliment Efremovich Voroshilov — November 6, 1925 to May 7, 1940.
Semen Konstantinovich Timoshenko — May 7, 1940 to July 19, 1941.
Iosif Visarionovich Stalin — July 19, 1941 to March 3, 1947.
Nikolai Aleksandrovich Bulganin — March 3, 1947 to March 24, 1949.
Aleksander Mikhailovich Vasilevskii — March 24, 1949 to March 6, 1953.
Nikolai Aleksandrovich Bulganin — March 6, 1953 to February 9, 1955.
Georgi Konstantinovich Zhukov — February 9, 1953 to date.

NOTES

I. SOVIET MILITARY ADMINISTRATION

1. The provisions of the Constitution of the USSR which are cited in the text, together with other constitutional provisions directly bearing upon military matters, are translated in Harold J. Berman and Miroslav Kerner, *Documents on Soviet Military Law and Administration* (Cambridge, Mass., 1955; hereafter cited as Berman and Kerner, *Documents*), no. 1.

2. I. I. Evtikhiev and V. A. Vlasov, *Administrativnoe Pravo SSSR* (Administrative Law of the USSR; Moscow, 1946), p. 151. The rank of marshal is bestowed by the Presidium of the Supreme Soviet.

3. N. Galai, "Vnutrennaia politika i sovetskaia armiia" (Domestic Politics and the Soviet Army), *SSSR sevodnia i zavtra* (The USSR Today and Tomorrow; Munich, 1953), pp. 56–63. The list of military leaders is drawn from this article with certain corrections. See also *Biuleten'* (Bulletin of the Institute for the Study of the History and Culture of the USSR, Munich), 1954, no. 1, pp. 51–52; no. 2, p. 36.

4. D. Fedotoff White, *The Growth of the Red Army* (Princeton, 1944), pp. 74–75. White relies for his description of the order of April 6, 1918, on Trotsky's *Kak voorushalas' Revolutsiia* (How the Revolution was Fought; Moscow, 1924). The text of the order of April 6, 1918, is cited in Wollenberg, *The Red Army*, p. 255.

5. Quoted by White, *ibid.*, p. 77.

6. Quoted by White, *ibid.*, pp. 78–79.

7. Order of the People's Commissariat for Military Affairs on the Creation of the All-Russian Bureau of Military Commissars, April 3, 1918, in G. D. Kostomarov and R. I. Golubev, eds., *Organizatsiia Krasnoi Armii 1917–1918* (The Organization of the Red Army, 1917–1918; Moscow, 1943; a collection of documents and materials), p. 156. The early history of the People's Commissariat for Military Affairs is described in Appendix II of the present volume.

8. See Merle Fainsod, *How Russia Is Ruled* (Cambridge, Mass., 1953), pp. 400–401.

9. See White, p. 232. J. H. Meisel and E. S. Kozera, *Materials for the Study of the Soviet System* (Ann Arbor, Michigan, 1950), p. 368, n. 2, refer incorrectly to the "abolition" of military commissars in 1924. The 1950 textbook on administrative law states: "The introduction of one-man control [by decision of the Central Committee of the Communist Party in March 1925] did not abolish the institution of military commissars, but changed their functions. The commissars were freed from obligatory supervision of front, administrative and economic activities of the commander and preserved the sole function of party and political guidance." (S. S. Studenikin, V. A. Vlasov, and I. I. Evtikhiev, *Sovetskoe Administrativnoe Pravo* (Soviet Administrative Law; Moscow, 1950), p. 235.)

10. Statute on Military Commissars of the Worker-Peasant Red Army, August 15, 1937, *Sobranie Zakonov i Rasporiazhenii Raboche-Krest'ianskogo Pravitel'stva SSSR* (Collection of Laws and Regulations of the Worker-Peasant Government of the USSR; hereafter cited as *Coll. Laws USSR*), 1937, no. 55, art. 233, translated in Berman and Kerner, *Documents*, no. 6.

The Political Administration of the Republic (PUR) was renamed the Political Administration of the Worker-Peasant Red Army (PURRKA) at some time between 1924 and 1929, but was nevertheless often referred to as the PUR thereafter.

11. *Cf.* A. I. Denisov, general editor, *Istoriia Sovetskogo Gosudarstva i Prava* (History of Soviet State and Law; Moscow, 1949), p. 396: "The military commissars helped to clear the army and navy of the intruders from the ranks of the Trotsky-Zinoview traitors, and to liquidate the influence of their treason in military work."

12. Edict of the Presidium of the Supreme Soviet of the USSR, August 12, 1940, *Vedomosti Verkhovnogo Soveta SSSR* (Journal of the Supreme Soviet of the USSR, 1940; hereafter cited as *Vedomosti*), no. 28, translated in Berman and Kerner, *Documents*, no. 7.

13. Edict of the Presidium of the Supreme Soviet of the USSR, July 16, 1941, *Vedomosti*, 1941, no. 33, translated in Berman and Kerner, *Documents*, no. 8.

14. Edict of the Presidium of the Supreme Soviet of the USSR, 1942, *Vedomosti*, 1942, no. 38, translated in Berman and Kerner, *Documents*, no. 9.

15. See Charter of the Communist Party of the Soviet Union, arts. 64–66, translated in Berman and Kerner, *Documents*, no. 10.

16. See Major General D. I. Ortenberg, *Partiino-politicheskii apparat vooruzhennykh sil Soiuza SSR* (The Political Organization of the Party in the Armed Forces of the USSR; Moscow, 1948).

17. "The regimental zampolit is usually a lieutenant colonel while the regimental Party bureau secretary is usually a major; the battalion zampolit is usually a major while the corresponding Party official is a captain." (Zbigniew Brzezinski, ed., *Political Controls in the Soviet Army* (New York, 1954), p. 15, n. 8.)

18. "The regimental Party organization is directed by a Party bureau (known as the Partburo), headed by a secretary who is elected by the regimental Party membership. The Partburo secretary is normally selected for his post by the divisional zampolit and proposed to the membership by the regimental zampolit." (*Ibid.*, p. 16.)

19. Ortenberg, p. 7.

20. *Ibid.*, p. 17. Ortenberg omits adding "company" to "regiment" and "battalion," since he was writing before the institution of the company zampolit in 1950 and after the elimination of the company politruk in 1943.

21. *Ibid.*, pp. 20, 22, 26. The Komsomols, or Young Communists, are not Party members, strictly speaking. Their organization parallels that of the Communist Party. Persons between the ages of fourteen and twenty-six are eligible to become Komsomols; membership in the Communist Party cannot begin before the age of twenty-four. While there are about seven million members of the Communist Party in the Soviet Union, there are some eighteen million Komsomols. Ortenberg states (p. 27) that in many battalions, companies, and platoons the Komsomols represent a majority of the personnel.

22. *Ibid.*, pp. 7 ff. A detailed study of the actual operations of Party organs in military administration is beyond the scope of the present work. Three monographs by former Soviet army officers contain valuable information on the subject. See Zbigniew Brzezinski, ed., *Political Controls in the Soviet Army* (New York, 1954); *Political Indoctrination in the Soviet Postwar Army*, Re-

search Program on the USSR Mimeographed Series no. 30 (New York, 1953; in Russian) [author's name not given]; I. Dmitriev, *Party and Political Organs in the Soviet Army*, Research Program on the USSR Mimeographed Series no. 36 (New York, 1953; in Russian).

23. Ortenberg, p. 14.

24. P. Kursov, "Trebovatel'nost' Ofitsera" (The Demand of an Officer), *Krasnaia Zvezda* (Red Star), September 4, 1953, p. 2.

25. Law of the Supreme Soviet of the USSR on the Organization of the Committee on State Security, April 26, 1954, confirming the Edict of the Presidium of the Supreme Soviet of the USSR on the Organization of the Committee on State Security of the Council of Ministers of the USSR, March 13, 1954, *Vedomosti*, May 12, 1954, no. 10. The edict of the Presidium has not been officially published, so far as a study of the issues of *Vedomosti*, *Pravda*, or *Izvestia* reveal.

26. The Ministry of State Security (MGB) was at first the Chief Administration of State Security of the MVD. It was a People's Commissariat briefly in 1941 and again from 1943 to March 1953 (renamed Ministry in 1946).

27. Brzezinski, p. 55.

28. *Ibid.*, p. 56.

29. *Ibid.*, p. 58.

30. *Ibid.*, p. 68.

31. Fainsod, p. 413.

32. Cited in Fainsod, p. 414.

33. Statute on the People's Commissariat of Defense, November 22, 1934, *Coll. Laws USSR*, 1934, no. 58, art. 430b, translated in Berman and Kerner, *Documents*, no. 2.

34. Studenikin, Vlasov, and Evtikhiev, p. 239. In 1950 the ministry was called the Ministry of War. A brief account of the organizational changes of the ministry is provided in Appendices II, III, and IV.

35. Statute on the People's Commissariat for Military and Naval Affairs of the USSR, November 12, 1923, *Vestnik rabochego i krest'ianskogo Pravitel'stva Soiuza SSR* (Journal of the Worker and Peasant Government of the USSR), 1923, no. 10, art. 301; Statute on the People's Commissariat for Military and Naval Affairs of the USSR, January 30, 1929, *Coll. Laws USSR*, 1929, no. 13, art. 105.

36. Statute on the Military Council of the People's Commissar of Defense of the USSR, November 22, 1934, *Coll. Laws USSR*, 1934, no. 58, art. 431, translated in Berman and Kerner, *Documents*, no. 3.

37. V. A. Vlasov, *Sovetskii Gosudarstvennyi Apparat* (The Soviet State Apparatus; Moscow, 1951), p. 344. The decree was apparently not published. Another source states that two Chief Military Councils were established in 1938 — one for the army and one for the navy — with Stalin in the former, and Zhdanov in the latter (*Bol'shaia Sovetskaia Entsiklopediia* (Great Soviet Encyclopedia; Moscow, 1951), VIII, 486).

38. See in particular Lieutenant Colonel Hittle, "Soviet Command and Staff Methods," *Combat Forces Journal*, July 1951, pp. 36–40; and *The Soviet Military Organization*, 1951 (a compilation of articles from *Army Information Digest*), published by Book Department, Armed Forces Information School, Fort Slocum, N.Y.

39. Statute on the Military Council of the District (Fleet, Army) of the

Worker-Peasant Red Army, May 16, 1937, *Coll. Laws USSR*, 1937, no. 31, art. 127, translated in Berman and Kerner, *Documents*, no. 4.

The words "military council" are a translation of *voennyi sovet*. Frequently the translation is rendered as "military soviet." The word "soviet," or council, is applied to many different kinds of Soviet governing organs, including the Supreme Soviet of the USSR, which is a kind of parliament; the Council of Ministers, which is a kind of cabinet; the city or village councils, which combine legislative, executive, and administrative functions; and military councils, whose functions are described below. The authors have retained the word "soviet" only for the Supreme Soviet and for the Soviet Union.

40. Edict of the Presidium of the Supreme Soviet on Martial Law, June 22, 1941, art. 2, *Vedomosti*, 1941, no. 29, translated in Berman and Kerner, *Documents*, no. 45.

41. Statute on the People's Commissariat of Defense, 1934, art. 9, translated in Berman and Kerner, *Documents*, no. 2. *Cf.* Decree on the Reorganization of the Local Organs of the People's Commissariat of Military and Naval Affairs, *Coll. Laws USSR*, 1925, no. 2, art. 18. On the subordination of the local organs of military administration (so-called local military commissariats) to the military council of the district, which was instituted after the 1934 statute, see Vlasov, *Sovetskii Gosudarstvennyi Apparat* (The Soviet State Apparatus; Moscow, 1951), p. 344.

Since the local military commissariats are not subordinate to the local governing bodies, they are exempt from the usual dual subordination of Soviet administrative bodies both to their administrative superiors and to the local governing organs. See Denisov, p. 14.

42. *Sobranie Uzakonenii i Rasporiazhenii Rabochego i Krest'ianskogo Pravitel'stva* (Collection of Laws and Regulations of the Worker and Peasant Government; hereafter cited as *Coll. Laws RSFSR*), 1917–18, no. 41, art. 518; no. 43, art. 528. *Ibid.*, 1922, no. 61, art. 786. *Coll. Laws USSR*, 1925, no. 62, art. 463. *Ibid.*, 1928, no. 51, art. 449. *Ibid.*, 1930, no. 40, art. 424. *Vedomosti*, 1939, no. 32.

43. *Coll. Laws USSR*, 1943, no. 12, art. 217. This law also exempted students in their last two years or last year of higher institutes or technical schools.

44. Decree of September 18, 1941, translated in Berman and Kerner, *Documents*, no. 12.

45. *Voennoe Obuchenie* (Military Training) [Journal of the Chief Administration of Universal Military Training], January 3 and 17, 1947.

46. *Ibid.*, February 14, 1947. A somewhat fuller translation is given in the United States President's Advisory Commission on Universal Training, *Report*, 1947, pp. 347–348.

46. The following description is taken from *ibid.*, pp. 348–349.

47. "Joint Decision of the Soviet Government and the Central Committee of the Communist Party concerning measures to be taken for reconstruction in the liberated regions," title X, *Krasnaia Zvezda* (Red Star), August 22, 1943, no. 198 (5569), p. 4; *ibid.*, December 1, 1943, no. 283 (5654), p. 1.

48. The following description is based in part on the United States President's Advisory Commission on Universal Training, *Report*, 1947, pp. 349–354, and in part on data furnished in *Za Oboronu* (For Defense), the former journal of the civil defense organization.

49. *Cf.* Evtikhiev and Vlasov, p. 161.

II. SOVIET MILITARY DISCIPLINE

1. The first Soviet disciplinary code was issued on January 30, 1919; the second on July 10, 1925; the third on October 12, 1940; and the fourth on June 1, 1946. The 1946 code was reissued in 1948 and in 1950. The disciplinary codes are hereafter cited as D.C. 1919, D.C. 1925, etc. The 1946 Disciplinary Code is translated in Berman and Kerner, *Documents*, no. 23.

2. The 1919 code contained seven chapters, besides the introduction, with a total of seventy-six articles. The 1925 code had seven chapters, with sixty-seven articles. The 1940 code had twelve chapters, with eighty-two articles. The 1946 code has sixteen chapters, with 144 articles, plus a large appendix containing regulations on arrest of servicemen.

3. Decrees of December 2, 1917, *Coll. Laws RSFSR*, 1917–18, no. 5, art. 80; December 29 (16), 1917, *ibid.*, no. 9, art. 138.

4. January 28 (15), 1918, *ibid.*, no. 17, art. 245. The term of enlistment was six months.

5. *Coll. Laws RSFSR*, 1917–18, no. 33, art. 446, translated in Berman and Kerner, *Documents*, no. 13.

6. *Coll. Laws RSFSR*, 1917–18, no. 41, art. 518.

7. The government enacted five decrees on desertion from 1918 to 1920. The first was on April 22, 1918, *Coll. Laws RSFSR*, 1917–18, no. 33, art. 443. The others were on December 25, 1918, *ibid.*, no. 99, art. 1015; March 3, 1919, *Coll. Laws RSFSR*, 1919, no. 9, art. 94; June 3, 1919, *ibid.*, no. 25, art. 287; April 8, 1920, *Coll. Laws RSFSR*, 1920, no. 26, art. 126.

8. The Bolsheviks had gained a considerable part of their original political strength in the representative military councils (soviets). See George Vernadsky, *A History of Russia* (rev. ed.; 1951), p. 254.

9. D.C. 1919, art. 3.

10. D.C. 1925, introduction, art. 4.

11. *Vedomosti*, 1939, no. 1, translated in Berman and Kerner, *Documents*, no. 14.

12. See Edict on the Procedure for Taking the Military Oath, *Vedomosti*, 1939, no. 1, translated in Berman and Kerner, *Documents*, no. 15.

13. D.C. 1940, art. 2.

14. D.C. 1946, art. 2.

15. The 1946 Disciplinary Code reverts to the style of the Imperial Code in dealing separately with the imposition of penalties upon officers. Further, after tinkering in previous codes with the definition of military discipline, changing its wording in every edition, the Soviets in the last disciplinary code have come back to the first sentence of art. 1 of the Imperial Code: "Military discipline consists in the strict and exact observance of regulations laid down by military laws." *Cf.* D.C. 1946, art. 1. Only a few articles of the Imperial Code were taken over by the Disciplinary Code of 1919 (*e.g.*, arts. 22 and 24), but their number gradually increased with the return to the prerevolutionary traditions. Quite a number of articles in the last code are almost identical with the Imperial Code (*e.g.*, D.C. 1946, art. 20, corresponds to D.C. 1869, art. 12; 19 to 10; 58 to 51; 59 to 52; 60 to 60; 62 to 59; 63 to 59; 66 to 58; 70 to 72).

16. Regulation of Service of Higher, Senior, and Middle Commanding Personnel of the Red Army, Order of the Military Council of the USSR, no. 225,

of 1928. This order codified the various earlier regulations. (Gsovski, *Soviet Civil Law* (Ann Arbor, 1948), I, 142–143.)

17. D.C. 1919, art. 10.
18. D.C. 1919, art. 15.
19. D.C. 1919, introduction, art. 6.
20. D.C. 1919, art. 44.
21. D.C. 1919, arts. 49–74.
22. Law of September 22, 1935, *Coll. Laws USSR*, 1935, no. 57, arts. 468, 469.
23. Edict on the Establishment of Military Ranks of Higher Commanding Personnel of the Red Army, *Vedomosti*, 1940, no. 5, translated in Berman and Kerner, *Documents*, no. 16. By an edict of 1942 guard ranks had been established for the newly restored elite guard units, *Vedomosti*, 1942, no. 20, translated in Berman and Kerner, *Documents*, no. 17.
24. Order of the People's Commissar of Defense, "On Military Saluting — Law for Military Personnel," *Krasnaia Zvezda* (Red Star), June 23, 1940.
25. Edict on the Procedure for Conferring Military Ranks on Servicemen of the Red Army, and Edict on the Division of Servicemen of the Navy into Rank and File, Petty Officers, and Officers, *Vedomosti*, 1943, nos. 28, 29, translated in Berman and Kerner, *Documents*, nos. 19 and 20.
26. January 6, 1943, for the army, *Vedomosti*, 1943, no. 2; February 15, for the navy, *ibid.*, no. 7. The former edict is translated in Berman and Kerner, *Documents*, no. 22. Gsovski states: "In the first days of revolution, epaulets became much more than a matter of uniform; they were commonly regarded as symbols of the old regime. During the civil war 1918–1920 the wearing of epaulets was a distinct mark of antibolshevik armies, nicknamed 'gold braid epauleters.' The volume of the *Soviet Encyclopedia* published in 1930 states that epaulets 'were abolished by the November 1918 Revolution as symbols of class oppression in the army.' In 1943 they were introduced again as 'emblems of military honor of the soldiers and officers of the Red Army' and 'supreme honorary distinctive marks of a warrior.' Moreover, ranks, uniforms, and epaulets were introduced for several categories of civil servants: for diplomats, public prosecutors, and railroad employees." (Gsovski, I, 143–144.)
27. See, *e.g.*, I. I. Evtikhiev and V. A. Vlasov, *Administrativnoe Pravo SSSR* (Administrative Law of the USSR; Moscow, 1946), p. 160, citing the 1946 Code of Internal Service; *cf.* S. S. Studenikin, V. A. Vlasov, and I. I. Evtikhiev, *Sovetskoe Administrativnoe Pravo* (Soviet Administrative Law; Moscow, 1950), p. 242.
28. D.C. 1946, arts. 3, 58. The obligation to salute was not specifically mentioned in the prerevolutionary 1869 code, but it was considered to be an essential part of the respect of servicemen (D.C. 1869, art. 3). It was always insisted on. However, a specific written legal requirement of the salute, as in the 1946 Soviet Code, is unusual and probably reflects a need for special emphasis of the duty after almost thirty years of desuetude.
29. D.C. 1940, arts. 26–29. These articles list the disciplinary powers of regimental, division, corps, and army commanders, respectively. Included among the powers of each is the right to bring charges against certain subordinate grades before the Officers' Court of Honor.
30. D.C. 1946, chap. 16, arts. 114–144.
31. D.C. 1946, art. 114. The Imperial Officers' Courts of Honor were likewise "to protect the dignity of the military service and to maintain respect for the officers' rank" (D.C. 1869, art. 130). Proceedings in the prerevolutionary Courts

of Honor were always *in camera*; now they are supposed to be public. Also the unwritten duty of an officer in prerevolutionary Russia to defend his honor by challenging his opponent to a duel seems to have disappeared, although it was rumored a few years ago that two famous Soviet generals were only dissuaded from a duel by the personal intervention of Stalin.

32. D.C. 1940, art. 14, lists "bringing charges against the delinquent before the Redarmymen Comrades' Court" as one of the disciplinary penalties which could be imposed upon privates.

33. Colonel Louis B. Ely, writing in 1949, compared the scale of pay in the Soviet and United States armies in terms of the factor of increase over the pay of privates. The Soviet equivalent of sergeant receives 4.3 times as much basic pay as the Soviet private; a captain 24.3 times as much; a general of the army 114.3 times as much. The corresponding United States figures are 1.8, 3.8, 15.2. (Ely, *The Red Army Today* (1949), p. 223.)

34. *Cf.* D.C. 1946, art. 17. *Cf.* Edict of the Presidium of the Supreme Soviet, July 24, 1943, *Vedomosti*, no. 28, translated in Berman and Kerner, *Documents*, no. 21.

35. See *supra* pp. 40–41.

36. D.C. 1919, arts. 4, 20, 22.

37. D.C. 1925, art. 5.

38. Prerevolutionary Russian military law permitted disobedience of orders in exceptional cases specially provided for by law (D.C. 1869, art. 2). The Code of Internal Service (1910 ed., art. 6) required subordinates "to obey their commander without reservation and to execute all their orders with the exception of criminal ones" (art. 6, par. 2).

Soviet military law has retained the traditional Russian distinction between "combat commanders" (*komandiry*) who are line officers in charge of combat units, and "service commanders" (*nachal'niki*) who are in charge of services; where both terms are used together, as in the provisions here under discussion, we have used the one word "commander" to embrace both.

39. Article 8 of the 1940 code appears as art. 6 of the 1946 code.

40. D.C. 1940, art. 8, par. 2.

41. D.C. 1946, arts. 18, 19.

42. D.C. 1940, art. 6, par. 2.

43. *Ibid.*, art. 7.

44. D.C. 1946, art. 7, par. 1.

45. D.C. 1940, art. 7.

46. D.C. 1946, art. 7, par. 2.

47. D.C. 1919, art. 48.

48. D.C. 1925, art. 32; D.C. 1940, art. 42.

49. D.C. 1946, art. 65.

50. D.C. 1919, art. 4.

51. D.C. 1925, art. 3.

52. D.C. 1940, art. 3.

53. *Ibid.*, arts. 4, 5.

54. D.C. 1946, art. 3.

55. *Ibid.*, art. 5.

56. *Ibid.*, art. 105.

57. *Ibid.*, art. 107.

58. *Ibid.*, art. 108.

59. *Ibid.*, art. 109. The terms "responsible" and "strictly responsible" do not seem to have a precise meaning.

60. D.C. 1940, art. 12.

61. D.C. 1940, art. 13; D.C. 1946, art. 18.

62. D.C. 1946, art. 19. The criminal code states that certain acts otherwise criminal are to be considered as disciplinary offenses if committed under extenuating circumstances. RSFSR Criminal Code, art. 193(2), par. b; 193(5), pars. b, c; 193(6), par. b; 193(7), pars. a, f; 193(14), par. b; 193(15), par. b; 193(16), par. b; 193(17), par. c; 193(18), par. b; 193(25), par. d; 193(29), par. b. The decision of a superior does not affect the duty of the investigating organs under the military criminal law. *Cf.* D.C. 1946, art. 20.

63. D.C. 1940, art. 9.

64. D.C. 1919, art. 44, stated: "Commissars and commanders have the right to impose the following disciplinary penalties: (a) reminder, warning, and reprimand, (b) personal reprimand in front of troops and in the order of the day, (c) extra detail up to ten days, (d) confinement to quarters for a period not longer than two weeks or detention in barracks for such period, (e) demotion to a lower command, in cases of platoon commanders and upon consent of the commissar, and (f) any other measures of a repressive character required by the circumstances and the situation and not contrary to the spirit and character of the Red Army."

65. D.C. 1925, art. 10.

66. D.C. 1940, art. 14.

67. D.C. 1946, arts. 23, 24, 25, 35, 39; D.C. 1869, arts. 13–20, 33–36.

68. D.C. 1946, art. 23. Seamen first class are included with corporals.

69. *Ibid.*, art. 24. Petty officers are included in these ranks.

70. *Ibid.*, art. 25.

71. *Ibid.*, art. 35.

72. *Ibid.*, art. 39.

73. D.C. 1925, art. 10 (a), par. 10.

74. D.C. 1946, art. 21.

75. D.C. 1925, art. 11.

76. D.C. 1940, arts. 51–65.

77. D.C. 1946, art. 73.

78. D.C. 1946, art. 67. *Cf.* D.C. 1940, art. 45.

79. D.C. 1946, art. 69. *Cf.* D.C. 1940, art. 47.

80. D.C. 1946, art. 60. *Cf.* D.C. 1940, art. 41.

81. D.C. 1946, art. 65. *Cf.* D.C. 1940, art. 42.

82. D.C. 1946, arts. 65, 102. But *cf.* D.C. 1940, arts. 9, 44 ("or if the imposition of the penalty is obviously wrong").

83. D.C. 1946, art. 66. *Cf.* D.C. 1940, art. 44.

84. D.C. 1946, art. 66, par. 2. *Cf.* D.C. 1940, art. 44, par. 3.

85. D.C. 1940, art. 78.

86. D.C. 1946, art. 79. *Cf.* D.C. 1940, art. 79.

87. D.C. 1946, art. 96. *Cf.* D.C. 1940, art. 74.

88. D.C. 1946, art. 97. *Cf.* D.C. 1940, art. 76.

89. D.C. 1946, art. 98. *Cf.* D.C. 1940, art. 76.

90. D.C. 1946, art. 101. *Cf.* D.C. 1940, art. 75.

91. D.C. 1946, art. 101. *Cf.* D.C. 1940, art. 77.

92. D.C. 1946, art. 108. *Cf.* D.C. 1940, art. 81.

93. D.C. 1946, art. 110. D.C. 1940, art. 82 established a much less complicated procedure.
94. D.C. 1940, art. 40.
95. D.C. 1946, art. 61.
96. D.C. 1946, arts. 26–34, 41–59. *Cf.* D.C. 1940, arts. 16–23.
97. D.C. 1946, arts. 114–144.
98. However, the 1940 Code of Internal Service (*Ustav Vnutrennyi Sluzhby*), which supplements the Disciplinary Code with detailed regulations concerning such matters as saluting, care of quarters, daily routine, interior guard duty, camping duties, hygiene, fire prevention, and other matters, states in art. 147 that the political director has the same right as the company commander to grant a pass to leave barracks after daily routine or after taps. A later edition of the Code of Internal Service, issued on July 24, 1946, was not available to the authors.
99. Brzezinski, pp. 59, 75.
100. *Ibid.*, p. 76.
101. Case of K., translated in Berman and Kerner, *Documents*, no. 33.

III. SOVIET MILITARY CRIMES AND PUNISHMENTS

1. The changes in Soviet military criminal law since 1917 have not found dramatic expression in a succession of new codes, such as the four Disciplinary Codes discussed in the previous chapter.

During the period of War Communism sporadic decrees were enacted dealing with military criminal law, such as the decree on the term of military service (*Coll. Laws RSFSR*, 1917–18, no. 33, arts. 443, 445), the decrees on desertion (*ibid.*, no. 99, art. 1015; *Coll. Laws RSFSR*, 1919, no. 9, art. 94, no. 25, art. 287; 1920, no. 26, art. 126) and the decree on revolutionary military tribunals (*Coll. Laws RSFSR*, 1919, no. 13, art. 131). The latter decree contained a detailed enumeration of crimes committed by servicemen. The first codification of military criminal law, however, was enacted in 1922 as Chapter 7 of the Criminal Code of the RSFSR (*Coll. Laws RSFSR*, 1922, no. 15, art. 153). Corresponding chapters were incorporated in the criminal codes of the other constituent republics. In 1924 a Statute on Military Crimes was enacted as the first all-union criminal law, required to be incorporated without change in the criminal codes of all the constituent republics (*Coll. Laws USSR*, 1924, no. 24, art. 207). This statute was revised in 1927 (*Coll. Laws USSR*, 1927, no. 50, art. 505) and has been amended in 1929, 1930, 1932, 1934, 1935, and 1940 (*Coll. Laws USSR*, 1929, no. 19, art. 265; 1930, no. 15, art. 159; 1932, no. 20, art. 117, no. 44, art. 259; 1934, no. 43, art. 335; 1935, no. 43, art. 359a; 1940, no. 18, art. 441).

In 1934 a statute on crimes against the state (some of which are under the jurisdiction of military courts) was substituted for the article on military treason (*Coll. Laws USSR*, 1934, no. 33, art. 255). The new statute provided the legal basis for the famous purge trials of subsequent years. It was introduced into the RSFSR Criminal Code as arts. 58 and 59, translated in *Documents*, nos. 25, 28.

2. Art. 193, sections 1 to 31, form Chapter IX of the RSFSR Criminal Code, translated in *Documents*, no. 24. Corresponding chapters in the criminal codes of other constituent republics are Ukrainian SSR, Chapter IX; Belorussian SSR, Chapter IX; Uzbek SSR, Chapter II; Armenian SSR, Chapter X; Turkmen SSR, Chapter IX; Tadzhik SSR, Chapter XII, Georgian SSR, Appendix.

The 1936 Constitution called for all-union criminal and civil codes (Constitution of the USSR, art. 14(u)). Although many attempts to draft such codes have been made since 1936, none have been adopted. There is apparently a widespread feeling that many parts of the existing republican criminal codes, including the military article, do not correspond to the present situation of Soviet society. In general, see Hazard, "Drafting New Soviet Codes," *American Slavic and East European Review*, VII: 32 (1948). The Supreme Soviet in 1951 intrusted a special committee with the preparation of a report on a new all-union criminal code. Agitation for the new code was renewed in 1953 after Stalin's death.

3. Decree of the Plenum of the Supreme Court of the USSR of December 31, 1938, in I. T. Goliakov, ed., *Sbornik Deistvuiushchikh Postanovlenii Plenuma i Direktivnykh Pisem Verkhovnogo Suda SSSR 1924–1944 g.g.* (Collection of Prevailing Decrees of the Plenum and Directive Letters of the Supreme Court of the USSR, 1924–1944; Moscow, 1946), no. 1. The decree states:

"Considering that in judicial practice there have occurred instances of incorrect application of arts. 58 (7), 58 (9), and 58 (14) of the Criminal Code of the RSFSR [translated in Berman and Kerner, *Documents*, no. 25] and of corresponding articles of the criminal codes of other constituent republics, the Plenum of the Supreme Court of the USSR instructs that according to the sense of these articles they may be applied only in those instances when the circumstances of the case establish that the accused acted with a counterrevolutionary purpose.

"In connection with what is here instructed, all explanations and decrees of judicial organs contradicting the present instruction shall be considered to have lost their validity, and in particular the explanation of the eighteenth Plenum of the Supreme Court of the USSR of January 2, 1928, 'On direct and indirect intent in counterrevolutionary crimes.'"

4. V. D. Men'shagin and Z. A. Vyshinskaia, *Sovetskoe Ugolovnoe Pravo* (Soviet Criminal Law; Moscow, 1950), p. 494. On the nature of criminal intent in Soviet law generally, see H. J. Berman, "Principles of Soviet Criminal Law," *Yale Law Journal*, LVI, 803, 818 ff (1946).

5. Chkhikvadze, p. 156.

6. *Ibid.*, p. 281

7. *Ibid.*, p. 281.

8. "If a socially dangerous act is not directly provided for by the present code, the foundations and limits of liability for it shall be determined according to those articles of the code which provide for those crimes most similar to it in kind." (RSFSR Criminal Code, 1952 ed., art. 16.)

9. A. N. Trainin, "Sistema obshchei chasti ugolovnogo prava" (System of the General Part of the Criminal Law), *Sovetskoe Gosudarstvo i Pravo* (Soviet State and Law), 1946, nos. 5–6, p. 8; V. M. Chkhikvadze, "Voprosy sovetskogo ugolovnogo prava v sviazi s proektom ugolovnogo kodeksa SSR" (Questions of Soviet Criminal Law in Connection with the Draft of the Criminal Code of the USSR), *Sovetskoe Gosudarstvo i Pravo* (Soviet State and Law), 1954, no. 4, pp. 59, 62. On the doctrine of analogy in Soviet criminal law see H. J. Berman, *Justice in Russia* (1950), pp. 27, 47; H. J. Berman, "Principles of Soviet Criminal Law," *Yale Law Journal*, vol. 56, pp. 803, 808 (1946).

10. See *ibid.*, p. 812, n. 44; Chkhikvadze, *op. cit.*

11. V. M. Chkhikvadze, *Sovetskoe Voenno-ugolovnoe Pravo* (Soviet Military Criminal Law; Moscow, 1948), p. 152.

12. Decree of the Plenum of the Supreme Court of the USSR, April 6, 1945, *Sudebnaia Praktika Verkhovnogo Suda SSR (Judicial Practice of the Supreme Court of the USSR*; 1945; hereafter cited as *Sudebnaia Praktika*), III (XIX), 3.

13. Chkhikvadze, p. 209.
14. *Ibid.*, p. 210.
15. *Ibid.*, p. 219.
16. *Ibid.*, pp. 213–214.
17. RSFSR Criminal Code, 1952 ed., art. 58(1)(a), translated in Berman and Kerner, *Documents*, no. 25.
18. Constitution of the USSR, art. 133, translated in Berman and Kerner, *Documents*, no. 1.
19. These crimes are defined in art. 193(20a), (21a), (22), and (24), but are also punishable under art. 58(1)(a), (b), and (c) of the RSFSR Criminal Code. See Chkhikvadze, pp. 276–292.
20. RSFSR Criminal Code, 1952 ed., art. 58(1)(c), par. 1.
21. *Ibid.*, art. 58(1)(c), par. 2.
22. Chkhikvadze, p. 309.
23. *Ibid.*, p. 306.
24. *Ibid.*, p. 317.
25. *Ibid.*, p. 319.
26. *Ibid.*, p. 318.
27. *Ibid.*, p. 325.
28. *Ibid.*, p. 328.
29. Translated in Berman and Kerner, *Documents*, no. 11.
30. Chkhikvadze, p. 330.
31. *Ibid.*, p. 336.
32. *Ibid.*, p. 343.
33. *Ibid.*, p. 360.
34. *Ibid.*, p. 361.
35. See Berman and Kerner, *Documents*, no. 14.
36. *Coll. Laws USSR*, 1932, no. 62, art. 360; *Vedomosti*, 1947, no. 19.
37. Chkhikvadze, p. 395.
38. *Ibid.*, p. 398.
39. *Ibid.*, p. 406.
40. This provision antedates the introduction of personal orderlies for higher officers.
41. *Vedomosti*, 1947, no. 20, translated in Berman and Kerner, *Documents*, no. 26.
42. *Ibid.*, translated in Berman and Kerner, *Documents*, no. 27.
43. Chkhikvadze, p. 422.
44. *Ibid.*, p. 424.
45. *Ibid.*
46. *Ibid.*, p. 427.
47. *Ibid.*, p. 447.
48. See H. J. Berman, "Principles of Soviet Criminal Law," *Yale Law Journal*, LVI: 803, 822 (1946).
49. Vsesoiuznyi Institut Iuridicheskikh Nauk (All-Union Institute of Juridical Science), *Ugolovnoe Pravo — Obshchaia Chast'* (Criminal Law, General Part; Moscow, 1943), p. 218.
50. Chkhikvadze, p. 225.

51. RSFSR Criminal Code, 1952 ed., art. 47.
52. Chkhikvadze, p. 247.
53. RSFSR Criminal Code, 1952 ed., art. 48.
54. Chkhikvadze, p. 249.
55. *Ibid.*
56. *Cf.* art. 193(2), (5), (7), (11), (14), (15), (16), (17), (18), (25), (29).
57. RSFSR Criminal Code, 1952 ed., art. 30.
58. *Vedomosti*, 1947, no. 17.
59. *Vedomosti*, 1950, no. 3.
60. RSFSR Criminal Code, 1952 ed., art. 58(1)(b).
61. *Ibid.*, art. 193(2)(d), (e).
62. *Ibid.*, art. 193(3)(c).
63. *Ibid.*, art. 193(4)(c).
64. *Ibid.*, art. 193(7)(d).
65. *Ibid.*, art. 193(7)(e), (8)(b).
66. *Ibid.*, art. 193(9)(a).
67. *Ibid.*, art. 193(10)(a), (b).
68. *Ibid.*, art. 193(10a).
69. *Ibid.*, art. 193(12)(c).
70. *Ibid.*, art. 193(13).
71. *Ibid.*, art. 193(14)(e).
72. *Ibid.*, art. 193(15)(e).
73. *Ibid.*, art. 193(17)(b).
74. *Ibid.*, art. 193(27)(b).
75. *Ibid.*, art. 193(28).
76. *Ibid.*, art. 193(3)(c).
77. *Ibid.*, art. 193(4)(c).
78. *Ibid.*, art. 193(17)(b).
79. *Ibid.*, art. 193(25)(b).
80 This edict was not published in the official journal of the Presidium. A statement of its provisions is found in I. T. Goliakov, ed., *Ugolovnoe Pravo, Osobennaia Chast* (Criminal Law, Special Part; Moscow, 1944), p. 44.
81. RSFSR Criminal Code, 1952 ed., art. 28, translated in Berman and Kerner, *Documents*, no. 34.
82. *Ibid.*, art. 28, n. 2.
83. Chkhikvadze, p. 253.
84. RSFSR Criminal Code, 1952 ed., arts. 31, 37.
85. *Ibid.*, art. 32.
86. See Berman, *supra* note 48, at p. 824.
87. RSFSR Criminal Code, 1952 ed., art. 32; Men'shagin and Vyshinskaia, p. 173.
88. RSFSR Criminal Code, 1952 ed., art. 33; Law on Universal Military Obligation, art. 30; translated in Berman and Kerner, *Documents*, no. 11.
89. Decree of the Plenum of the Supreme Court of the USSR of January 7, 1943, in I. T. Goliakov, ed., *Sbornik Deistvuiushchikh Postanovlenii Plenuma i Direktivnykh Pisem Verkhovnogo Suda SSSR 1924–1944 g.g.* (Collection of Prevailing Decrees of the Plenum and of Directive Letters of the Supreme Court of the USSR 1924–1944; Moscow, 1946), no. 146.
90. *Cf.* RSFSR Criminal Code, 1952 ed., art. 31(f).
91. *Ibid.*
92. *Ibid.*, art. 40.

93. RSFSR Code of Criminal Procedure, 1953 ed., annotation to art. 389, p. 104.

94. *Ibid.*

95. This fact is known to one of the authors, Mr. Kerner, through his service with the Czechoslovak army in the Soviet Union in 1943 and 1944. The Czechoslovak military courts applied the official Soviet tables of appraisal.

96. Chkhikvadze, p. 236.

97. This law was not published in the official publications of the Presidium of the Supreme Soviet or the Council of Ministers. It is referred to in various Soviet writings.

98. Chkhikvadze, p. 238.

99. A former Soviet military procurator writes: "The number of people in a penal battalion was not constant. It always fluctuated and at times reached absolute zero. For example, in the autumn of 1943 the penal battalion of the Fiftieth Soviet Army moving in the direction of Mogilev on the Belorussian front, achieved the dimensions of a brigade. During November and December the unsuccessful attacks of Soviet troops against the sector of the Twelfth Army Corps of the Fourth German Army cost the penal battalion of the Fiftieth Army very heavy losses. Its numbers, which at the beginning of this offensive reached 5000 persons, were reduced, despite continual replacements, toward Jaunary 1944, as a result of the losses incurred, to 300 men." (N. Semenov, *Sovetskii Sud i Karatel'naia Politika* (The Soviet Court and Penal Policy; Munich, 1952), p. 128.)

100. *Ibid.*, pp. 127–128.

101. Petr Uranov, "Ni shagu nazad" (Not a Step Backwards), *Novoe Russkoe Slovo* (The New Russian Word), New York, November 19, 1951.

102. RSFSR Criminal Code, 1952 ed., art. 53; Men'shagin and Vyshinskaia, p. 196.

103. RSFSR Criminal Code, 1952 ed., art. 28, note 2.

104. The 1945 and 1953 edicts on amnesty are translated in Berman and Kerner, *Documents*, nos. 40, 41. There had been two previous amnesties in 1938, one in 1940, and one in 1944 (*Vedomosti*, 1938, nos. 1 and 6; 1940, no. 25; 1945, no. 1). All four were far more limited in scope. The amnesty of January 24, 1938, in celebration of the twentieth anniversary of the Red Army, was applicable to servicemen sentenced to deprivation of freedom for three years or less, unless for state crimes, and to servicemen who had received suspended sentences. The amnesty of April 10, 1938, was applicable principally to ex-prisoners who had voluntarily remained to work on the construction of the Moscow-Volga canal. The amnesty of July 16, 1940, was applicable to all citizens sentenced to fines ("corrective-labor tasks") and lighter penalties who had fought in combat against the Finns. The amnesty of December 30, 1944, was applicable to persons who had left their jobs in war industries without authorization, in violation of the Edict of December 26, 1941, but who had returned voluntarily or who would return prior to February 15, 1945.

From 1918 to 1927 there were eleven amnesties; from 1928 to 1932 there were none (*Malaia sovetskaia entsiklopediia* (Small Soviet Encyclopedia; 1933), pp. 326–327). From 1933 to 1936 there were amnesties in certain localities in celebration of the fifteenth anniversary of their joining the federation of Soviet republics.

IV. SOVIET MILITARY COURTS AND PROCEDURE

1. The structure of the Soviet judiciary is laid down in Chapter IX of the Soviet Constitution, arts. 102–117; see translations in Berman and Kerner, *Documents*, no. 1. On the basis of these provisions the Judiciary Law of the USSR was adopted by the Supreme Soviet of the USSR on August 16, 1938. (*Vedomosti*, 1938, no. 11, translated in part in Berman and Kerner, *Documents*, no. 42.)

2. Judiciary Law of the USSR, arts. 53–62, translated in Berman and Kerner, *Documents*, no. 42. Special Camp Courts, established during the war by an apparently unpublished edict of the Presidium of the Spreme Soviet of the USSR of December 30, 1944, are not mentioned in the subsequent 1947 edition of the Judiciary Law. Golunskii and Karev list them in an enumeration of special courts. (Golunskii and Karev, *Sudoustroistvo SSSR* (The Judicial System of the USSR; Moscow, 1946), p. 117.)

3. The organization and jurisdiction of the Supreme Court of the USSR is outlined in arts. 63–77 of the Judiciary Law of the USSR, translated in Berman and Kerner, *Documents*, no. 42. Article 77 provides that the Plenum shall sit at leat once every two months. The number of judges and of people's assessors varies at different times. (Two people's assessors sit with a single judge in cases in which the Supreme Court has original jurisdiction.) Judges and assessors are chosen by the Supreme Soviet of the USSR for a five-year period. On March 19, 1946, the Supreme Soviet chose sixty-five judges and twenty-five people's assessors (*Vedomosti*, 1946, no. 10). On March 10, 1951, the Supreme Soviet chose seventy-eight judges and thirty-five assessors. Of the seventy-eight judges, fourteen were women, and of the thirty-five assessors eight were women.

4. Golunskii and Karev, p. 136.

5. Edict on the Introduction of Martial Law to All Railroads, *Vedomosti*, 1943, no. 15, translated in Berman and Kerner, *Documents*, no. 47

6. Statute on Military Tribunals and the Military Procuracy, art. 2, translated in Berman and Kerner, *Documents*, no. 51.

7. N. Semenov, *Sovetskii Sud i Karatel'naia Politika* (The Soviet Court and Penal Policy; Munich, 1952), p. 92.

8. Golunskii and Karev, p. 141. *Komendant* is also listed; it might be translated as "provost."

9. Military judges belonged to the category of service command officers, as distinct from combat command officers. The ranks go through the entire military scale. Ulrikh, who was President of the Military Division of the Supreme Court of the USSR for many years prior to his death in May 1951, had the rank of Colonel General. (Ulrikh was not listed among the judges chosen on March 10, 1951.)

10. The institution of people's assessors is used throughout the Soviet judicial system generally. See USSR Constitution, art. 103; Judiciary Law of the USSR, arts. 9–14, 31, 39, 49, 55, 56, 68, 70, 72. See also RSFSR Code of Civil Procedure, art. 24(a).

The 1936 Constitution called for the popular election of people's judges and people's assessors. Such elections were not held, however, until 1949. A former Soviet officer states that "assessors, as a rule, are usually soldiers or officers elected in the regiments at general assemblies." (P. Zorin, *Soviet Military Tri-*

bunals, Research Program on the USSR Mimeographed Series no. 50 (New York, 1954, in Russian), p. 11.)

11. Golunskii and Karev, p. 178.

12. Translated in Berman and Kerner, *Documents,* no. 46.

13. "All cases of crimes committed by servicemen, as well as crimes committed by persons liable to military service during training courses irrespective of the article of the criminal code under which the crime falls, shall be placed in the jurisdiction of military tribunals." (Edict of the Presidium of the Supreme Soviet of the USSR, December 13, 1940, *Vedomosti,* 1940, no. 51.)

14. The edict of the Presidium of the Supreme Soviet of January 27, 1944, "On the Responsibility of Officers and Enlisted Men of the Military Guard of Enterprises and of the Military Fire Guard of the NKVD of the USSR for Service Crimes," which states that the responsibility of the named classes under military law "shall be established for wartime," has retained its validity in peacetime, according to a footnote appended to it in *Spravochnik po Zakonodatel'stvy dlia Sudebno-Prokuratorskikh Rabotnikov* (Handbook of Legislation for the Procuracy; Moscow, 1949), I, 29.

15. *Coll. Laws USSR,* 1930, no. 57, art. 601.

16. *Ibid.,* 1934, no. 36, art. 284.

17. *Sotsialisticheskaia Zakonnost'* (Socialist Legality), 1948, no. 5, p. 55. *Cf.* Case of Chadaeva, translated in Berman and Kerner, *Documents,* no. 31.

18. Decree of the Plenum of the Supreme Court of the USSR of February 18, 1943, *Sbornik Deistvuiushchikh Postanovlenii Plenuma i Direktivnykh Pisem Verkhovnogo Suda SSSR 1924–1944 g.g.* (Collection of Prevailing Decrees of the Plenum and Directive Letters of the Supreme Court of the USSR, 1924–1944; Moscow, 1946; hereafter cited as *Sbornik 1924–1944*), no. 11.

19. *Ibid.* Citizens in units of the people-in-arms (*narodnoe opolchenie*) were declared subject to the Statute on Military Crimes and under the jurisdiction of military tribunals. Decree of the Plenum of the Supreme Court of the USSR of July 28, 1941, *Sbornik 1924–1944,* no. 8.

This decree was modified shortly thereafter as follows: citizens in units of the people-in-arms were declared to be subject to the Statute on Military Crimes and under the jurisdiction of military tribunals if they were enrolled in units of the Red Army; or, under appropriate articles of the Statute of Military Crimes, if upon leaving their work and awaiting enrollment in the Red Army, they violated the laws on military service. Otherwise they were declared to be subject to the general courts. (Decree of the Plenum of the Supreme Court of the USSR of October 11, 1941, *ibid.,* no. 9.)

20. The edict of December 26, 1941, establishing the jurisdiction of military courts over unauthorized quitting of war-industry enterprises, fell into disuse after the war, apparently owing to the narrower interpretation of "war industry." It was mentioned as late as 1948 in textbooks on labor law, but since 1949 has been omitted altogether from such textbooks and from compilations of legislation for procurators. From 1945 on, Soviet writings have emphasized that the law of June 26, 1940, which makes the unauthorized quitting of a job punishable by the civilian courts, is the basic law governing this crime. The edict of December 26, 1941, was published in the 1947 and 1950 editions of the RSFSR Criminal Code, but together with the law of June 26, 1940, and other laws imposing penalties for unauthorized quitting, has been omitted from the 1952 edition.

21. *Coll. Laws USSR*, 1934, no. 12, art. 78, no. 36, art. 284, translated in Berman and Kerner, *Documents*, nos. 28, 44.

22. RSFSR Code of Criminal Procedure, 1953 ed., art. 36. See the Case of S., *Sudebnaia Praktika* (1948), III, 13.

23. The edict on martial law was repealed by two laws. See *Vedomosti*, 1945, no. 71, and *Sbornik Zakonov SSSR i Ukazov Prezidiuma Verkhovnogo Soveta SSSR 1945–1946* (Collection of Laws of the USSR and Edicts of the Presidium of the Supreme Soviet of the USSR, 1945–1946), p. 180, translated in Berman and Kerner, *Documents*, nos. 49, 50.

24. *Coll. Laws USSR*, 1934, no. 12, art. 78.

25. Golunskii and Karev, pp. 138, 143–144.

26. *Ibid.*, pp. 144–145.

27. *Coll. Laws USSR*, 1926, no. 57, art. 413; as amended in 1928, 1929, 1930, 1934, 1935, and 1940. *Ibid.*, 1928, no. 19, art. 161; no. 33, art. 291; no. 34, art. 298. *Ibid.*, 1929, no. 13, art. 106; no. 39, art. 336; no. 50, art. 444; no. 70, art. 655. *Ibid.*, 1930, no. 47, art. 485; no. 49, art. 509. *Ibid.*, 1934, no. 12, art. 78; no. 36, art. 284. *Ibid.*, 1935, no. 43, art. 359a. *Vedomosti*, 1940, no. 51. (Translated in Berman and Kerner, *Documents*, no. 51.)

Article 28 of the statute provides that procedure in all military tribunals shall be governed by the procedure applicable to provincial (*i.e.*, regional) courts under the codes of criminal procedure of the constituent republics. Several of the relevant provisions of the RSFSR Code of Criminal Procedure are translated in Berman and Kerner, *Documents*, no. 52.

28. Translated in Berman and Kerner, *Documents*, no. 45.

29. The Special Board of the MVD has a legislative basis in 1934 and 1935 statutes which provide that it shall be presided over by the People's Commissar of Internal Affairs of the USSR, with the Deputy People's Commissar of Internal Affairs of the USSR, the RSFSR People's Commissar of Internal Affairs, the Chairman of the Chief Administration of the Militia, and the People's Commissar of Internal Affairs of the constituent republic in which the case arose, as members. The statutes further provide that the Procurator General or his deputy shall be present at sessions of the Special Board and that he may protest a decision to the Council of People's Commissars of the USSR. *Coll. Laws USSR*, 1934, no. 36, art. 283; 1935, no. 11, art. 84.

30. RSFSR Code of Criminal Procedure, 1953 ed., arts. 466–473, translated in Berman and Kerner, *Documents*, no. 53.

31. See H. J. Berman, *Justice in Russia* (1950), pp. 199–291, 306–308.

32. *Ibid.*, pp. 210–215.

33. *Ibid.*, pp. 168–173.

34. Statute on Military Tribunals and the Military Procuracy, art. 21, translated in Berman and Kerner, *Documents*, no. 51.

35. RSFSR Code of Criminal Procedure, 1953 ed., arts. 466–470, translated in Berman and Kerner, *Documents*, no. 53.

36. *Ibid.*, arts. 471–473, translated in Berman and Kerner, *Documents*, no. 53.

37. *Cf.* Edict on Military Tribunals in Localities under Martial Law, translated in Berman and Kerner, *Documents*, no. 46.

38. Golunskii and Karev, p. 186.

39. M. A. Chel'tsov, *Sovetskii Ugolovnyi Protsess* (Soviet Criminal Procedure; Moscow, 1951), pp. 412–413.

40. RSFSR Code of Criminal Procedure, 1953 ed., art. 136.

41. *Ibid.*, art. 112.
42. *Ibid.*, art. 111.
43. *Ibid.*, art. 206.
44. *Ibid.*, art. 305.
45. *Ibid.*, art. 212.
46. *Ibid.*, arts. 413, 414.
47. N. Semenov, *Sovetskii Sud i Karatel'naia Politika* (The Soviet Court and Penal Policy; Munich, 1952), pp. 96–97.
48. Chel'tsov, p. 413.
49. RSFSR Code of Criminal Procedure, 1953 ed., arts. 277, 282, 288, 304.
50. *Cf. ibid.*, art. 23(6).
51. Semenov, pp. 98–99.
52. Chel'tsov, pp. 414–415.
53. *Ibid.*, pp. 316–317.
54. Golunskii and Karev, p. 192.
55. RSFSR Code of Criminal Procedure, 1953, ed., art. 55, art. 381, par. 2. The latter provision omits mention of disabled persons but states that "the provincial court shall be obliged to admit or assign a defense counsel if the accuser is admitted to the trial." Trial in military courts is governed by the code provisions regulating trial in provincial — now called regional — courts. See n. 27 above. *Cf.* the Case of Muzykin and the Case of Gvanii, translated in Berman and Kerner, *Documents*, nos. 54, 55.
    The "accuser" (*obvinitel'*) may be a member of the procuracy (the prosecutor) or the injured party. RSFSR Code of Criminal Procedure, 1953 ed., art. 50. (In Soviet law, as in continental European systems generally, the complaining witness may be awarded civil damages in the criminal action; he may thus appear both as "accuser" and as plaintiff.)
56. RSFSR Constitution, art. 115. *Cf.* USSR Constitution, art. 111.
57. D. S. Karev, "Ugolovnyi Protsess — Ugolovnoe Pravo" (Criminal Procedure — Criminal Law) *Sovetskoe Pravo vo Vremeni Velikoi Otechestvennoi Voiny* (Soviet Law in the Time of the Great Fatherland War; Moscow, 1948), Part II, p. 194.
58. *Cf.* Gsovski, I, 876–909.
59. See Semenov, pp. 102–104.
60. USSR Constitution, art. 49(c).
61. RSFSR Code of Criminal Procedure, 1953 ed., arts. 413, 414.
62. USSR Constitution, art. 113.
63. *Ibid.*, art. 114.
64. *Ibid.*, arts. 115, 116.
65. *Ibid.*, art. 117.
66. Golunskii and Karev, p. 176.
67. *Ibid.*, p. 168.
68. *Ibid.*, p. 177.
69. See Major General of Juridical Service I. M. Zarianov, "Podgotovka voennykh iuristov" (The Preparation of Military Jurists), *Uchenye Zapiski V.I.Iu.N. Ministerstva Iustitsii SSSR* (Transactions of the All-Union Institute of Juridical Science of the Ministry of Justice of the USSR; Moscow, 1945), Issue IV.
70. According to Zarianov, the following textbooks were published by 1945: Chkhikvadze and Savitskii, on Military Criminal Law; Studenikin and Lunev, on Military Administrative Law; Karev, on Military Tribunals. The following

were ready for publication: Vinogradov, Pobezhimov, and Lunev, on Soviet Military Administrative Law; Chkhikvadze and Gertsenzon, on Statistics of Military Tribunals; Avdeev, on Medicine in the Procedure of Military Tribunals; Korovin, on International Law. The only book on the subject available in this country, so far as the authors know, is Chkhikvadze, on Military Criminal Law (1946). Chkhikvadze, a Colonel of Juridical Service, was the head of the Military Law School at the time of the publication of the book.

V. AN APPRAISAL OF THE SOVIET SYSTEM OF MILITARY LAW AND ADMINISTRATION

1. *Sudebnaia Praktika Verkhovnogo Suda SSSR* (Judicial Practice of the Supreme Court of the USSR), 1946, IV (XXVIII), 3, translated in Berman and Kerner, *Documents*, no. 38.

2. *Ibid.*, 1945 V (XXI), 6; translated in Berman and Kerner, *Documents*, no. 30.

3. *Ibid.*, 1946, IV (XXVIII), 4; translated in Berman and Kerner, *Documents*, no. 31.

4. *Ibid.*, 1944, III (IX), 8; translated in Berman and Kerner, *Documents*, no. 33. See p. 63 *supra*.

5. *Sbornik Postanovlenii Plenuma i Opredelenii Kollegii Verkhovnogo Suda Soiuza SSR, 1944* (Collections of Decrees of the Plenum and Decisions of the Divisions of the Supreme Court of the USSR, 1944; Moscow, 1948), p. 44.

6. *Ibid.*, 1947, IV, 14; translated in Berman and Kerner, *Documents*, no. 54.

7. See Berman, *Justice in Russia*, pp. 199ff.

APPENDIX II

1. The decree of November 8, 1917, establishing the Council of People's Commissars, is translated in J. H. Meisel and E. S. Kozera, *Materials for the Study of the Soviet System* (Ann Arbor, Michigan, 1950), p. 22.

2. D. Fedotoff White, *The Growth of the Red Army* (Princeton, 1944), p. 33.

3. The decree of November 8, 1917, named V. A. Ovseenko (Antonov), N. V. Krylenko, and F. N. Dybenko as members of the committee. See Meisel and Kozera, p. 22.

4. White, pp. 432–433.

5. B. Tal', *Istoriia Krasnoi Armii* (History of the Red Army; Moscow-Leningrad, 1928), p. 38.

6. Decree of the Council of People's Commissars on the Organization of the Worker-Peasant Red Army, January 28 (15), 1918, reproduced in part in G. D. Kostomarov and R. I. Golubev, ed., *Organizatsiia Krasnoi Armii 1917–1918* (The Organization of the Red Army, 1917–1918; Moscow, 1943; a collection of documents and materials), pp. 24–25.

7. *Ibid.*, p. 25.

8. The Red Guard was an industrial workers' militia which came into being after Lenin's return to Russia in the spring of 1917 and which is considered to have been a decisive force in the Bolshevik seizure of power. White, p. 17.

9. Quoted by White, p. 33.

10. Of the original three-man committee, Ovseenko remained on the All-Russian Collegium and Krylenko was on the All-Russian Supreme Staff; Trotsky was on the All-Russian Collegium and, as People's Commissar of Military and Naval Affairs, was on the Supreme Military Council; Podvoiskii was on the All-Russian Collegium and also on the All-Russian Supreme Staff. *Ibid.*

11. White, pp. 38, 39.

12. Order of the Supreme Military Council on the Establishment of Military Districts, March 31, 1918, art. 1, in Kostomarov and Golubev, p. 100.

13. *Ibid.*, art. 2.

14. *Ibid.*, art. 3. The Military District Committee, under the chairmanship of the military leader, consisted of the following: (a) two political commissars, (b) delegates from the regional Soviet, (c) the commander of the district staff, (d) the commander of the district economic administration, (e) the commander of the district artillery administration, (f) the commander of the district military-technical administration, (g) the commander of the district military-sanitation administration, (h) the commander of the district military-veterinary administration, (i) a representative of the district aviation center, and (j) a representative of the district automotive center.

15. *Ibid.*, art. 4.

16. *Ibid.*, arts. 5, 7, 8.

17. Decree of the Council of People's Commissars on the Institution of Small Rural District, County, Provincial, and District Commissariats for Military Affairs, April 8, 1918, quoted in Kostomarov and Golubeva, p. 156.

18. White, p. 35.

19. In 1924 the power of Trotsky as People's Commissar for Military and Naval Affairs declined, and his subordinate, Mikhail Frunze, emerged as the

de facto head of the commissariat. In January 1925, Trotsky resigned and Frunze became People's Commissar. Frunze died on October 31, 1925, and he was succeeded in November by Kliment Voroshilov.

20. Studenikin, Vlasov, and Evtikhiev, p. 235.

21. Service in the standing army was for two consecutive years, in the terri-torial forces for a total of two years spread out at intervals over five years.

22. *Cf.* Towster, *Political Power in the USSR 1917–1947* (New York, 1948), pp. 288–291.

23. *Sobranie Uzakonenii i Rasporiazhenii Rabochego i Krest'ianskogo Pravitel'stva* (Collection of Laws and Regulations of the Worker and Peasant Government) 1921, no. 22, art. 135.

24. *Coll. Laws USSR*, 1925, no. 2, art. 18.

INDEX

Abandonment of field of battle, 73, 85, 140. *See also* Battle crimes

Abandonment of sinking warship, 85. *See also* Battle crimes

Absence without leave, 68, 73, 90, 94, 99, 150, 152ff. *See also* Desertion; Failure to report for duty

Abuse of authority, *see* Official crimes

Academy of Sciences, 127

Administrative order, crimes against, 106

Aggravating circumstances, 72, 87, 90, 149, 150, 151, 152. *See also* Extenuating circumstances

Air force, 10, 27, 32, 175

Allowances, 96, 125, 145. *See also* Pensions

All-Russian Bureau of Military Commissars, 14, 181. *See also* Commissars, military

American military law, 129, 130, 149

Amnesties, 3, 95, 169, 193

Analogy, doctrine of, 2–3, 69ff

Antonov, *see* Ovseenko

Appeals and Protests, 3, 101, 102, 103, 111, 112, 113, 117, 122ff, 125, 158–159, 160, 196. *See also* Cases; Courts, military

Aralov, S. I., 172

Armenian SSR Criminal Code, 189

Artem'ev, Colonel General P.A., 10

Assessors, 104, 105, 113, 194, 195. *See also* Courts, military

Avdeev, 198

Bagramian, Marshal I. Kh., 10

Basistyi, Admiral N. E., 10

Battle crimes, 73, 84–85, 150, 152

Belorussian SSR Criminal Code, 189

Beria, Lavrenti P., 2, 9, 160

Bogdanov, Marshal S. I., 10

Border and Internal Guards, *see* MVD troops

Briukhanov, N. P., 172

Brzezinski, Z., 182, 183, 189

Budenny, Marshal S., 10

Bulganin, Marshal Nikolai A., 8, 9, 10, 11, 12, 45, 179

Camp courts, 101, 103, 194. *See also* Corrective labor camps

Cases, officially reported: Case of Chadaeva, 153–155, 168, 195; Case of Golubeva, 153–155, 168; Case of Gvanii, 170, 197; Case of Il'in, 169; Case of K., 63, 156, 168, 189; Case of Muzykin *et al.*, 161–162, 170, 197; Case of Poliakov, 168; Case of S., 196; Case of Zatyk, 152–153, 169

Cases, unofficially reported, 62–63, 140, 141, 143–144, 170

Central Executive Committee, 95, 173, 176. *See also* Supreme Soviet of USSR

Chel'tsov, M. A., 96, 119, 196, 197

Chief Administration of State Security, 22, 183. *See also* Ministry of Internal Affairs; Security agencies

Chief Inspectorate, 27, 32. *See also* Ministry of Defense

Chief Military Council of Ministry of Defense, 26. *See also* Military Council of Ministry of Defense

Chief Political Administration, 8, 10, 16, 17ff, 21, 23, 27, 31, 32, 33, 126, 134, 175. *See also* Communist Party; Ministry of Defense; Political Administration of the Republic (PUR)

Chkhikvadze, V. M., 69, 71, 72, 76, 77, 78, 80, 82, 83, 84, 86, 87, 88, 94, 95, 96, 190, 191, 192, 197, 198

Chuikov, Colonel General Vasili I., 10

Civilian property, crimes against, 91, 138, 145

Civilians, crimes against, 91

Civilians, jurisdiction of military courts over, 64–65, 72, 106–109